Deborah Frances-White is the creator and host of the hit podcast *The Guilty Feminist*. She is a stand-up comedian best known for her BBC Radio 4 show *Deborah Frances-White Rolls the Dice* which won the Writers' Guild Award for Best Radio Comedy. She is also a screenwriter and regularly speaks in businesses about diversity and inclusion.

Deborah Frances-White

THE GUILTY FEMINIST

From our noble goals to our worst hypocrisies

virago

VIRAGO

First published in Great Britain in 2018 by Virago Press
This paperback edition published in 2019 by Virago Press

1 3 5 7 9 10 8 6 4 2

Copyright © Deborah Frances-White 2019

The moral right of the author has been asserted.

A CIP catalogue record for this book
is available from the British Library.

ISBN 978-0-349-01012-0

Typeset in Garamond by M Rules
Printed and bound in Great Britain by
Clays Ltd, Elcograf S.p.A.

Papers used by Virago are from well-managed forests
and other responsible sources.

Virago Press
An imprint of
Little, Brown Book Group
Carmelite House
50 Victoria Embankment
London EC4Y 0DZ

An Hachette UK Company
www.hachette.co.uk

www.virago.co.uk

*For Monica and Philippa, remarkable
women who've shown me over and over
how to turn fantasy hour into reality hour.*

*And for Gina, my rock, and Tom,
my anchor. Without you two, I'm
just some ideas in bed. Xx*

Contents

Introduction

What is a Guilty Feminist?

*I'm a feminist but when I was choosing a new
headshot, I asked my husband, 'Does this photo of
me look a bit "Dove campaign for real beauty"?'
And he said, 'No, darling, you look lovely,' and
I thought, 'Well, that campaign's failed.'*

What is a guilty feminist? In 2015 I described myself as a 'guilty feminist' for the first time, because I lived with the knowledge that my beliefs were firm but my feelings existed on a trampoline. My goals were noble but my concerns were trivial. I wanted desperately for women to be taken seriously in leadership roles all over the world, but I also wanted to look good sitting down naked. I knew that even thinking there was a 'good' way to look in any posture didn't chime with body-positive, twenty-first-century feminism where we were all meant to love our bodies as if they were our dying grandmothers, and that any criticism of them could be seen as disloyalty to the sisterhood.

I felt like a fraud for saying defiantly in an internet debate that, as a woman, my chief role was not to be decorative; and then later that day crying actual tears on finding that my favourite dress was tighter than usual because I'd put on weight. I could deliver a power seminar on charismatic leadership techniques for senior women in a law firm and the next day make an apologetic phone call to a comedy promoter in which I 'hoped I was not bothering him', speaking as fast as possible in my lady voice, as 'I was sure he was very busy', when it was obvious I'd just woken him from an afternoon nap.

This troubled me especially because so many more of my conversations with women were moving away from *Sex and the City* territory and towards gender equality. Something was in the air. Hillary was running for the White House. *New York Magazine* pictured thirty-five of Bill Cosby's accusers on its front cover. Gloria Steinem dedicated her book to the doctor who illegally performed her abortion in 1957, naming him as a hero. A tidal wave of change was coming and I wanted to be on the crest of it, but I worried I wasn't good enough.

I confessed my feelings to fellow comedian and friend Sofie Hagen. She and I had a series of lunches that year which had started as jokes, shop talk and revelations about our love lives, but had drifted into feminism. I showed Sofie my hypocrisies on the grounds that she'd show me hers. Because we were both comedians, council zoning required that these insights be shared with the world, through the medium of podcasting, and *The Guilty Feminist* podcast was born.

For the uninitiated, a podcast is radio that no one stops you making because you put it on the internet yourself. Please let me reassure you that whether you live in a delightfully secluded cave not cursed with Wi-Fi and have never heard a minute of this podcast, or you binged the whole thing in a week and cross the days off on your calendar until the next episode comes out, I wrote this book with you in mind.

When Sofie and I committed to admitting our double standards out loud, a part of me feared we'd be shunned by the club, that the 'proper' feminists we knew would roll their eyes at our embarrassing admissions. We weren't just making these confessions to our BFFs four margaritas into a Friday night, we were recording them for distribution. We screwed up our courage and hoped that other women identified with our inadequacies and aspirations.

It turned out we weren't the only ones living with contradictions. Women responded in droves. Many have written to tell us that they'd previously felt unable to call themselves feminists but now they knew they wanted to and could. Others said the show had acted as a valve for their guilt – a place they could laugh off things that didn't matter or that they were working on. They realised they didn't have to be perfect or even consistent to be a force for meaningful change. The emails I receive, which tell stories of women activated by *The Guilty Feminist* to apply for PhDs, lodge sexual harassment cases, start talking to their high school students about gender equality or even report sexual assaults, can always be boiled down to two statements: 'Because I listened to the podcast, I have decided to say yes,' or 'Because I listened to the podcast, I have started to say no.' I do not take credit for the boldness of these listeners. I think a big part of their conviction comes from hearing our live audience laughing and agreeing and commenting. It makes individual women feel like they have an army behind them when they speak up in a meeting, fill out a funding application or tell a catcaller he's just not cool.

We've had some luck with our timing. More people listen to podcasts now than go to the cinema on a weekly basis. Just when feminism was facing the onslaught of Trump, Weinstein and the worst excesses of Twitter, people were turning to podcasts for information, inspiration and entertainment.

I'm overwhelmed at the response from our audience, who turn out in droves for the show and queue, tweet and email to tell us what the show means to them. I'm also convinced that if I'd attempted to pitch a broadcast comedy show with 'feminist' in the title in December 2015, the industry would have responded with a polite refusal and an assurance that feminism isn't a ratings winner. I am amazed and thrilled to say that *The Guilty Feminist* podcast has had 50 million downloads in just over two years. While internet neutrality exists, artists can find their audience and audiences can find their jam.

For readers who've not heard the podcast, it's a comedy show in which we explore themes that feminists need to tackle head-on – from nudity to body capability and from power to democracy. Each episode features stand-up, discussions with guests and also weekly challenges. Thanks to this aspect of the podcast, I have thrown myself out of a plane, posed naked for a life-drawing class, led a feminist discussion group with a class of teenage boys at an inner-city school and directed a short film like a boss.

The guests and I always start each episode with one-liners that begin, 'I'm a feminist but . . .' These are true confessions about times when our actions and values have spent time apart. They're usually playful, silly things that don't really matter. It's the equivalent of using a loofah in the shower to slough off anything you don't need, but for your gender equality headspace. Here's one of mine: I'm a feminist but when my four-year-old nephew insisted on me putting on my wedding dress and watching *Beauty and the Beast* with him, I also put on my tiara, which he had not requested.

In autumn 2016 Sofie Hagen left the podcast to go on to other exciting projects, but I'll always be grateful we first sat down together at lunch and said, 'I'm a feminist but . . .' I hope that, in continuing the show with other comedians and in writing this book now, I'm shooting (even if it's in a scattergun way) for a life of 'I'm a feminist and . . .'

For readers who know and love the *Guilty Feminist* podcast, I hope you find this book has plenty of new takes on much-loved themes which challenge us daily, with some requested favourites down on paper for the very first time.

For every reader, I hope this book will reflect this mix of comedy and more thoughtful discussion and challenge you to leave the house, take up the space and time you deserve, find your most unapologetic and persuasive voice, begin to truly trust yourself and communicate that self-belief to the room, create your own microclimates for success, shine a bold, strong light on other feminists and strike out fearlessly for gender equality – exfoliating unnecessary guilt as you go.

This book also intends to include as much as possible. It looks at the intersections between gender, race, sexual orientation, disability and gender identity and how those advantage and disadvantage groups and individuals in society. It includes trans-women as women. A 2016 survey by the consumer insight agency J. Walter Thompson Innovation Group discovered that 48 per cent of Generation Z (people born mid-1990s to mid-2000s) identify as 'completely heterosexual', compared to 65 per cent of millennials. In addition, 56 per cent of these same young people said they know someone who goes by non-traditional gender pronouns like 'they/them/ze' and the same percentage shopped for themselves in both men's and women's clothing shops. Seventy per cent of Gen Zs in the survey supported gender-neutral lavatories as opposed to 57 per cent of millennials. The future isn't binary and this next generation won't form two orderly camps. We need to build a world for these young people who are more comfortable with their own fluidity and don't see gender or sexuality as fixed. The world they want to live in doesn't conform to gender norms and that's a good thing because it doesn't demand that they 'act like a lady' or 'man up'. This book is unapologetically part of that trend. The right side of history is calling us in.

I am using terms in current style guides as directed by the communities in question. I use 'people of colour' and 'women of colour' to describe non-white people because it is the term currently used by the social justice movement and recommended by the *American Heritage Guide to Contemporary Usage and Style* (Houghton Mifflin, 2005). Although it began in America, it has become universal and I use it because feminist leaders and influencers in non-white communities do. It is often abbreviated to POC or WOC on the internet.

I use 'queer' as is increasingly standard, to mean 'non-normative' and as an umbrella term for sexual and gender groups who are not heterosexual and/or not cisgendered.[1]

I use 'non-disabled' not 'able-bodied' because most often it is society's attitudes and infrastructure that disadvantage those whose bodies function differently and because this is recommended by disability activists.

If you identify with any of these groups and prefer alternative terms, switch them out as you read and know that I've gone with the most current accepted terms, at the time of writing, to be as respectful as possible to the communities I'm writing about.

Why guilt and feminism sometimes go together ...

We've all been raised in a patriarchy, and our feelings have been shaped by this, starting in our childhood. While our adult minds might be far beyond thinking our worth lies in having

---

1 Cisgendered refers to people whose gender identity matches the gender they were assigned at birth.

Jennifer Aniston's hair, Jennifer Lopez's arse and being liked by everyone everywhere all of the time, deep down inside it's easy to feel that things will be better if we can only live up to what the billboards want for us.

Just because we've been hardwired to be self-critical and distracted by meaningless, unattainable goals doesn't mean we aren't feminists. It's one reason we need feminism! We're allowed to acknowledge, to try to reverse and even laugh at our own cultural brainwashing while we tackle the big stuff. We need to create a space for ourselves to be and grow. I don't wish to lower the bar for feminism by saying, 'I'm a feminist but ...' *but* I've realised over the last few years of engaging with this and talking to women that, for many of us, feminism has become another thing to feel guilty about.

Women are trained to feel guilty when their kids are in the after-school club because they are working back-to-back nursing shifts – and guilty that they've dropped out of the half-marathon they were running for their teentrepreneur charity because they've got severe period pain – and guilty for being late to their mother's birthday dinner because they've been helping their friend through a messy break-up – and guilty for enjoying sexual submission because it feels like they shouldn't be getting pleasure from some kind of *Handmaid's Tale*-style scenario, as surely that's what feminists are meant to be fighting against in the first place?

Not all individual women feel these things, but I know that many do, because when I talk about them on stage, the largely female audience laugh in recognition. (One advantage of doing stand-up comedy is that you can identify trends without surveys. If the audience don't laugh, it might mean you're on your own.) Also, women often approach me after shows in the bar to tell me they labour daily in a guilt soup and are tired of it. Are most men judging their best efforts as failures?

Is it common practice for guys to attack each other savagely on Twitter for not being sufficiently nuanced in the language they use around the brotherhood? Are boys encouraged to look at their achievements and aspirations as wanting?

Proper, dedicated, lived-and-breathed fuck-the-patriarchy feminism is a wonderful thing for the empowerment and elevation of women everywhere. But what if we're not there yet? What if we know the bits we know and are embarrassed by the bits we feel we should know and don't? What if we fear we will die at ninety-five, still wanting desperately to have smooth legs and a flawless forehead and without having read *The Bell Jar*? What if we tell our best friend that she's strong, powerful, clever, beautiful and that she should never accept that loser guy who treats her like she's disposable – and then immediately sext our sexist ex? What if we are at base camp, and the summit looks like it's crowded with better feminists than us?

This book is about starting today and challenging ourselves to a series of small but meaningful changes. We don't have to be perfect to dare ourselves to be better. Taking power and finding strength is a positive, potent thing to do. Learning to live with our contradictions and love ourselves anyway is a noble goal in itself. Laughing at the gap between where we want to be (Maya Angelou) and where we are (My God, I Can't Believe I Just Said That) can be cathartic, joyful, bonding and just as empowering as celebrating our achievements. If we can dare to put our bag of guilt down for an hour to play and laugh, we might find that, when we pick it up, we don't need all of it any more.

Equally importantly, I want to explore in this book how guilt can be an invisible gatekeeper that stops us fully including ourselves in rooms of influence – and stops us including others. Stepping forward and making ourselves central in circles where we have any amount of influence is the first step in including other women in those places. To include ourselves we have to look at how welcome we feel inside our own bodies and how to use them to signal our power and confidence to the world. We will explore how to be confident and take up the space we deserve in classrooms, boardrooms, hospital rooms, living rooms and even hotel rooms. We will look at our willingness to conform or to flaunt our differences, how potent a tool language can be and our ability to create boundaries. We will examine the identity of the enemy in the feminist fight and ask how our protests can be more than sound and fury and truly lead to meaningful change. We will even ask how some of our guilty pleasures have hidden feminism packed inside of them.

Many people now define feminism as individual women being able to make individual choices. But feminism is not about whether you personally wear high heels or not. Wear them if you want. Don't if you don't. If you wear them regularly and want to check in to make sure it's your actual conscious choice rather than what your brain has been persuaded to see as normal through lifelong submersion in the patriarchy, you can try giving heels up for a few months and then putting them on again, so you have room to make a comparison. That way, you can assess whether being taller is a sensation you enjoy, or if high heels are just painful and unfun, and proceed with the rest of your life accordingly. Either way, it's not much to do with feminism. That's just learning about what makes you happy.

You turning up to a party in trainers or a kitten heel isn't going to make the world a safer, better-represented, more liberated place for women to live in. You could argue that your choices about heels, make-up, romcoms and career help to create an empowered headspace important for your feminist agenda. If so, start to assess your life step by step and work out who you are and how much more dangerous you could be if you got fearless and ferocious. But really and truly, *it's how different the world is because you are in it* that's the feminist part.

So, feminism and us. Guilt and all. Let's begin.

Part 1

How We Got Here

What's Feminism For?

I'm a feminist but some days even my
life doesn't pass the Bechdel Test.[1]

When I was a teenager, my family became Jehovah's Witnesses. In that religion, as in many, feminism was not encouraged or even allowed. Men were 'the head of the household' and women were 'in subjection'. I always struggled with my place in this small-scale patriarchy.[2] I was a pious Bible student but had a great deal of trouble with the misogynistic, homophobic and xenophobic texts in the Bible. Although known as a hard-working, faithful Jehovah's Witness girl (I was devotedly dowdy), I was once told by a young 'brother' in my congregation, 'No man will take you on because you wouldn't be a submissive wife.' Well spotted,

---

1 The Bechdel Test is a test invented by Liz Wallace, popularised by Alison Bechdel, asking whether a film or other work of fiction includes two named female characters who have a conversation with each other about something other than a man. Over half of films fail this test.
2 Patriarchy literally means 'rule of the father', and today refers to the male-dominated power structures in which we live. It encompasses the large social capital and privilege that men, as a group, are invested with and the way that marginalises and excludes women.

Brother Darren. I would not. When I realised that I was an atheist and left the religion, I knew that equality for women was something I believed in and wanted to fight for. To be clear, this does not mean I don't respect feminists with a faith but my experiences in an extreme religion have led me to be alert to sexism within religion. I'm aware that some contemporary religions go to great lengths to eradicate their patriarchal heritage.

I applied to go to university (further education was also discouraged by the religion, so my ambitions had stalled while I was still a practising Jehovah's Witness), but it was 1997 and 'feminist' was a word that came before 'studies' – something to write essays about rather than a way of life. It wasn't something we talked about much as young women in the Junior Common Room. It was a time of 'Girl Power' and ladette culture in Britain, where I had taken residency. Girl Power meant the freedom to drink, swear and watch porn like the boys, without ever asking if 'like the boys' was something we all wanted to be.

It was my impression that too much focus on gender inequality was perceived as an unwillingness to take personal responsibility for your place in society. It felt like we had to shut up and pretend we were on a level playing field, because we didn't want to be accused of complaining. In this regard, the brave new world I'd stepped into was disappointingly reminiscent of the cult I'd just left. Back then, I wasn't sure if 'feminist' was a word that I could or should use as my own. I wasn't alone.

Many women I knew then, and still others I know now, didn't or don't identify with the word, fearing that if they own it, it will make them appear militant or man-hating. Some feel guilty if they use the word, worrying that it excludes men. Some women feel marginalised from the feminist movement and find it's just another place for them to feel 'less than' because of the way they've been treated. Their experience of feminism is what is sometimes called 'white feminism' – movements for 'equality' within the feminist movement that effectively mean that when white, straight, cis, non-disabled women have as much power and privilege as their powerful male counterparts, the job is done. Some women feel ashamed if they don't call themselves feminists, anxious that they're betraying the sisterhood.

It's important to know what the word means, whether we're trying it on for size or we've worn it proudly for years, while perhaps forgetting to check in with its full history. So I've written a beginners' guide to feminism in this chapter and tried to make it brief, amusing and accessible. The history of feminism is none of those things, so wish me luck. If you feel like I'm teaching suffragettes to suck eggs, skip this section or read it to check I got it right.

Feminism is a combination of social and political movements with a common goal to define, develop and demand political, social and fiscal rights for women. I'm sorry to tell you that a man coined the term. Charles Fourier, Utopian French philosopher, came up with the word. Of course he did. It was 1837, when no one listened to women. I'm willing to bet his girlfriend coined it half an hour before, but no one took it seriously until he said it and then mansplained it to her. He didn't have a wife because he thought that traditional marriage was damaging to women's rights. He was also queer positive, socialist and thought we could make our everyday work erotic. Where's Charles Fourier on Tinder when you need him?

Feminism isn't one thing. It's been through lots of waves, existed in many guises and today is a collection of tribes, frequently in disagreement with each other.

Feminists are often categorised by their points of view on

how best to gain equal ground, and I find it helpful to think of feminist tribes in terms of board games:

Mainstream feminists try to carve out legal rights and social breakthroughs for women within the existing sexist system. Today's mainstream or liberal feminists often focus on individual choice to reject or conform to traditional gender roles, while arguing on behalf of women over issues such as reproductive rights, parental leave, sexual harassment, sexual assault and domestic violence. They have a pragmatic approach favouring changes that can be made in the short to medium term, using existing legal procedures and power structures.

Basically: 'If we all team up together we can get the top hat, the car and the boot and buy Trafalgar Square, Bond Street and some train stations and start chipping in for some houses. We can play Monopoly as well as the old boys' club, and yes, we might be ten thousand years behind in the game, but with some luck from the Community Chest and the occasional Get Out of Jail Free card, we can catch up because we're terribly clever and much more motivated. We might not win but we can bloody well stay on the board.'

Radical feminists tend towards a view that the patriarchal capitalist system will always oppress women and that power will never be shared and must be taken. Some radical feminists see a complete dismantling of the system and the constructing of a new one as the only viable solution to gender inequality.

In short: 'Fuck this shit. We are not playing your stupid, unfair game so stop trying to give us the iron and telling us to Pass Go and accept £200 that you're just going to take away when we hit your Mayfair hotels. You want to play Monopoly? Well, we want to play Equality. We don't care if we go to jail. We definitely don't want to win Second Prize in your stupid Beauty Competition.'

Separatist feminists (a much rarer breed) subscribe to a sort of radical feminism that believes women must separate themselves from men entirely and start over. They believe that women need to remove themselves from heterosexual relationships, at least for periods of time, suggesting celibacy for straight women. This isolation denies the system valuable female resources and allows women to author our own structures.

To summarise: 'We've tipped up the board and are playing Jenga in our fort. Don't come in. You can't play.'

Parasite feminists use the opposite approach, feeling that women need to feed upon the patriarchal system, bleeding dry its resources and using them for our own ends.[3]

Their approach is, 'I see you have Mayfair and Park Lane. I'm taking them and putting four of my hotels on them, collecting rent and charging you for loitering. What do you mean, that it's not fair? Nothing you've ever done has been fair. Fair's not possible till we steal from you what you've stolen from us. Oh look, we've landed on Free Parking. Give us everything you've got, mofo. We've just changed the rules.'

There are many more schools of feminism that you can research and find board game metaphors for, but this gives you an idea. Most varieties of feminism want the same thing – equality of influence, power and resources for women – but each faction thinks its methods for reaching those goals are best. Some feminists get frustrated that we seem to be letting the male-favouring status quo build more hotels on Park Lane and Mayfair while we argue about the best way to pass Go and the right way to mortgage our Waterworks.

*

3 I learned about parasite feminism from Jesse Jones, an Irish artist who created a remarkable Parasite Feminist Institution for her exhibition 'No More Fun and Games' which piggy-backed the facilities of the predominantly male collection at the Hugh Lane Gallery in Dublin in early 2016.

Feminism is also defined in 'waves', or generations, because every time we win or lose a point, the struggle changes.

First-wave feminism has its roots in the social revolutions of the 1700s. If you're overthrowing a government, you start to think about your place in both the old and new order and now the subject of 'fair' is on the table, you want a piece of it. Socialist ideals took an awfully long time to take. Society had been feudal and autocratic for a very long time. First-wave feminism includes the terrifyingly brave suffragettes, who chained themselves to railings, blew up buildings, set fire to landmarks and were force-fed horribly in prison, all so we would have the right to vote for Donald Trump and Brexit. I'm glad they're dead and don't know this.[4]

Second-wave feminism came about after women had gained the right to vote in most Western countries and had been granted (or had snatched) some extra autonomy, overalls and tractors during the world wars due to a lack of men on the ground. Then they were expected to get back in the kitchen and make the patriarchy a sandwich in the 1950s. The 1960s is a famous period for women's liberation, synonymous with bra-burning, which some people say never happened, but actually did once. I've seen a picture.[5] Second-wave feminists – many of them women of colour, Jewish women and queer women, a fact that is often shamefully forgotten – made incredible strides in the perception of appropriate roles for women in society and gave women a loud voice and permission to ask for more rights,

---

4 The suffragettes were themselves problematic in that many of them were both classist and racist and mostly acting in the interests of well-to-do white women, but their idea was larger than their intentions and so I am very thankful they didn't give up when the democratic process failed women.
5 Bras, girdles, tweezers, stilettos and other 'instruments of torture' were thrown in burning rubbish bins at the 1968 Miss America Protest in Atlantic City.

representation and influence. They made massive headway in reproductive, parental and employment rights. They even made everyone stop saying 'When the judge enters everyone must stand for *him* ...' because they pointed out that if we always default to a male pronoun, we always expect a male judge. Now we say 'them', but most of us still picture a bloke most of the time. Everything takes ages.

Third-wave feminism embraced **intersectionality**, a term coined in 1989 by civil rights activist Kimberlé Williams Crenshaw. Intersectionality examines the intersections of different systems of oppression such as race, sexual orientation, class, gender identity and disability. In short, it's harder to be a black, queer, broke, deaf woman than it is to be a rich, straight, non-disabled, middle-class white woman, and if feminism doesn't address that, then it's part of the patriarchy. Intersectionality is constantly asking us to check our privilege(s) and create more platforms for marginalised women and those who identify as neither male nor female. The language can feel like a minefield and the culture can be pretty lively, so while it's good to take criticism on board it's best not to take it too personally.[6] It's a crucial next step for feminism. Without it, feminism will probably die, because it's not supporting those who most need it.

Fourth-wave feminism is like the third wave but with added Twitter and podcasts. That's right, patriarchy – the feminists have taken control of the means of production.

Fifth-wave feminism is forming itself now. All we know so far is that it is about action. It will promote the ideas of the intersectional movement from the third wave, which will allow us more of a mainstream, influential platform. It will take the social-networking capability of the fourth wave and use it to

---

6 I still take it personally sometimes, but I try to let it go within half an hour.

organise and galvanise and turn hashtags into consequences.
Women who have never marched before are joining those who
have marched hard for a long time. Women are responding to
Trump and Brexit and the environment those major political
surprises have created, with angry get-up-and-go. Movements
like Me Too and Time's Up are gaining ground in a way that
is having real-life, financial consequences for high-profile men
who have abused their power to sexually harass and assault
women. The intention is now to forge systemic change across
many industries and institutions that have accepted abuse and
protected perpetrators. The fifth wave is a global army that
crowdfunds and realises proper, permanent changes can be
made with the right strategies.

Inclusion – who feels she can say 'me too' and who feels it's not for her?

Feminism has meant different things to various women in a
multitude of times, countries and communities. Women are
not a monolithic group, and individuals often radically disagree even within their own collectives about the best methods
or the real purpose of feminism.

The way I see it, there is one thing that every brand of feminism has in common. Feminism has always been a request,
or demand, for inclusion. Inclusion is a watchword of the
second decade of the twenty-first century and in recent waves
of feminism, but it's nothing new. Inclusion is the foundation
of society. Inclusion is the reason human beings are the top
of the food chain. One person cannot beat a lion in a fight,
but twelve people can outsmart a lion. Including each other
is the basis of our survival. The cost of complete exclusion is
our mental health. If you're Tom Hanks on a desert island you
have to make a volleyball-head to talk to, so you don't start to

hallucinate. Inclusion is vital to humanity. So, the question can only ever be: who is included and why? Women have been routinely excluded in places of power and influence. Socially, they've been included tentatively and conditionally. You only have to look at the comments section under any article about feminism online (and I seriously recommend you don't do that) to see that many people now feel that women are far more included than they should be. Some people see female judges, CEOs and even heads of state and think that if there ever was a struggle for women to be included, there isn't one now, and it turns out that there are many and various ways to say that in well under 280 characters.

These people argue that women today are sufficiently included and have enough influence and opportunity, so that any observable inequality is down to individuals and not structures. 'Surely if more women were funny, we'd see them on television comedy panel shows.' 'If a woman works hard enough in the Western world she can be anything she wants to be, and it would be unfair for her to be given any further advantage.'

Why should we have women's networks in politics, scholarships for teenage girls wanting to get into film school or gender targets in Silicon Valley? First, it seems highly unlikely that after around ten thousand years of exclusive male domination, women could possibly have caught up in the last hundred years. There isn't enough positive discrimination in the world to make up for slavery, colonisation and the slaughter of indigenous peoples to somehow equalise the racial advantage gifted to white people, and it is important for Caucasian people to get that and live as if that's true. I am not putting race and gender on a par, but in a parallel way, it's hard to know how anyone can watch *Mad Men*, featuring the historically accurate, misogynistic business practices of the incredibly recent

1960s and come to the conclusion that we've somehow levelled out the playing field in a few decades.

Most industries include many more men than women in their decision-making processes. One way to make up for a huge historical handicap and include more women is to create quotas. It seems like an easy solution to create mandatory requirements to include women and men equally within industries or sectors – and even bring these into law when it comes to politics or positions of real influence. Sometimes this does happen. For example, in 2016 Germany enforced quotas requiring that corporations based there make their boards at least 30 per cent female. Previously most companies averaged 20 per cent.

There was a horrified outcry about this quota, as there always is when the topic arises. Even many feminists worry that it makes the women promoted feel token and creates a counterproductive resentment among men. Sometimes women feel guilty accepting a seat at the table where a quota exists, as if they're taking something they haven't earned. Other women become understandably defensive and explain why this apparent unfairness to others is really correcting structural bigotry. Some men and women get angry about quotas and speak of them as if undeserving women are taking away men's hard-earned jobs at gunpoint.

It is the very existence of, and terms used in, the debate about quotas that I think really highlights society's blindness to the exclusion of women and overinclusion of men, and the need to examine history and society closely to identify our unconscious bias.[7]

To be clear, I don't have a particular agenda here, and I am

---

7 If you don't think you have any prejudices you're unaware of, then try the Harvard Implicit Association Test at Harvard.implicit.edu. It's an eye-opener!

not recommending quotas in all industries. I think targets are valuable everywhere and quotas are appropriate sometimes, but my views on this aren't especially relevant. What I am examining here is how the fear and fury about quotas highlights the landscape of gender inequality when it comes to men, as a group, being fast-tracked to the VIP suite and women being left out in the cold.

What is never mentioned in these hysterical debates is that historically quotas have been the norm. The gender quota for voters in general elections was 100 per cent male and 0 per cent female in the UK until 1918. In Switzerland, the quota for voters in general elections was 100 per cent male and 0 per cent female until 1971. Even more implausibly, in one canton of Switzerland women were not able to vote on local issues until 1991!

The quota for practising medicine in the UK was 100 per cent male and 0 per cent female until 1862, when Elizabeth Garrett Anderson did an extraordinary amount of agonising work and overcame an insufferable amount of rejection to find a loophole in the system and qualify as a doctor.[8] She found a college that had forgotten to specify 'men only' in their charter as it appeared too obvious to mention, like saying 'no zebras need apply'. Therefore, they couldn't refuse her. She passed with the highest marks in her class, but even so the loophole was closed so that no further women could qualify until 1876. Despite her outstanding grades achieved in difficult circumstances, no hospital would hire her, so she had to set up her own private practice, which eventually thrived after a cholera

---

8 Dr James Barry, who pre-dated Elizabeth Garrett Anderson, was an Irish British military surgeon whose assigned gender at birth was female. It is not clear whether James was a woman living as a man to fulfil her career ambitions or whether he was a transgender man. Either way, she or he was a remarkable historical figure but not one who interrupted the quota system.

epidemic meant that patients were willing to put aside their gender-based prejudices. To get a full medical degree in addition to her licence to practise medicine, she had to go to Paris, where they were open to female students, and *learn French* well enough to study there first. In 1873 she became an exception to the British Medical Association's 100 per cent male quota system, which excluded all other women for the following nineteen years.

In 1909, the same Elizabeth Garrett Anderson ran for Mayor of Aldeburgh and won. Guess what the gender quota was for mayors in 1908? You're correct. It was 100 per cent male, 0 per cent female. Amazingly, she won an election without being allowed to vote for herself.

The gender quota for lawyers was 100 per cent male and 0 per cent female in the United Kingdom until 1922 when Ivy Williams was admitted to the bar. She had completed her law degree at Oxford University in 1903. Why the huge gap between finishing her degree and becoming a lawyer? Well, the gender quota for students able to graduate with a degree was 100 per cent male and 0 per cent female. Women could study at Oxford and pass the exams with flying colours, but they weren't included in the graduation ceremony and were denied their degree. When Ivy was finally granted her first-class Oxford degree in December 1919, she joined the Inner Temple one month later and was subsequently called to the bar two terms early.

The gender quota for actors in England was 100 per cent male and 0 per cent female until Charles II worried that acting like girls would turn young men gay and decreed that women should play female parts. It wasn't only homophobia, it was also practicality. Charles had been inconvenienced when a play he was watching was brought to an unscheduled halt because an actor playing a female part needed a shave, so he changed the law. The first woman allowed on stage in England was Margaret Hughes, who played Desdemona in *Othello* in 1662.

In 1776, when the American Revolution gave birth to a democracy, nearly every state created a voting gender quota that was 100 per cent male and 0 per cent female, with John Adams warning against 'the despotism of the petticoat'. New Jersey, however, permitted all persons to vote who had fifty pounds and had resided in the state for one year. This meant that free black men, free single black women and single white women[9] had the right to vote and did so in large numbers. However, in 1808 a quota was *introduced* that meant voters had to be 'free white men'. That all-white quota lasted till 1870 when African American men were able to vote, and the all-male quota remained until 1920 when both black and white women could vote. (In reality, in many parts of the country African Americans were unable to exercise their right to vote until the 1960s, and in some states considerable efforts are made to exclude people of colour even now. It is not an official quota system but practical exclusion, and amounts to the same thing.)

In the late 1950s, the gender quota for American astronaut candidates was 100 per cent male and 0 per cent female. After some men had gone into space, Jerrie Cobb broke the all-male quota in the early 1960s with twenty-four other female pilots when NASA allowed them to go through the physical and psychological evaluation as part of the First Lady Astronaut Trainees programme. Jerrie ranked in the top 2 per cent of all the astronaut candidates (regardless of gender), which is no surprise as she had been teaching men to fly planes at nineteen

---

9 Not married women. Their husbands were seen to vote for them. Their household had a say.

years of age and had gone on to set world records for speed, altitude and distance. She was told by NASA that she'd be the first woman in space and was celebrated on television.

However, America wasn't ready to let its all-male quota go. NASA cancelled the women's programme in 1963. A congressional hearing upheld this decision, during which astronaut John Glenn testified that, 'Men go off and fight the wars and fly the airplanes,' and added, 'The fact that women are not in this field is a fact of our social order.' (You might remember John Glenn as 'one of the good guys' in the 2017 movie *Hidden Figures*.) Jerrie left NASA and returned to flying, and was named Pilot of the Year by her colleagues. She also went on to do extraordinary humanitarian work. America did not allow a woman into space for a further twenty-one years.

In 1998, John Glenn got back in a rocket at the age of seventy-seven and was lauded as the 'oldest man in space'. When sixty-seven-year-old Jerrie petitioned to go too, arguing that the opportunity had been denied her originally in part due to Glenn's sexism, her request was refused. She begged and said that she would seriously accept a one-way ticket to space. John Glenn got to go without her. Jerrie Cobb turned eighty-six this year. I wouldn't mind betting she still gets there.

When people get angry about gender quotas setting a target for 30 per cent women on boards, or one woman on a panel show of five to seven men, we need to remind them that positive discrimination was alive and well and 100 per cent in men's favour for thousands of years. Current quotas aren't even beginning to redress the balance.

You may notice two things about the women who break all-male gender quotas. First, they are usually exceptional in their field and breathtaking in their determination because they have to be in order to break the almost impenetrable patriarchal strongholds. Second, they are almost always white.

This is because the patriarchy favours white women the way it favours men.

If you don't believe me, look at Trump's cabinet. Look at pretty much any room of influence in the West. Predominantly male. Predominantly white. Colonialism is too vast and horrendous for the scope of this book, but it is important to note that even in populations that are made up entirely of people of colour, white Westerners have usually dominated the resources of the land or people at some point, and white tourists are treated as special almost everywhere we go.

Women of colour who do things before white women are often 'hidden figures' in history. For example, the first woman admitted to the District of Columbia Bar, and the first woman admitted to practise before the Supreme Court of the District of Columbia was an African American woman called Charlotte E. Ray. Charlotte, who left law school in 1872, was held up as a precedent for women in other states who wanted to take the bar exam. Charlotte didn't last long as a lawyer, because a combination of racism and sexism meant she couldn't get a job and her own practice was boycotted. She had to go into teaching even though she was said to be 'one of the best lawyers on corporations in the country'. She was also a suffragist and helped to get white American women the vote.

It is important for us as feminists – whether radical, liberal, guilty or otherwise – to recognise that women, as a group, aren't on a level playing field any more than men and women are.

The history of American patents is a great place to get some insight on the interplay between race and gender because innovators are leaders in their fields and patent offices keep excellent records.

On 31 July 1790, Samuel Hopkins was the first person to be issued a US patent. It was for a process of making potash, an ingredient used in fertiliser, and the patent was signed by President George Washington.

Nineteen years later, Mary Kies became the first woman to receive a patent for her method of weaving straw with silk in 1809.

Twelve years later, the first African American to receive a patent was Thomas L. Jennings, for innovative dry-cleaning equipment in 1821.

Sixty-three years later, the first African American woman claimed a patent: Judy W. Reed, for an improved dough-kneader in 1884.

When I first wrote this list, I did not notice that I had described these individuals as 'the first person', 'the first woman', 'the first African American' and 'the first African American woman' because that is how they are listed in the history books. The further away you are from being a white man, the less you are seen by society as being a neutral 'person'.[10] That's pretty devastating, isn't it?

In fact, this is a list of the first Caucasian man, the first Caucasian woman, the first African American man and the first African American woman to be granted a patent and everything about our environment makes it easy to forget that. It is significant that while Samuel Hopkins is to be found on sites about patents, Mary Kies is usually referenced in lists of historical women, Thomas L. Jennings can only be found in resources about African Americans and I read about Judy W. Reed in an article entitled 'Uncovering History's Black Women Inventors' (because, depressingly, 'uncovering' is almost always required to find the achievements of women

---

10 Signifiers include gender, race, sexual orientation and disability. A native American man in a wheelchair or an Asian transgender woman will be defined by their visible distance from the dominant group.

of colour). Innovators, and leaders who are not white men, live in the margins of history and the specialist sections of the library.

You will also notice that the first white woman was included in the inventor's process a full seventy-five years before the first woman of colour. This is an anecdotal example, but one that's part of a pattern. White women are often included before and instead of men of colour, but men of colour are usually included before and instead of women of colour. Feminism is a fight for equality, so we've got to notice when the power gap benefits us (if we are white, straight, cis or non-disabled or a combination of any of these) as well as when it fails us.

The patriarchy – and why you might be part of it

Just like we can't fully embrace feminism (even guilty feminism) unless we know its origins and history, we can't understand why we're stuck with the patriarchy unless we know how it came to be. It's a common misconception that men have always had the upper hand, but it is widely accepted by academics that hunter-gatherer societies in Africa, where the human race began, were mostly egalitarian.[11]

We know this because many hunter-gatherer societies have survived uninterrupted to this day. Twentieth-century anthropologists studied tribes in various remote locations in Asia, South America and Africa. Almost always in these tribes, women and men share influence and resources and neither gender is seen to be superior. The hallmark of these societies

---

11 Lee, R. B. (1988). 'Reflections on primitive communism'. In T. Ingold, D. Riches and J. Woodburn (eds), *Hunters and Gatherers*, vol. 1, 252–68 Oxford: Berg.

is decision-making which is egalitarian and consensual. The reason the patriarchy doesn't feel right to many of us is that it is not how our brains evolved to survive and thrive. Women didn't evolve to be oppressed by men and men didn't evolve to dominate and mansplain. One of humanity's closest relatives, the chimpanzee, operates in a dictatorship run by the alpha male. Palaeoanthropologists often theorise that the reason human beings developed language, community and even human consciousness was to resist alpha male dominance.[12] It's possible that what separates us from the animals is actually feminism. That's a t-shirt waiting to be made if ever there was one.

Hunter-gatherer tribes were less hierarchical than our society. There's evidence that labour was divided among our woke ancestors and that leadership was fluid, depending on the nature of the task and the skills of the tribal member. Resources were shared and childcare was a gig for the whole family. Hunters and gatherers traditionally work about forty hours a week, with parenting equally shared. It is not always the case that men do the hunting, either, in case your unconscious bias was kicking in. While women typically gather, Aeta women (from the Philippines), for example, hunt in groups and have a 31 per cent success rate as opposed to 17 per cent for men. When Aeta men and women join forces, they come back from 41 hunts out of 100 with food for the tribe. Our hunter-gatherer ancestors were, and their contemporary counterparts are, kicking our capitalist arses for gender equality. There are diversity and inclusion directors in investment banks weeping at the targets that nomads are hitting.

---

12 Erdal, D.; Whiten, A. (1994). 'On human egalitarianism: an evolutionary product of Machiavellian status escalation?' and Boehm, Christopher, *Hierarchy in the Forest: The Evolution of Egalitarian Behavior* (Harvard University Press, 2001).

What went wrong? Well, the plough really screwed women over. The gather was traditionally more reliable than the hunt, though the hunt was celebrated because it was more dangerous and protein gave the tribe a boost. This meant that female gatherers (as was the norm) offered the tribe more economic stability. We were the more reliable breadwinners. When humans started growing food, women couldn't plough, because we lacked the upper-body strength necessary for pushing early models, especially when pregnant. This made us dependants rather than valuable contributors. Also, staying in one place meant people could build permanent structures to live in – and so the kitchen was invented. At this point it made sense for childcare to be managed by the person staying indoors so the children wouldn't distract the one growing and farming the food.

The biggest driver in the construction of the patriarchy was the ability to acquire property. If you are nomadic, possessions are a nuisance. It's easy to want more coffee tables and stand-ard lamps in your house, but as soon as you have to cart them around an airport you want to be shot of them. Ever bought a Persian rug while travelling through the Middle East? That's how our nomadic forebears felt about luxury goods. They couldn't preserve food, so they caught and gathered what they needed and walked on unencumbered, letting the area replenish like the environmentally friendly human beings that they were.

Once we put down roots, we started to want stuff. And once we had stuff, we started comparing it with our neigh-bours' stuff, like a very early 3D Facebook. Anything a wealth creator kept in his house became property to be shown off and bragged about, including his wife and children. If you weren't contributing to the bank account, you were in the bank account, which is why it's traditional for fathers to give their daughters away at weddings.[13] That's when men started to make the decisions, take the best resources for themselves and use their physical strength like our chimpanzee cousins, to oppress and abuse. In other words, capitalism has rarely been a friend to feminism.

Thousands of years of pastoral life gave way to the Industrial Revolution, which meant social status was determined by even more readily available material things. This reinforced a woman's place as sexually objectified property. She was to be kept inside the home, where she could be controlled and where she looked after the rest of her husband's possessions and cared full-time for his offspring. Women working outside the home for money was a sign of poverty and need. A man of means could and should keep his wife as a cherished possession, and having her do anything except needlework and make babies was a sign of his failure to provide and control.

This meant the power structures and economic models were created entirely in the absence of women, and they were purposefully created, in part, *to exclude women*. White men (in their own countries and globally through empire-building) created a tribe of ownership and influence and they got used to deciding how much pie there was and dividing it as they saw fit. There was nothing motivating that homogenised group to offer women and other marginalised groups more opportunity, say and representation. Even when individual white men acted as allies, the structures didn't support those actions.

Let me tell you a story that starkly highlights the staying power of the patriarchy. In the 1930s, Andriy Stynhach, a

---

13 I'm a feminist but because my father had sadly passed away before I got married, and I love ceremony and tradition, I had a family friend give me away. I don't think anyone at the wedding mistook me for Ivan's property. Also I gave a speech, because I'm not so hung up on tradition I'm letting a man speak for me.

research scientist, established that high doses of progesterone can inhibit ovulation. Sorry, gang, it was again a man who discovered this, but please bear in mind that the plough had put us into the kitchen and we weren't yet readily welcomed into labs. Why have you never heard of this man – the father of the pill? Well, because governments and pharmaceutical companies had no interest in funding or developing his discovery.

In 1939, Russell Marker, a professor at Penn State University, worked out how to synthesise progesterone out of Mexican yams. This meant an oral contraceptive pill was possible. Great news. Why isn't the pill called the Marker? Because no one – not Penn State University, not one pharmaceutical company, not one government – was interested in developing such a pill.

The patriarchy had no interest in allowing women to determine if and when they conceived, even when it was clearly a huge money-making opportunity – which is usually the patriarchy's favourite thing. The social cost was too high. The turkeys weren't going to vote for Christmas, especially if it came with an advent calendar in which each window contained a sweet that could magically give women choice, and the freedom to walk out the door.

In 1951, a reproductive physiologist called Gregory Pincus, who had founded the Worcester Foundation for Experimental Biology, went to a fancy Manhattan dinner party held by the vice president of Planned Parenthood. He sat next to a woman called Margaret Sanger, whose name might ring a bell. She was the founder of the American Birth Control Movement. She helped Pincus get a small grant to start research. He and his lab partner, Min Chueh Chang, resurrected the experiments done in the 1930s (which had been shelved) and found that all that stood between women and the pill was funding. That funding was denied, because the patriarchy is no fool.

Margaret Sanger wrote to Katharine Dexter McCormick,

a wealthy philanthropist and feminist. Katharine Dexter McCormick gave Pincus fifty times his previous budget for research and together they employed John Rock, head of gynaecology at the Free Hospital for Women in Boston.[14] He'd been using similar methods in reverse, to encourage fertility. They combined forces and after various trials, invented the contraceptive pill, which appeared on the cover of *Time* magazine in 1967.

Without feminism, we would never have had the pill. It was driven and funded by women because the patriarchy knows what's good for it: women in the kitchen making no choices and having little influence outside the domestic sphere. If that had not been better for male power structures, we would have had the pill in the 1940s. Imagine the ways history might be different if we'd had freely available contraceptives during the Second World War.

To be clear, individual women choosing to be full-time carers of children is in no way supporting patriarchal structures. Raising children is vital, fulfilling, difficult and very real work that is not to be minimised. Women and men creating warm family home environments, caring for elderly relatives and disabled loved ones is necessary, underappreciated and usually unpaid work. Some people can't or don't need to work for money, and there is no reason why everyone should. But a system that restricts the contributions of women as a group, making female influence exceptional, drives a self-serving, male-dominated system.

The availability of the pill was the first death knell of the patriarchy. My definition is conveniently alliterative: the

---

14 The Free Hospital for Women in Boston, Massachusetts was originally built so poor women could receive free treatment, but soon gained such an excellent reputation other women wanted to go there and it extended its scope.

patriarchy is the blip in history known as the pastoral life – the time between the plough and the pill.

In the last few years, feminism has become a word synonymous with any choice that a woman makes. Occasionally, if I tell someone about the concept of 'I'm a feminist but …' they respond, 'But the whole point of feminism is that you can do whatever you want and you're not restricted by anyone else's idea of how to be a woman.' If that were true, feminism wouldn't be worth having. Just do anything, any time, any how, any way, without questioning, growing, learning from others or building strength or endurance? Where's the value in that?

Some choices women make are not feminist. Feminism is about creating change and emboldening women as a group. If you choose to take an afternoon off to go to a protest for some kind of fight you really believe in, then yes, you're supporting a feminist cause. But what if you're a white woman and the march happens to be made up of 90 per cent white women and you're looking for your friends in the crowd and you thoughtlessly barge in front of a South Asian woman who, unbeknown to you, is feeling a little ignored or alienated in the crowd?

Now imagine the way you might feel at a different march where the gender split was 90–10 male to female. Imagine if a really loud, tall man pushed in front of you and didn't see you there. Imagine if he cut across your path to get to his friends and you got pushed to the kerb while he and his friends all laughed together. That was the way some women of colour reported they felt at the January 2017 Women's March.

It is a choice to be a man who talks over women, mansplains, manspreads and denies male privilege. Men who refuse to acknowledge their advantages could take the time to listen, look around them, have a think, do a cursory Google and start to notice some of their own patterns and the power structures they benefit from. If they continue to tell us that they worked hard to get what they've got in life and no one gave them a free ride, and claim that women don't want the kind of responsibilities that go with being in power roles, then we see those men as choosing to put on blinkers and benefiting from their privilege while living in denial.

The world doesn't have to hand every man a million pounds in cash for most of its structures to put men as a group front and centre. But here's the thing: the men it mostly favours happen to be white, straight, cis and non-disabled. On the great Venn diagram of privilege, if you share any of those identities with the guys in charge, congratulations, you've won one or more of life's lotteries. If you've already mounted an argument in your head about why that doesn't apply to you, despite your sharing one of those qualities with the chaps who've made the decisions, laws and handouts, then the most likely explanation is that – just like the men who don't see their advantages – you don't want to look. It's not that the patriarchy is creating advantages with you in mind, it's that it's in their interests to service white, straight, cis, non-disabled people first and best, because that's the queue they're in for access, rights and opportunity.

Those who've been in power for generations have created a system that favours themselves, because human beings with access to the chocolate box have a habit of taking out the salted caramels and leaving the orange ones nobody likes. Remember – the patriarchy won't sponsor a pill that doesn't celebrate the baby-making status quo. In addition, it's easy for human beings to think that everyone else has the same needs as they do. If you've never needed a wheelchair ramp, you have to have the empathy to imagine or notice someone else struggling to have their needs met in a building designed to meet yours.

Individual powerful people who are female, queer, disabled, not white or a combination of these things, have to fit into existing patriarchal structures and are usually required to homogenise in a way that makes changing things for others in their tribe difficult. Women have to act like one of the boys to be accepted on a building site or on the trading floor. Gay people have often closeted themselves to be able to advance in business and in some industries and nations still have to, to survive. The more of these identities you share, the more likely you are to be marginalised, demoralised and/or criminalised by the power base.[15]

Money also plays a huge factor. A person who is upper middle class, rich and has extra smarts or talent will pretty much be guaranteed to find many doors open to them. Success is almost a certainty. A person who is rich and has an average IQ and no special sporting or singing prowess will probably do very well in life. Someone who is rich and not very clever, talented or charming will do just fine. They'll be supported by their family, their family's connections and the world's assumption that people who look wealthy are usually good at things.

Someone who is poor but academically gifted, or a genius at football, or very good at acting, might break through if they work extremely hard, knock on many doors and get the attention of some influential allies. If a person is poor and of average IQ and has no special gifts, they will end up where they began in life. They will die earlier and in worse health than their middle-class counterpart. If a person does not have

---

15 When I heard Kimberly Bryant, the CEO of Black Girls Code, speak, she said, 'Black girls are routinely marginalised, demoralised and criminalised', and it rang so true and stuck with me, hard. I now see these three verbs manifest everywhere.

an aptitude for school, sport or music and has no money at all, they will end up in a worse place than where they started out. They have a better than average chance of going to jail or becoming homeless.

Feminism must recognise that class and cash, for example, matter, because they advantage some of us and disadvantage others of us the same way that gender does. I am a woman, so if I were to get into a physical fight with a man I would probably lose, whether that man were black or white. However, I am a white woman, so if I were to take a black man to court, he would probably lose, because being white gives you extra plausibility in the eyes of the law. If you dispute this, imagine right now that I am passing a black man on the street and a police officer walks by and I shout, 'That man stole my phone!' You know that the police would spring into action. Now imagine that situation is reversed and the black man accuses me of theft. The police would probably hesitate because their unconscious bias would tell them that white people are usually wealthier than black people and white women do not steal phones from black men. They'd likely question that man and his motives before they approached me. If they did question me, they'd likely do it in an apologetic or polite manner.

This effect is neutralised if you add fame to the mix. Bill Cosby, for example, has the extra credibility of celebrity which trumps the usual pattern of race privilege. The word of fifty-eight women in the public domain and Cosby's own testimony that he gave a woman Quaaludes and had sex with her when she was unconscious was not enough to get a jury to agree that he was guilty. Assumed credibility in the eyes of the law and public opinion is a tent pole of privilege that is often over-looked. Sometimes it is a direct result of other random elements like whiteness, maleness or age, but it almost always comes free with titles and fame. The Very Right Reverend and Professor

Emeritus gigs come with keys to the executive washroom and the presumption of innocence.

Privilege and oppression are complicated. This is why Kimberlé Crenshaw developed a language for talking about the intersections between them. I am white. I am effectively a straight woman (with some pansexual tendencies but not enough to call myself queer in any way that would bring me oppression). I am cisgendered. I am not disabled. When I was growing up, my family wasn't rich, but nor were we poor. We always had lots of books in the house and were encouraged to read and study. I experienced being broke after I joined a cult where I was limited in the hours that I could do paid, secular work. I had my electricity cut off and, at times, didn't have enough money for food. However, I am aware that broke and poor are not the same thing. Having no money and having no hope and no way out of poverty are very different things. I have always lived in peaceful countries and have never had to run from war, occupation or climate change.

Overall, on the Venn diagram of life's opportunities, I am very privileged, so I need to redress the balance. 'Guilty' feminism is a great place to blow off steam about things that don't really matter, but this is important. We can't say, 'I'm a feminist but I don't recognise where inequality favours me', because then we're really saying, 'I'm not a feminist at all'. For this reason, I've asked respected colleagues who are black, of South Asian origin, queer, trans and disabled to speak about their experiences to educate all of us, no matter how many intersections of oppression or privilege we cross. I say this only because it is important that society starts to make this a norm: I've paid them to do it.[16] It is essential for everyone to understand that education

---

16 Some contributors requested their fee go to the charity or cause they represent.

is a valuable commodity and that if we ask women of colour, queer women or disabled women to share their experiences and insights, we should pay whatever we can, whenever we can, especially if our venture is profitable. It is not a privilege for them to appear in a book or to have 'exposure'. It is a privilege for readers to learn about their experiences if we have not lived them ourselves and necessary representation if we have.

I interviewed Jessamyn Stanley, Zoe Coombs Marr, Susan Wokoma, Bisha K. Ali, Reubs Walsh, Becca Bunce, Amika George, Mo Mansfied and Leyla Hussein and featured a piece from Hannah Gadsby. These conversations will be woven into various chapters of this book to make the read representative of more life experiences. In doing so I hope to bring the perspectives of black, Asian, queer, trans and disabled women so that we can all understand better the challenges feminism presents to others. It's important to understand that doors that might be routinely open to you, are padlocked to someone else.

Making change

Men in all cultures (and especially white men in white-dominated cultures) have benefited from exclusive inclusion for thousands of years. The quota system worked in their favour until really very recently. We could also call this the patriarchy. The patriarchy, for those who hear this word bandied around and aren't quite clear what it is (and are not reading the footnotes carefully) is a combination of intersecting systems run by men which grant them privilege, authority, social capital and power and often exclude or exploit women.

The patriarchy is also the male-authored, male-dominated fabric of society which advertises male views, skills and quality as superior and frames history and delivers social commentary through a male lens. The patriarchy oppresses all marginalised people regardless of gender, so it's not great for poor or working-class men and it even makes rich, straight, white guys conform to macho ideals of how men should behave, asking them to suppress their emotions and toying with their mental health. The patriarchy gifts power to those who misuse it and obscene amounts of money to those who don't need it. The patriarchy sucks. In the following chapters, I'll explain how it sucks in more detail.

Where women have been included, they've had to fight so hard for it, it brings tears to your eyes. Change is painfully slow, but it's happening. In 2015, the leadership of the United States Patent and Trademark Office was taken by a woman for the first time. Michelle K. Lee is also the first person of colour to take the role. Michelle was thought to be a truly outstanding candidate, who had built her own television as a child. Her recent achievement inspires hope.

Today 51 per cent of GPs in the UK are female, something Elizabeth Garrett Anderson, the first British female doctor, may never have imagined possible. It is now normal for society to include women as doctors and for women to include themselves in medical training. The male-dominated system did not make way for Elizabeth and those who came after her. Feminism is responsible for that. Feminism is the best tool we have for making sure women are included in positions of influence and innovation. It's not perfect and it's not cohesive, but it's responsible for all the changes we have made to date.

The women who requested, demanded and shed blood for inclusion have enabled women today to feel that the medical profession is somewhere they belong and something that girls are entitled to work towards. This does not mean that women equals feminism. Florence Nightingale was, by all accounts, a terrific nurse but she wasn't keen on women becoming doctors and preferred them to train as nurses. In fact, she fell out with her close friend Dr Elizabeth Blackwell, the first female American doctor, over this issue.

Elizabeth Garrett Anderson did not just achieve her goal to become the first British female doctor and enjoy being the exception to the rule and use it to make herself feel more important than other women. She set up a teaching school to train as many women as possible in medicine. That school still exists today and is part of University College London. She did not just make her own space; she changed the whole environment of medicine and made wonderful things possible.[17]

Those who challenge and change the male-dominated power structures are responsible for feminism.

Feminism does its job for each generation, and each decade society declares that the job is done. But the statistics demonstrate that the patriarchy still exists and that feminism is still a necessary force. In 2016 the percentage of female CEOs of Fortune 500 companies dropped from 5.5 per cent to 4 per cent. *Dropped.*

In 1995, 11.3 per cent of national parliamentarians were female, globally. In June 2016 that percentage had risen to 22.8 per cent. At this rate, it'll be 2045 before we get to 50 per cent. That seems like a great year to set a science fiction film, not a reasonable goal for equal representation for equal taxation.

The gender balance is so poor for positions of control and influence that we have to accept either that straight, white men are better at everything or that things are unfair. They are the only options. If we do not believe that straight, white men should almost exclusively decide on the future of our economy, environment and social structures, and create the habitat in

---

17 She also fought for the vote and died one year before she saw it granted. Her sister was the famous suffragist Millicent Fawcett recently honoured with a statue in Parliament Square.

which the small number of women who break through work, then we need feminism.

Many people disagree. What about asking those same people if women should be considered for positions of influence and if roles should be granted on the basis of merit rather than gender? Some of them would admit that women have valuable insights from their diverse life experiences and that including those views would improve the quality of decisions made in government, stories told in films and moves made by large corporations. It's possible many would concede that white men left to their own devices have tanked the economy any number of times, caused almighty death tolls in their quest for conflict and are driving our precious environment off a cliff.

If enough people can see that the world could be better and fairer, and certainly couldn't be any worse if women were given a fair crack of the leadership whip, what stands in our way? Why do we make gains in gender representation at such a glacial pace?

The answer is that the patriarchy has nothing to gain and everything to lose if all genders are given a say.[18] And since at least some privileged women can choose (thanks to the pill) if, when and how we have and care for children, the patriarchy has had to come up with other excuses not to include us. We are not suited to leadership. We are too emotional. We are the wrong kind of emotional. We may want to leave occasionally to give birth and breastfeed. We are too focused on our children and don't give our careers 100 per cent. We are not confident enough. If we were good enough, we'd have got there on merit.

---

18 It is important to acknowledge that there are more than two genders, and that some people identify as non-binary, which means they are neither male nor female.

But what is ignored is that the institutions to which we need to gain access, in order to have power and influence in the current system, are created by and for men. This means women are often looked at with suspicion when we walk through the door, and the working environment is concrete rather than plastic, so it is fundamentally unable to cater for diversity.

Men generally have bigger feet than women, but bigger shoes are not objectively better. The structure and fabric of most industries mean that women have to work in clown shoes, and sometimes that means we trip over our feet. It's okay to ask parliaments, banks, law firms, charities and comedy clubs to make changes to accommodate the half of the population that deserves a place there. They had to build ladies' loos in the House of Commons when women first became MPs in 1919. Why does that have to be where the changes stop? We feel guilty asking for change because we've been trained to fit in and be accommodating and not make a fuss. Guess who trained us to do that? The patriarchy.

The political landscape of 2018 is a pretty scary place for women. Many parts of the globe are violent, punitive, oppressive places for women to exist. The relatively progressive United States of America currently has a president who was caught boasting on tape about sexually assaulting women and laughed it off as 'locker room talk' while on the campaign trail. Lots of (mostly white) women voted for him. (White men voted for him too, but women are the only ones expected to have known better. White men get a free pass for 'furthering their own interests'.) He is constantly photographed making momentous decisions that affect the political, environmental, fiscal and reproductive climate for women, while surrounded overwhelmingly by old white men.

Brexit means the United Kingdom is going to lose a great deal of legislation created to protect gender equality and women's rights. We will have to request, and in some cases demand, those rights back. It feels as if this is a time when feminists need to get on the same page, or at least agree to work in tandem on a series of complementary pages. This is a great time for women who haven't yet come to feminism to learn about it, embrace it and use it to influence, debate, fight and win rights and representation for our generation and the next.

We need feminism right now, and we don't just need it from the most self-assured, academic, gung-ho, self-sacrificing, full-time, right-on feminists. We need them and we need them badly. But we also need an army of feminists in every office, hospital, school and shopping centre. We need an army of uncertain, amateur feminists who don't let the fact that their favourite song is by R. Kelly and they're addicted to *The Bachelor* put them off making a difference. It's going to take a lot of us to show up and include ourselves in the existing patriarchal structures and have the courage to change them. It's going to take a tribe of mainstream feminists, radical feminists and guilty feminists to make the brave moves required. Many more of us will have to take up space, ask for time and assume and, if necessary, demand inclusion for ourselves and, crucially, for others.

Just as individual women choosing full-time parenting don't feed the patriarchy, individual women in boardrooms don't feed feminism. Women have to amplify and endorse other women they believe in, the way men have endorsed other men for thousands of years, which is why they own the Monopoly board and a man is almost always the banker. The patriarchy is not a bunch of individual men, each one serving himself. It's structural advantage. It's a system fighting for the status quo. Feminism is a system fighting for change.

In 2016 I heard legendary second-wave feminist Gloria Steinem speak and she said of feminism: 'A movement needs to be moving somewhere. Where are we going?' It feels to me like feminism stopped moving for a while because it was underpowered and underfunded. Recently it has been dramatically jump-started. Let's be honest, most feminists feel guilty, because most feminists are women and women have been trained to feel guilty because it maintains the status quo. Guilt makes us feel ashamed and when we are ashamed we feel less entitled to take action. We could spend our whole life trying to remove the guilt, or we could accept it as the distraction it is and crack on with the fight. Guilty feminists unite – we're moving. Let's ride this incoming fifth wave like we stole it from the patriarchy and they're not getting it back.

Part 2

Now We're Here, What Do We Do About It?

Drink the Kool-Aid – Just One Calorie

I'm a feminist but once when getting on a light aircraft from Cape Cod to Boston, I was publicly asked to declare my weight and I lied by twenty pounds, endangering my own life as well as the life of the pilot, the other passengers and a Border Collie that was along for the ride.

What the papers say

I read that a survey found that 97 per cent of women have negative thoughts about their bodies every single day. I didn't believe it.

Three per cent of women like their body? That seems high. Are they pretending? That was my first deep gut response. Who are these women who are happy with their bodies and can go all day, getting dressed and undressed, glimpsing themselves in mirrors and shop windows and never ever wishing they looked different? I don't think I know these women. Even those of us who are consciously trying to like our bodies report a long hard battle with the disdain we've had for them.

Why is that a concern to feminism? Isn't it trivial? Who cares if we're dissatisfied with our thighs? Haven't we got more important things to be getting on with? 'Sure, sure. We've been brainwashed by billboards. Blah, blah, blah.' Shouldn't we accept that we'll always be on a diet, and work on getting more female MPs into the cabinet? Well, no. It's important that as individual women we start to truly sort this out for ourselves emotionally. We can't simply buy wise feminist texts about beauty myths and diet industries and let them pile up dustily in our loo, next to our bathroom scales and under our magnifying mirrors, where daily we obsess about cosmetic perfection. Body-positive messages have to be not only intellectualised but also internalised into our actual bodies, where they're needed. It's crucial, because otherwise we will continue to carry the delusion that the primary purpose of a woman is to be decorative and desirable. Everything about our environment, the media and the patriarchy is sending us daily messages that we are ornamental property like a flash car, a pretty painting or an attractive sofa with a matching ottoman. This is why I want to address it up top. Our attitude to the very stuff we are made of determines how powerful a feminist – guilty or otherwise – we can be.

Remember how the plough turned us from economic equals, or even superiors, into owned goods to be traded from our fathers to our husbands for a dowry price? (At least, that's the short version.) That's why we feel this need to be 'good to look at'. We need to look youthful so we will be a top pick in *Which?* magazine's Deal of the Month section and someone will want to buy us. That feeling never seems to go away, even if women are happily single with no interest in finding a partner, married with six children or menopausal, because – again – capitalism is no friend to feminism.

Once the marketplace worked out that it could sustain our desire to look like a pretty piece of stock in Harrods' window, it started to bottle that promise and sell, sell, sell. What all the potions, perfumes and pills are marketing is the same thing – possibility. The possibility that we can be turned into the shiniest, most desirable bit of kit in the shop and not end up on the two-for-one rack in the Boxing Day sale. The structure is designed to make the stock feel competitive. We look at other women's thighs, eyes and highlights and worry that ours are subpar. We are our own gocompare.com – checking out the competition and giving ourselves a one-star review.

Look at the language society uses to describe promiscuous women. She's cheap (when she should be expensive). She gives it away (when she should make them pay). Every time we criticise our body, we objectify it and commodify ourselves. We make ourselves public property. This is a big problem for women as individuals and for feminism.

It's not that men don't care about their appearance or worry about their weight or hair loss. Of course they do. But men are not constantly given signals by their environment, the media and their families that their looks are their first and most important asset. The patriarchy gave us this burden, and it gave men the encumbrance of being the sole breadwinner when we left the nomadic life behind and they took on the responsibility of the plough. At this point men were rated on their ability to create and store wealth and any skills, talents or smarts that would allow them to do this. Boys are encouraged to run fast, talk fast and think fast – all good skills for stockpiling cash. Physical appearance is one of many features that can give men status, but it's by no means the first or most important.

Almost every week some horrendous viral article claims

that women will be less sexually attractive if we are funny, less desirable if we're cleverer than the man we're dating or that we will emasculate our husbands if we earn more or have a higher-profile role.

Here are a few examples.

From a pop psychology magazine . . .

New Research Explains Why Smart
Women Intimidate Men[1]

A low-brow website . . .

Why Funny Chicks Can't Get Laid[2]

And a national broadsheet newspaper . . .

Female Breadwinners: How Earning
More Can Poison Your Marriage (But
not in the way you'd expect)[3]

Some of the articles are aimed at men, to reframe how they feel about the woman they're already with.

How to Date a Woman Who Earns More
Than You: If You're in a Relationship With
a Woman Who Has the Power Financially
You Might Feel Emasculated[4]

---

1 *Psychology Today*, 22 September 2016.
2 *Blunt Monkey*, 30 August 2011. An article for the release of *Bridesmaids* about how no one fancies the cast.
3 *Daily Telegraph*, September 2014.
4 *Men's Fitness*, April 2017.

Not only are we told that it's of paramount importance to be pretty, we're told that being funny, clever and successful can actually detract from our worth. This implies that being pretty, and nothing else, is better than being pretty and talented. This is why teenage girls are sometimes encouraged by their peers to 'play dumb', sit out of sports to avoid getting sweaty or laugh at boys' jokes rather than go for the gag. Try as I might on Google, I couldn't find one article that claimed humourless men with low IQs and large overdrafts were more desirable partners.

When I did an internet search for 'women don't find clever men sexy', the first three articles listed were: *Men don't Fancy Clever Women Unless They're Very Attractive* (Daily Mail)[5], *Why Men don't Like Funny Women* (The Atlantic)[6] and *Do Men Really have a Problem with Witty Women?* (The Telegraph)[7]. Google flipped my search because it figured I'd made a mistake or it just had no relevant material for me. I did find an article in *Men's Health* magazine titled *Women are Happier with Less Attractive Men Says Science.*[8]

All this means that women, as a group, are at a significant disadvantage – and my adolescent experience gives me a particular perspective on this. As a young Jehovah's Witness I was told to cease my education and not to prioritise a relationship or children or a mortgage because Armageddon was coming, and what was urgent was spreading the good news so that others could be saved. Despite being a book-smart teenager who'd only been introduced to the religion at fourteen years of age, I acted against my own self-interest and deep desire to get a degree and become a writer and performer.

---

5 *Daily Mail*, 5 August 2016
6 *The Atlantic*, 19 November 2015
7 *The Telegraph*, 10 March 2015
8 *Men's Health*, September 2017.

I chose to make ridiculous, self-destructive choices which roadblocked my love life, career and financial opportunities. I had been in the path of so much propaganda I started to feel deep in my bones that this was my only option. I threw away a chance at a functional, exciting life at the age of sixteen when I tore up my university application form.

I did this because I was a member of a cult. I call the Jehovah's Witnesses a cult because they ban friendships outside the organisation and the punishment for breaking the rules or even just disagreeing with the doctrines is shunning, which means you must conform or you'll find yourself alone. I think that similarly, and in some cases just as dangerously, women are invited into a cult at the age of twelve (or even younger), where we are brainwashed to believe that unless we adhere to arbitrary and unachievable cosmetic standards we have little value and further, that attributes such as intelligence and talent can diminish our value. Consequently, we act in ways that inhibit, limit or even damage ourselves for this Cult of the Body that insists we drink the low-cal Kool-Aid.

If we do not take measures to fight this indoctrination, we walk into a pitch at a funding meeting and allow our male competitors to have a serious advantage. We enter the room inside our own body, which we have learned to see as an enemy. We have, that morning, while preparing for the presentation, looked in the mirror and said negative, hateful things about our own breathing, living, warm being. This may have happened out loud and with full angst and emotion. I've certainly cried in front of the mirror, abandoning outfit after outfit as unflattering and hateful on what I saw as my stupid, fat, ugly body. It may have happened imperceptibly quickly, like a daily ritual we don't even remember. Just a flicker of dissatisfaction as we check in with all the ways in which our body is different from the ones we see on prime-time television.

We have walked into a meeting, at odds with ourselves, uncomfortable inside the only vehicle we can drive. If we are secretly feeling miserable and useless because we have put on half a stone again, and old because we have not had time to touch up our roots, we cannot possibly be as central, included and confident in that room as our older, fatter, greyer male counterpart who sees his body as either a perfectly good example of the genre or entirely irrelevant in a work context.

It is more difficult to convince the room that we deserve the funding for our film, scientific study, academic research, start-up, charity or passion project if we have spent the morning telling ourselves that we don't deserve breakfast because we are not deliberately underweight, like many of the women we admire in American sitcoms. We cannot confidently point to the work we have done if we dislike the arm we are pointing with because we have learned in a women's magazine that it has a 'bingo wing' and with only fifteen minutes of weight training daily that we've been 'too lazy' to do, that could be eradicated.

When we give out micro-signals betraying we are uncomfortable in our own skin, then the funding is less likely to go to us. These factors are working in tiny increments, but they're working hard every single day. We have to take our bodies on dates, to parties, to parent–teacher meetings, into negotiations and job interviews. We need to take them on marches and protests. These are places we need to be seen, heard and respected if we are going to make the sorts of strides that feminism requires us to in the twenty-first century.

It's easy to feel that unless we are conforming to the doctrine of the perfect body we will be isolated and alone. Many women see themselves as outsiders from the club and self-exclude from various social situations because they feel they look nothing like the billboard ideal and never will, so they need to 'withdraw from the race'. When I left the Jehovah's Witnesses, I surrounded myself with people who thought differently from my religious friends, which was an easy way to acclimatise to a new life. How can we get out of the body club when almost everyone is in it and there is no one to save us? We need to gently wake up and save ourselves.

You might think I'm overdramatising the situation but 97 per cent of us do not like our bodies, so something is going on.

What if we took time to deconstruct these feelings and retrained our brains to see ourselves as contributors, not belongings? What if even a chunky minority of us started to realise that it's not our responsibility to be ornamental? What if an influential, infectious few of us decided that we weren't for sale – even psychologically – and understood that the root of our insecurities is patriarchal and that we don't have to participate?

That doesn't mean we can't be attractive, feel desirable and enjoy decorating ourselves. None of this stops us being athletic, flexible, strong and fast. In fact, I think the liberation of the need to advertise ourselves is the very thing that allows us to nourish, move and accessorise our bodies with freedom, flair and joy. What if we could love our bodies just as they are, while getting to know their new capabilities? What if we could enjoy our sexuality without inhibition and genuinely see ourselves as hot as hell? What if we weren't tempted to pay others for permission to love ourselves? Well, that might screw the patriarchy right up.

Me and my guilty body

I want to tell you that I have it sussed by now, and I'm pretty sure that's what you want to hear. The truth is that – unsurprisingly, given I'm writing a book like this, containing a chapter like this – I'm a Humpty Dumpty feminist. Used to be fat. Now a bit broken. No amount of men could put me together again. I'm well aware that my only chance at a fix is all the Queen's forces and all the Queen's Zen – and the bad news is, I'm the Queen. Let me tell you how I ended up this way.

When I was a Jehovah's Witness adolescent, exploring my own body came under the heading 'sins of the flesh'. Masturbation was 'gross uncleanness' and a sin you would be expected to confess to the elders,[9] which is enough to put a teenage girl off trying it even once. I was entirely unathletic and sedentary by nature anyway, but had I been tempted to enjoy moving my body the Watchtower Society[10] would have discouraged it. Gyms weren't banned, but they were frowned upon as 'worldly places' where people went to make their bodies 'showy' and 'sexually attractive'. First Timothy 4 v. 8 was often quoted by the elders: 'Physical training is beneficial for a little; but godly devotion is beneficial for all things.'

A friend of mine wanted me to train for a triathlon with her, but her father found out and wouldn't allow it because competitive sports were discouraged. Professional sporting careers were right out.[11] Yoga wasn't allowed because if you let your mind go blank 'the demons would get in'. You might think I'm exaggerating, and I wish I were. All this created an atmosphere in which I didn't look at my naked body getting in and out of the shower. I didn't dress it to show it off because you were only meant to 'court' a young 'brother' with a 'view to marriage', and I didn't want to get married. I was still a child and far more Sandra Dee than Rizzo.

---

9 Elders are self-appointed 'older men' in the congregation who have a teaching and judicial role.

10 The Jehovah's Witnesses are owned and run by the Watchtower Society.

11 Neither Venus nor Serena Williams are official, baptised Jehovah's Witnesses. Some families would be too strict to let their kids watch Wimbledon on television, much less participate in it.

My body was changing, developing breasts, curves, pubic hair and starting to ovulate, and throughout that metamorphosis, I looked away. I've heard stories of other people seeing their pubic hair growing in for the first time and being fascinated or embarrassed. I honestly have no memory of it happening.

The elders told us that our bodies were a pathway to vanity and sin, but my greatest fear was that my body wasn't. I suspected that my body would lead me nowhere dark or dangerous because no one would ever be attracted to it.

Consequently, I ignored it. All the normal vices explored by young people like booze, drugs and sex were banned. Even close, tactile friendships weren't the done thing. Knocking on doors in the heat was extremely dull and unstimulating and young people were expected to do this full-time in lieu of university. The work was unpaid, so we had part-time minimum-wage jobs to pay our bills. This left us with little free time, no cash and zero thrills. The only legal, affordable high was sugar, so I put on weight.

I lived in an Australian beach town where being fat made you unattractive at best, invisible at least and a target of derision at worst. Although I was frightened of my body, I did have a deeply submerged longing to be desirable, because the cult couldn't eradicate the billboards which had been erected to cause doubt in young women like me. I also hated being larger than necessary. I was already bigger than most women, being five foot nine and a half and having a relatively large head, broad shoulders and sizeable hands and feet.

Once, when working in a jewellery store as a teenager, I offered my wrist to a colleague who wanted to check that a bracelet was about 'the right size for a woman'. He laughed and said, 'Not you! Your wrists are big, like a man's!' I was so devastated, I walked out of the shop without a word and without my bag. Looking back, he was clumsy and thoughtless (and, I now realise, pretty transphobic in his assumptions about what a 'woman's' wrist should look like). He was also trying to flirt with my petite manager, but I thought it was about me, and I put that experience, with others like it, in a bag and carried it with me wherever I went.

I hated seeing myself in photographs next to other girls because I always felt like Gulliver next to their Lilliputian frames. I used to joke that I could dwarf national monuments in holiday pictures. I didn't like taking up space and getting in people's way. I had been trained to think that women were meant to be petite, and that was something my skeleton would never allow, so my aim was to be as small as possible. When I meet podcast listeners, they sometimes say with surprise, 'You're not particularly tall or large. The way you talk about yourself, I was expecting you to be a giant.' Not that it would matter if I were, but I'm not Gulliver, although that's my self-imposed family nickname. I'm just a regular, tallish woman. At the moment, I'm around a British size 12 to 14. I suspect I think I'm bigger than I am, but I still have carry-on baggage, even if I've got rid of most of the suitcases.

I went on the crazy crash diets my friends were recommending in the 1990s. Fruit till lunchtime. Nothing but fruit all day, every day for a month at a time. Only meat and salad. Only meat. Only salad. Only things that cavepeople would eat. Only specific combinations of food groups, only before 6 p.m. I totted up calories, carbs and anything else they told me to, like the Count from *Sesame Street* only with an eating disorder. I have made myself throw up a number of times after overeating. I have taken diet pills of various kinds. For many years I celebrated every time my body got smaller, and then was furious with it when I stopped eating a largely grape-based diet and hungrily had a croissant and discovered I had got bigger again. I'm sure this played havoc with my metabolism.

I have felt guilty for believing that other women should be allowed to take up space in the world and be whatever shape they are while I have, in the past, punished my own body for not conforming to standards I despise. I'm a feminist but I probably like your body more than mine. If you have suffered or are suffering from this right now, you probably feel lonely, but you are far from alone. You are lonely at the most crowded party in the world.

What are you not eating?

Most Western women have a troubled relationship with food. I'm going to go further and say that I think almost all of us have some kind of low-level (or more severe) eating disorder. Many of us are self-medicating with sugar, cheese or bread. Lots of us are routinely overeating because we have decided food is the enemy that stops us from being our best self, but since we find it impossible to limit our diet to dirt and string, then we might as well eat a whole cake to demonstrate to ourselves how pointless it all is.

Others of us are relishing the control with which we can avoid food. Not eating doughnuts becomes its own achievement. Juicing things we used to enjoy tasting, and swiping left on bread even when hungry, is how we prove we are getting the job of being a woman right. Lots of us oscillate between the two.

I realised a couple of years ago that almost every time I met a woman for coffee or even a business meeting, the conversation would begin with the question, 'What are you not eating?'

A: You've lost weight. What are you not eating?
B: I'm not eating carbs.
C: Well, I'm not eating sugar. I completely cut it out and

I feel so much better. It wasn't to lose weight. It was for health reasons, but I've actually lost a stone.

A: Well, you look amazing. What about you, Susan? What are you not eating?

D: I'm not eating Mondays and Wednesdays.

This is only a very mild parody of a conversation I've had hundreds of times over the years. Whether the women are thin or fat or somewhere in between, nearly every conversation is food-obsessed.

The accompanying conversation is almost always about exercise:

A: I'm doing hot yoga now. It makes such a difference.

B: I just cycle everywhere and go to British Military Fitness twice a week.

C: I prefer Bob's Boot Camp because it's got great music and I'm in pain for days afterwards, so I know it's working.

A: I've got a friend that swears by Soul Cycle, but she goes on about it so much it puts me off.

C: Oh god. That's the worst. Why does everyone have to tell you about their exercise regime?

These irony-free conversations are pernicious, and I'm a feminist but I admit I still have them even though I try not to. The reason I'm attempting to give them up for Feminist Lent is that they play right into the methods of a high-control group. Cults don't work if they're policed from the top down. The membership has to keep disseminating the beliefs to each other. They need to keep the disinformation going from one devotee to another and back again. They operate on individuals shaming themselves and each other.

When I was a young cult member, if one of our friends was engaging in 'worldly', unpermitted behaviour like secretly going to a rock concert or wearing a short skirt on the weekend, another of us would report that 'sister' to the elders out of genuine concern. Think Orwell's *1984* in dowdy frocks. We'd encourage each other to keep 'serving Jehovah', and personal lapses were treated with praying, shame, masses of guilt and promises not to disappoint Jehovah again. I see this same behaviour from women, including myself, when it comes to eating and exercising.

Women use language like 'I fell off the wagon' or 'I was good today' or 'I've been terrible this week'. There is even a popular dieting group that has a food group known as 'sins' spelled 'syns', like that's fooling anyone. I've had women ask me to accompany them to the gym to make sure they go (as if they need to be nannied), or tell me they're more likely to go hard in a Zumba class because there they have to dance like *everyone*'s watching. Most of us are paid-up members of this high-control group.

The fat-positive movement seeks to break this arduous pattern and some of its advocates do great work in creating a peaceful, alternative space that allows women to celebrate their bodies. Inevitably, some branches of fat-positive culture create another cult with different rules. I've had friends confide in me that they've started eating mindfully and doing yoga for their mental health and general well-being and have felt the ire of their fat-positive friends when they started to get smaller and stronger. I've read articles saying that fat celebrities who lose weight are selling out and contributing to a dehumanising of the 'fat community'.

Any group that is trying to dictate other people's habits or attitudes towards their own arms, legs, heart and stomach is damaging. Some anonymous anorexia clubs on the internet share information about the best way to self-starve and some (not all!) fat-positive groups aggressively seek to shame people for the almost inevitable results of nourishing, cardiovascular self-care. Being positive about your body doesn't mean hiding from its power and limiting its potential. It means having a personal relationship with it and one that acknowledges that all our bodies and psyches are different. What makes someone else feel healthy and happy might not be right for us, so body positivity can't be a team sport in the same way that feminism is. The body is highly personal. So why can't we just find out what our body needs and do it in a clinical way?

When male friends or husbands of mine want to lose weight, I've seen them approach it as a science. They want to lose fifteen pounds, so they need to take in x calories and expend y. I know not all men have such a straightforward relationship with food, but it is not uncommon for men to be able to diet and exercise with some boredom but little emotion. They might share an exercise app with a mate, but for straight men at least, a cult-like culture seems to exist only in bodybuilding gyms.

It is hard for my husband to understand why something as simple as fuel intake (which is how he sees it) is such an emotional topic, but he wasn't eating nothing but pineapple for a week when he was sixteen, getting light-headed at step aerobics, then feeling miserable on the beach because deprivation and hunger hadn't magically transformed him into a petite blonde with tiny hips. Why would the thought of dieting make him cry? He's never deliberately vomited so he could look better in a party dress, so why would he feel like throwing up when he hears the words 'calorie controlled'?

The pattern that is a damaging part of the cult of the female body is this: every diet book bought, every chocolate finger denied, every gym joined is a *contract* the mind is making with the body. It is not to fuel, energise and nourish.

'If I eat this salad, if I don't eat this box of Quality Street, if I get up early and go for a run – you will change for me. You will get smaller, thinner and tighter.' If we keep our side of the bargain and manage to sustain these behaviours for even a short time and our bodies do not change fast enough, we get angry with them. 'What's the point of treating you well,' we shout at them, 'if you're not going to change?! I have one night out with friends, after all I've done for you this week, and now you're a pound heavier again! You've let me down. I might as well fill you with Ben & Jerry's and never move you off the sofa again, you ungrateful bitch. It's all you deserve. Just get bigger and slower as far as I'm concerned. You're not worth it.'

Imagine a romantic relationship where your partner treated you that way. 'I'll run you a bath and make you dinner . . . if you change. I'll send you romantic texts . . . if you get smaller. I'll give you a back rub, I'll save all the Netflix for you . . . as long as you're lighter at our weigh-in at the end of the week. Don't let me down.' 'What?! Look at all I've done for you! You've not changed? You're the same?! Worse? You're two pounds heavier? I have one Sunday lunch out with friends when I'm not supervising you and making sure you stick to your diet regime, and you gain two pounds! Why do I bother trying for you? You're disgusting. You must hate me. It doesn't matter what I do for you, you'll never be what I want you to be. Never.'

If your partner was talking to you like that, your friends would tell you to pack a bag and get the hell out. They would stage an intervention. How is this an acceptable way to black-mail and emotionally abuse our own bodies?

If you relate to these feelings and emotions, if you're con-stantly depriving or overfeeding your body, if you don't enjoy living in it, looking at it or moving it, it's time to take your body to couples counselling and restructure your relationship with it. You cannot break up with your body, like it's a bad boyfriend or girlfriend. Othering it will only lead to unhappiness because you're handcuffed together like a mismatched couple in a 1940s screwball comedy, no matter what you do. Your body can't make the relationship emotionally healthy without you.

You're in the driver's seat. You've got to start over and make a new arrangement with what's keeping you alive. It is so worthwhile doing this, and I know that only to the extent that I have done it. I am, very much, a work in progress. I'm still walking towards this place, but every step I take towards it makes me feel happier and more powerful.

All the Queen's forces

We have to start treating our bodies as if we love them, because it is an act of internalised misogyny to hate our female bodies. Even if they are larger or smaller than we want them to be or they give us pain, or have cellulite, or we think our toes are weird. We have to nourish and nurture them as if we like them, before we actually do. We have to start with actions and let feelings catch up.

This is true of so much of feminism. Sometimes striking out and doing the brave thing that's in line with the values we aspire to, even though we feel like guilty hypocrites, is the only way to make progress. We have to negotiate our salary, though it makes us feel nauseous, or send the email saying, 'No, I don't have time,' even though we are sitting at the computer screaming, 'Please don't stop liking me!' We have to insist that another woman is brought into a decision-making process, even though the all-male committee is rolling all ten of its eyes.

The most important question is: what does your body need now? Is it hungry? Is it thirsty? Is it sad? Is it bored? You need to sit quietly, close your eyes and ask your body how it feels and what it needs. The first time you ask your body this, your brain might cut in and answer on its behalf, because your body has probably not been allowed to speak for many years. Your brain might claim your body wants chocolate, because your brain has long decided that is your body's greedy, sugar-craving, never-ending, self-destructive agenda. Your mind will brainsplain to your body what it wants and play the patriarchal oppressor to your body's actual needs and desires.

When I was in a cult, I was told that without the organisation, I'd quickly fall into fornication. When I left, I discovered this was nonsense. Turns out they don't call it 'getting lucky' for nothing. All sorts of dark behaviours were anticipated and attributed, by the men running my religion, to the 'untrustworthy heart'. I was told that I shouldn't trust myself or put myself in environments where I might be tempted. Similarly, we are seduced with the idea that left to our own devices we'd want all the sugar, all the time. Advertisements frequently feature women eating chocolate alone, in the bath, in a secluded field or hiding it from others in the house. The only adverts that feature women eating chocolate in public are those where the women discuss the surprisingly low number of calories in the treat. Memes circulate on the internet that depict women as cake and wine addicts and women tag each other and share them declaring, 'This is who I am! Someone who can't be trusted near a Victoria sponge and a bottle of Chardonnay for fear I'll overfeed my body as if it is some sort of rubbish bin.'

Your body probably does like chocolate, cake and chips. Sure. But it's not all it wants all the time. It doesn't want unlimited portions. The body cult is feeding us a lie along with our ice cream and we are eating it up with the same spoon. It is a myth sold to us by the sugar industry that we can't stop eating M&Ms, and it's fake news from the diet industry that we need constant expensive supervision to provide the discipline that our runaway bodies lack.

If you listen to your body and don't let your brain answer, it might want lots of ice cream at first, if you've denied it shame-free sweets for a long time. But if you keep listening at every meal and in between, pretty soon it will want generous portions of nutritious, lovely food. It doesn't want three baguettes in one sitting. It doesn't want all the sugar. It doesn't like being overfull. It doesn't want to go to bed hungry. It doesn't like feeling nauseous and sleepy in the middle of the day. Your brain is screwing your body up with denial and excess, with starving and bingeing, because it's been messed up by your mum, your PE teacher, your best friend from school, your magazine subscription for teenage girls, MTV and that guy you inadvisably slept with at Glastonbury who made that comment about your stomach.

The messages of the body cult are in the pop song on the radio we wake up to, the packaging on the low-fat spread we have for breakfast, the writing on the bus we get to work and the Facebook feed we scroll through a dozen times a day. We've lived in a Derren Brown show-style experiment since birth, trying to subliminally convince us we are hungry all the time and constantly want foods with very few nutrients. Why on earth would our bodies ask for that? Our bodies want to survive and thrive.

Our patriarchy-trained brains should not be running this particular show. Our brains are good for reading maps, learning French verbs and writing strongly worded emails to our MP, but they are just appalling at knowing what food we need. Our brains can be controlling, oppressive and sometimes abusive.

When we start listening to our bodies, most of us discover that we've learned to dull other emotions by activating our taste buds. That's okay. People do things for good reasons. When I was a young Jehovah's Witness, having a chocolate milkshake was a useful strategy to dampen the pain and get some fleeting pleasure when I had nothing else. That strategy is no longer useful to me. It's an old pattern which I now have permission to let go of and leave in the past. I have started to tune back in to my body and feel where the tension is, where the pain lives and the difference between sadness and hunger.

If you had a child who came to you and said, 'I feel sad,' you'd be unlikely to reply, 'Say no more. Just eat this whole packet of biscuits and swallow those feelings while you're at it.' Likewise, if a child said, 'I'm hungry,' you probably wouldn't say, 'You've had a kale salad and a tiny piece of tuna and the book says you can't have anything else till 6 p.m., so distract yourself with water and self-loathing.'

It might take months to unpick the co-dependent, scrambled, controlling relationship between your mind and your body. For some of us it will take years, and we will never ever be a hundred per cent at peace, but we can make huge strides forward and along the way understand that the residue of shame and guilt we carry is natural. That doesn't mean we have to shrug and give in to our conditioning. We don't have to keep buying products that promise we will like ourselves tomorrow just because we will probably never be cured of this way of thinking. If your eyes are bad at seeing long distance, you can know they'll never be fixed and wear glasses to see more clearly. We can create metaphorical glasses for our messed-up minds when re-examining our bodies. When things seem out of focus, we need to remind ourselves to put those glasses on.

All the Queen's Zen – busting a move for feminism

Have you seen the movie *Room*, about the woman who is kidnapped and kept in a dark room with her son? Some of us are doing a *Room* to our bodies and keeping them tied down like hostages who are desperate to be free. Our bodies want to move within their capabilities and the more they move, the more they want to move. Some disabilities make movement difficult – or harder at some times than at others. Whatever our access to movement, we do not want it to be limited by patriarchal forces signalling that we need to bound around like young women on the beach in tampon commercials or not at all.

We need to get to know our bodies so that we can bust a move for feminism. I can think of no one better to take us there than inspirational yoga teacher, fabulous body-positive femme and Instagram legend Jessamyn Stanley. Jessamyn is from North Carolina, was the sixth guest on *The Guilty Feminist* podcast and was the first teacher to get me into a headstand. She uses yoga to move past mental and emotional barriers. Her classes provide a body-positive approach to yoga which celebrates bodies and encourages students to ask 'How do I feel?' rather than 'How do I look?'

Hello, Jessamyn Stanley. How would you describe yourself? Some people call you an Instagram yoga inspiration or a body-positivity guru.
I teach yoga, I write, but more than anything, I'm just a practitioner – definitely not a guru!

I think you've been a very important role model for young people, because you are a sort of icon of body positivity. Have you always been positive about your body?

The more time I spend in the body-positivity community, the more I realise how the people who are allowed to stand on the platform of body positivity often still fit very traditional, patriarchal beauty standards. When you're in the real community, there's a lot of pushback against bodies that strike against the norm. And I think for that reason people see me as being a great example of someone who has a body that's socially unacceptable but has consciously chosen to own it.

I had a terrible relationship with my body my entire life. It is a work in progress. I learned to abuse my body from a very young age, verbally and emotionally. The most negative conversations we have about our bodies are with ourselves. I'm just going to be in a permanent state of recovery for the rest of my life!

What advice would you have for somebody who really does not like her body, and who every day looks in the mirror and thinks, 'This isn't good enough'?
I would ask that person to look within themselves and say, 'Where is that statement coming from?' They should, just for the fun of it, think, 'What if I'm actually perfect? What if everything about me, even the perceived flaws, even the things that I think could be better, is perfect?' And if that could be the case, then they should eliminate everything from their life that doesn't allow them to understand that truth, because that's all it really is.

What about somebody who fears exercising because they fear how people perceive them? What advice would you have for somebody who would like to go to a yoga class but feels like, 'What if I'm the fattest person there?'

This is a topic that I talked about in my book *Every Body Yoga*. It's one of the most common questions I get about being physically active. Running is a great example. You're running and people are shouting things at you – I've experienced this. So what? How long are you going to be worried about what other people think of you? Are you going to spend your entire life not doing things because you're worried about how other people are going to perceive you?

And the reason that other people say those things about you is because that's what they're thinking about themselves, and when you start to understand that dynamic, you realise it's about them, not you.

Can you tell us about being body positive? Is it the same as being fat positive?

I think of fat positivity and body positivity as being two different things. To me, the fat-positivity community is much more radical. If you are being body positive, the most important thing is to listen to what's going on within yourself.

When you taught me yoga you talked about loving your body today and every day and that really appealed to me. There are times when I've felt that the message from the fat-positive movement was that you kind of let the sisterhood down a bit if you lose weight because you're conforming to a stereotype.

Eating is a practice, like yoga is a practice. Thinking about the things that you put into your body is something that every human being needs to do. Food is the fuel for this very expensive machine you have, that you only get one of, that breaks down very easily and isn't getting any younger. Why wouldn't you pay attention to what you're putting in it?

So, can you make changes to your habits and your body while being body positive and fat positive?
Yes: you need to pay attention to what your body tells you. After three decades of life I realised that dairy does not make me feel good. I love cheese so much! I would just sit around eating nacho cheese all day, but it makes me feel awful. So at what point do you just say, 'I'm just not going to do that any more'? It doesn't have anything to do with beauty standards or losing weight. I have to ask, 'What makes me feel good?' Vegetables make me feel good because they come from the earth and I come from the earth. That transcends this need to fit into a specific body box.

I've noticed that the closer my body gets towards a billboard standard, the more easily I can get into that really very dangerous headspace of, 'Oh, if I just made a few more changes, I'd arrive.' It's like, the closer you get, the more critical of yourself you become.
I totally agree. If your body does start to look more in line with these socially acceptable standards, you then have more pressure: 'Well, I'm almost there, so if I just did XYZ things ... ' Even people who do literally look like they could be on magazine covers still feel this way. And I think it's because we are not taught to celebrate our differences. We're taught to fit in.

The main issue is thinking, 'The way that I was born, the way that I showed up on this planet, the way that the world has shaped me – that's not good enough.' We live in a society of quick fixes, like, 'I'm going to do yoga for, like, a month, and I'll drink juices and I'll meditate for five minutes a day, and then magically after all that I'm going to be totally okay with myself,' and that's not how it works.

When I watch you, I see you doing all these incredible graceful moves and your strength is so extraordinary.
This is something I hear a lot. It's like, 'Wow, you're so strong. You're so much stronger than I am'. And really all I do is take my yoga medicine. I just practise.

The real issue why people think 'I can't do that' is that our perception of ourselves is generally so low. And I know this because there are still poses where I'm like, 'Oh man, it's out of my range for XYZ reason' – and is it really? No, it's not. It's just about understanding that it's not automatic. It takes time.

The first thing, in order to get anywhere with any pose – and that includes just sitting still with your eyes closed – is to breathe, and that is the step that many people ignore. As long as you can inhale and exhale, even if you need a machine to help you do that, that's all it is.

That's why I think yoga can be a feminist act – because the connection with the self, the trusting of the self, is what is eroded by the patriarchy. It feels to me like the diet industry memes are saying, 'You cannot be trusted alone with food because your body wants you to eat more than it needs, and unless you police it with this diet club, these scales, these apps, you cannot trust your body.'
It's really important to note that the diet culture exists to make money. It's a 'cult-ure'.

Oh wow. A 'cult-ure'. Yes!
They want to make people feel unsafe and like they need to look for the answers somewhere else. 'You don't know how to live your life, you don't know how to exist on this planet because you yourself are flawed.' That's how you can sell diet clubs, diet food, diet drinks, based on that core idea.

I think it's our responsibility as humans to turn away from the idea that we need anyone other than ourselves to understand ourselves. So if you say, 'Hmm, do I want to eat a full dozen doughnuts?' the answer is, 'Probably not.' No human body wants that. It's about being intuitive and looking within yourself as opposed to looking outside yourself for the answer.

I like going to a yoga class rather than practising on my own, though, because I last longer and I can just focus on the breathing and the physicality. If I do it at home alone, I'm inclined to do twenty minutes and then stop. I get that, but that's actually a very Western model of education in general, but especially of a fitness education. Everyone facing the teacher and moving together is characteristic of Western fitness culture. It's good to learn to do it on your own too and just be with your mat and your breath and if you quit after twenty minutes every time, listen to your body and find out why.

That's interesting, Jessamyn. The yoga class where everyone faces the teacher and the teacher has the answers is Western. Do you think that even the fat-positive movement and the body-positive movement are Western forms of finding safety in conformity, and is that a little bit like the guided yoga class?

Exactly. I think it's very dangerous to rely on the opinions of other people in order to feel strong as an individual. I think that it's great to have the support of others, and I think that there is strength in numbers, but ultimately you can't learn about yourself through another human being. It's always just going to come down to you understanding yourself and that your opinion is all that matters.

Okay, but how do I like my thighs more? I don't want to be a 5'2" petite blonde, because that's not who I am. But I do not like my thighs, and I don't think they are changeable!
It's about accepting where the hate is coming from. Because the hate is something you own and you are the only one who can release it. Everybody has a thing, whether it's their nose or their belly or their upper arms, so stop thinking that it should be different. It is exactly as it needs to be now. And if it changes, it changes. Maybe your thighs like the way that they look, and just because they don't look the way that some magazine editor thinks they should does not mean that they're not beautiful and worthwhile.

As an African-American woman, I know you're very aware of cultural appropriation.[12] **How can we address this when it comes to yoga?**
Appropriation is happening to some degree if your practice has an origin in any culture that is not your own. So,

---

12 Cultural appropriation or misappropriation refers to the adoption of elements of a marginalised culture by a dominant culture without proper acknowledgement, payment or respect.

the most important thing to do is to know that's what you're doing, know that imperialism and colonialism is the reason you feel comfortable doing that. Start to accept that privilege and try to understand it. That's the first step that I'm pretty sure 99 per cent of practitioners are not doing. Everyone is just trying to pretend like they're not the problem. It becomes a grab-bag situation where people are like 'I'm just going to take this iconography, and this chanting, and this white way of dressing, and it's all fine, because – yoga . . . namaste.' That's just not how it works. That's somebody's cultural identity.

I heard an Indian woman who has practised yoga every day of her life say that she feels that the Om connects all humanity and transcends culture as a greater truth like pure maths or musical harmony – which I thought was a really lovely way to look at it. We can be respectful of its origins and also celebrate its greater human truth. I feel like the most important thing is to see that, to understand that, and then see that the truth of yoga, the looking for the light and dark within yourself, that knows no culture. That is a truth that has been found in so many different practices for thousands of years on all continents.

Do you have an 'I'm a feminist but . . . '?
I'm a feminist but I believe feminism is rooted in white supremacy.

We need to stop talking about the body we wish we had and start caring for the one we've got, by taking it out to run around and play or stretch it as far as it wants to go. We can withdraw from what Jessamyn calls the 'cult-ure'. Let's create a network of women who reframe what the media and perfection-marketers are telling us and stop drinking the low-cal Kool-Aid. We don't have to live in the patriarchy's body cult. We've got our own warm, wonderful bodies to live in. They'll take us all the way to the revolution if we can only learn to see them as they are – beautiful, powerful and all ours. If we begin to like our bodies, the next step is understanding that how we take them into rooms can determine how included we feel, which leads us – as guilty feminists – to confidence.

I Just Had a Thought – I Don't Know if It's Worth Mentioning

I'm a feminist but once I left a party without talking to a single person except for apologising to a man who'd stood on my foot.

The story of Al and Bob

Imagine a social experiment, the kind they used to do in the 1960s before ethics had troubled the psychology community very much.

You have identical twin boys, and you call one Al and one Bob. When they're five years old you start giving them pocket money for tidying away their toys. Every week you give Al a pound and Bob 78 pence. If Bob complains, deny it. Tell him he's imagining it. If he shows you the evidence and insists that it's unfair, tell him Al is just that little bit better at helping out.

Bob will probably start to work harder to show that he's as good as Al. Al might start to coast, having been validated by his parent and seen hard evidence in his piggy bank that he's better. No matter how much effort Bob puts in, insist he's not quite as capable as Al. Occasionally, when Bob has excelled, taking the whole afternoon to double-check his homework, fold the laundry and handmake you a card telling you how much he loves you, give him the full pound and say, 'See, Bob, this just shows you can do it when you put the work in! You have to try harder.' Don't do this too often. Just enough for Bob to think that success is possible and keep him striving for it.

You want Al to hear, 'You're amazing. You're a natural!' every day.

When Al and Bob turn six, put news of a pay rise to £1.20 a week in Al's birthday card. Bob's card should be empty. If Bob asks why his pocket money isn't going up, say, 'You need to demonstrate why you deserve it, Bob. Where's your evidence?'

When they're seven, tell the twins it's time one of them became the toy cupboard supervisor, deciding where things go and checking if the games are organised. The other will answer to his brother, and do the actual tidying. Interview them both. Notice that Al comes to the interview with more swagger and an attitude like he's got it in the bag. Give the kid a high five and a fizzy drink. Bob might be more detailed in his answers and overexplain himself nervously in the interview. Do nothing to relax him until he starts to look defeated.

When you give Al the job, congratulate him and tell him he's got natural leadership skills. Give Bob feedback, too. Explain to him that although he was well prepared for his interview and you appreciated his PowerPoint presentation, there was a certain something missing. Tell him he needs to be more like his brother. That he's lacking a certain ... confidence. Issue Al a commensurate pay rise as befits his new role. There's no reason for Bob to get more, as he's effectively doing the same job as before, even if it will take a little longer.

On their ninth birthday, after Bob has been working under Al's often critical supervision for two years, get the boys to rate their skills and abilities. Al will almost certainly give himself a five-star rating for organisation, self-determination, creativity and overall ability. He'll probably tell you that he's confident he's ready to take on more responsibility. Bob may well mark himself down on his general ability and will almost certainly feel that he has no management experience and that his leadership skills are lacking. His morale might be quite low, so reiterate that confidence is important and that you're expecting to see him develop the kind of can-do, know-it-all attitude that his brother exudes. Offer to give him some special after-school confidence training while Al plays *Minecraft* and eats ice cream.

On their tenth birthday, ask the twins if they'd like some pets. When they excitedly say yes, introduce them to Bitsy and Ditsy, two adorable baby hamsters, and tell them they are absolute equal owners of the fluff-balls. As they rush to stroke them, explain that Bob will have to do 90 per cent of the feeding, grooming and hutch-cleaning. Bob may see this as a new job opportunity and ask how much he'll be paid. Explain that hamster care is worthless but needs to be done relentlessly without pay.

When Al's friends come over he'll want to proudly play with the hamsters and show them off, but it's key that he should do little of the actual work. If you see Al refilling their water bowl, loudly say to someone else, 'Isn't Al a great hamster-daddy? Look at him, babysitting the hamsters,' and make sure he hears it. If Bob complains about the extra workload or falls behind in his toy-tidying role, say, 'Well, that's the price of "having it all", Bob. Remember, you're the one who wanted the hamsters.' If Bob complains that Al wanted the hamsters too, say, 'Did he? Or did he just say that to make you happy, Bob?'

Let's roll out this experiment with a whole generation of twin boys. A few Bobs will get angry and grow up to do better than their brothers because they have something to prove. A small number of Bobs will be gifted with so much more natural smarts or talent that they'll sail past their brothers regardless.

As a trend, though, twenty years from the beginning of this social experiment, twin boys called Al will be more confident, greedy for leadership roles, sure of themselves and convinced of their own opinions than their brothers called Bob. It will be an Al's World, not a Bob's World.

People always say that women should be more confident, but confidence is the product of our experience. Lack of confidence is one more thing to feel guilty about, and constantly telling women we are under-confident isn't likely to propel us swaggering through the biggest doors in the land, shouting, 'We've arrived'.

When people tell us to be more confident, they are suggesting that we should behave counter to our experience. They are suggesting we speak up in meetings as if we haven't been spoken over, present our best work as if we haven't been patronised in the past and pitch ideas as if they haven't been stolen before. They are telling us to act like Al, even though we've been treated like Bob. Fake it, Bob, till you make it like Al. This isn't the worst advice in the world, but it's important to acknowledge that there's a reason why women often reveal their anxiety while men swagger about.

People can lack confidence in multiple areas, not just their careers. However, I notice that women most often complain about a deficit of confidence in their workplaces. I've seen a woman charge up to her kid's teacher at the school gate to demand her child be put into a higher maths set and then say, 'I couldn't possibly ask for a meeting with my boss's boss. It's just not me to do something that bold.' I've seen a woman give a hilarious speech at a wedding of 150 mostly strangers, and then claim she'd be too nervous to go on a panel to talk about a topic on which she is an expert. No woman who opens a conference call with, 'I just had a thought and I don't know if it's worth mentioning' tells her children to put their shoes on that way.

I'm not saying no woman lacks confidence on Tinder or at parties. I'm saying that companies and industries that have been constructed for men, by men, often seem impenetrable to women who are confident elsewhere. Once I said to a male friend who declared he intended to direct a film, 'How do you know you'd be a good director?' He said, 'Because I'll be a brilliant director.' That's not an answer! It's a display of confidence. I'd love to direct a film, but a big part of me says, 'What if you take all that money and return nothing? Don't do it!' And a big part of him says, 'You need no evidence but the feeling inside that you're awesome.'

This is by no means the first or only reason why women made up just 7 per cent of the total directors for the top 250 films in 2016, which was 2 per cent down from the previous year.[1] There are other factors such as discrimination, unconscious bias and patriarchal power structures, but to combat these we need more confidence than we've ever had.[2]

Some caveats before we get into the gladiatorial ring of confidence:

1. These are just trends! Men are taller than women. That's an observable pattern. That doesn't tell you anything about Rupert Murdoch and Jerry Hall. Similarly, we

---

[1] Statistics from the San Diego State's Center for the Study of Women in Television and Film.

[2] To combat unconscious bias, Tropfest (a short film festival in Australia) introduced anonymous judging of entries for the first time in 2017 – removing the identifying details of the film-makers for the preliminary rounds – and the proportion of female finalists shot up from around 5 per cent to 50 per cent.

all know individual women who display more confidence than individual men but we can also identify gender trends.

2. Sometimes young women have had more of an 'Al experience' than a 'Bob experience'. There's no need to discourage millennials or Gen Zs, but be warned – seen from a distance a glass ceiling can look like the sky.

3. If you're a woman of any generation who feels like an Al and you don't know what other women are talking about when they complain about sexism, good for you. But the Bobs aren't making it up and your experience is counter to the norm, which is great for you but doesn't eradicate the problem.

4. Confidence isn't everything. There are any number of articles that suggest women don't apply for jobs unless they have 100 per cent of the advertised skills, whereas men assume they need only 60 per cent.[3] The origins of this statistic are dubious, but women regularly share it as a trend they recognise. The conclusion is always that women should be as confident as men. My suggestion would be that men stop talking their way into roles they're not qualified for like, for example, President of the United States of America, and driving the whole thing off a cliff to the detriment of the rest of us. How about men and women both go up for roles they can basically do, with some room to grow, and we meet in the middle at 80 per cent? Confidence without substance is just recklessness.

---

3 This statistic has been debunked because no one can find the source material. It was cited as a study but seems to be an anecdote: http://www.huffingtonpost.co.uk/curt-rice/how-mckinseys-story-became-sheryl-sandbergs-statistic---and-why-it-didnt-deserve-to_b_5198744.html.

5. Cultural differences are a factor, but the trend for a gender confidence gap seems to hold within different countries around the world. American women are often perceived as confident in the UK because displays of bravado are less blatant here in general. Those same women will still be trying to get a word in edgewise back in Silicon Valley.

What is confidence anyway?

I know why I lacked confidence after I left the Jehovah's Witnesses. I'd been in an environment which had discouraged me from following my talents and thinking for myself. When I came out of the bunker, I wasn't a bright-eyed Kimmy Schmidt, I was a nervous, damaged young woman trying to fake it and failing. I didn't like telling people I'd been in a cult because I didn't want them to see me that way. Years later when I came out to a close friend, she said, 'I wasn't sure what had happened to you but I knew something was wrong. I thought you'd been raped because of the way you interacted with men.' In truth, I had never even been kissed. I just radiated fear of the world. I was frightened of men because my life had been ruled by them and because I was scared of sex and anything that might lead to it. You wouldn't know that now if you listened to my podcast or saw me perform. A lack of confidence isn't something you're stuck with. It's a temporary state of mind.

Some women do not know why they lack confidence, and they beat themselves up because they feel they should be confident. Even if they do all their growing in a female environment or an environment which has overtly told them that they can do and be anything they want, they sometimes report that they still apologise three times in an average sentence.

It's not like there's only so much confidence to go around.

Where do some people get their confidence from? How do other people end up with so little? And why does this so often end up dividing along gendered lines? What is confidence when it's out in a limo with RuPaul, anyway?

The word 'confidence' comes to us from the Latin root 'confidere', which means 'to have trust'. A confidence man is a trickster. To share a secret is to break a confidence. *Self-confidence* means you trust yourself.

When most people think of confidence they think of this quality. Someone who trusts themself walks into rooms as if things will go right for them. If they've done something 99 times, they trust they can do it the hundredth. There are two components to self-confidence. One is that you trust in your ability to do something. The other is that you can communicate that trust to the room and *get others to trust in you too*.

This part is a display of micro-signals which expresses the idea: 'I am anticipating a successful outcome of this endeavour'. Sometimes it's the natural result of knowing from experience that you've got a high chance of success. Sometimes it's a performance for other people, to cover up uncertainty. One reason we sometimes suffer from 'impostor syndrome' is that we see other people's displays of confidence and assume it reflects a genuine inner certainty. We feel every single secret doubt, paranoia and insecurity of our own – and never suspect others might be feeling the same.

But there's a second kind of confidence, that for some people goes without saying. This has nothing to do with how successful we think we will be at accomplishing a task. It's how certain we are that we will be included in a group. I call this *tribal confidence*.

If you're trying paintballing for the first time, you might have no reason to believe you'd be good at it, but if you're on your own hen night you will be certain that the group will include you regardless. In fact, you'll be central to proceedings, so your skill won't really matter.

If, on the other hand, you're trying paintballing for the first time on your office awayday in the first week in a new job, and you're the only woman on the team, and everyone else on your side is boasting about their skills, you might start to wish you'd practised because your inclusion in the group might depend on your hand–eye coordination. What if the Software Development Team loses to Sales and Marketing because you keep screwing up? What if you're a better shot than your boss and it pisses him off?

Sometimes our confidence in our ability to do things we know we're good at (our personal confidence) wobbles if we're in a group where we feel our inclusion or belonging depends on that skill (we are lacking tribal confidence). You were a champion paintballer at uni, but now you're trying out for the National Paintballing Major League and you start to doubt yourself and miss easy shots. In other words, you may trust yourself, but if the tribe doesn't demonstrate its trust in you, you can begin to doubt that you should be trusted. You can enter a room feeling like an Al but the group keeps sending signals you're a Bob.

Most people haven't ever broken their confidence down this way, and I'd encourage you to analyse it when you feel nervous. Am I truly doubting my abilities (personal confidence), or am I doubting this room, this group, this date, this friend, this employer, this mother to accept, include or validate me (tribal confidence)? What is the source of the lack of trust? Am I projecting a lack of tribal trust based on past experience, or is it clearly there? If I up the demonstration that I trust myself, does the tribe relax and follow suit, or double down and tell me, 'Girls aren't good at this kind of thing', overtly or covertly? I have heard women of colour talking about the disconnect between the abilities they know they have and those that others assume they have which is incredibly frustrating and a waste of their talents.

People who have almost always known inclusion may be much less affected by tribal confidence. They have built up reserves of trust like money in the bank. 'I've done this before, so this'll be a walk in the park,' Als think. 'Everyone will like me because they always do.' This is because they have been raised with the trust of senior people in their tribe so new tribes don't faze them so much. They've got a home base. Or alternatively, 'I haven't done this before, so I have no need to be good at it first time around.' In either case, they have no lack of tribal confidence so they bathe happily in personal confidence. And one of the most obvious ways in which people assemble themselves into tribes is by gender.

You probably don't notice how much confidence you gain from your gender tribe until you walk into a room and find you're the only woman or the only man.[4] Then you might feel a little less comfortable. I notice that many men feel less comfortable in rooms with a majority of women than women do in rooms of men. This is because women are experienced at being in the minority, especially in business contexts. It isn't remarkable for me to be the only woman on a comedy bill, or for a female lawyer or mechanic to be the only woman at the table or in the workshop. When I speak at women's professional

---

4 A non-binary person is often the only person of their gender in the room and so do not be surprised if they're routinely more nervous than other people, or conversely, if they take huge responsibility for their personal confidence because they have learned to live without tribal confidence unless they are in gender-queer spaces. That won't be the experience of every gender-binary person of course, and this effect will diminish as future generations feel more comfortable with gender fluidity and more non-binary people are visible in society.

networks, a senior male ally is often asked to give an introduction. Almost always he will joke about how unsafe he feels or how he might say the wrong thing or how unusual this is for him. Really? Welcome to our world, buddy. What he doesn't realise is that as odd as it is for him to be in a room full of women, it's just as odd for us to be in the majority. Any woman in a male-dominated profession has to store up extra reserves of personal confidence because tribal confidence is usually in short supply. We've all felt a lack of trust based on nothing except our gender. Men who don't even know us sideline us, patronise us and assume we'll pour the tea.

Children can already identify with their gender tribe when they are very young. This is probably part nature, part nurture. My friend's little girl, Daisy, who was still learning to talk, was asking her mother, 'Mummy's a girl? Daisy's a girl? But Daddy's a boy?' Her mother's response was, 'That's right, darling,' but she told me she was secretly thinking, 'Well, we don't want to impose gender identity on others, sweetheart.' We agreed that gender fluidity is a hard concept to explain to a two-year-old.

Daisy is simply trying to make sense of the world and is finding ways to create categories and tribes. 'People who live in my house.' 'People who go to my nursery school.' 'People who are children and people who are grown-ups.' 'People who are in the girl tribe, like me.' Transgender people often report the experience of being misgendered as children and feeling they were being marshalled into the wrong tribe. Our brains create tribes and categories all the time, as we grow. We identify with tribes where we feel we fit in – or at least won't stand out – because it can make us feel safe.

One way of learning how to operate and discover what the tribe will reward (or what will allow us to stay within it unnoticed) is to follow the typical behaviours of members of our tribe. If little girls see female teachers timidly coming into rooms, saying, 'Mr Johnson, I think the choir has booked this room for practice today, but only if you're not using it. We'll make do if you are,' then they note it and role-model it. Boys do the same if they frequently see male teachers saying, 'All right – everyone out of the room now, it's time for choir practice. Thank you, Miss Andrews. See you next week!'

They will unconsciously spot patterns and norms in their environment, on television and YouTube. They will learn how their tribe behaves and mimic their gestures, verbal cues and ways of entering a room. If Peppa Pig's father is always at the steering wheel of the car, that seeps in. Children start to understand when the tribe trusts people like them and when it doesn't, and they may extrapolate and have less confidence because of what they witness.

At school and at play, we are quickly pushed into gendered tribes. Boys wear shorts and girls wear skirts. Boys build towers and girls dress dolls. We are encouraged to behave differently. If we don't fit into our gender tribe (as transgender or non-binary people will tell you), it can be painful. I recently worked with ShaoLan, the inventor of Chineasy, a method for English speakers to learn Mandarin. She said that the Chinese character for gender, broken down into symbols, means 'the birth of your heart', which I thought was a lovely way of explaining gender. It isn't the birth of your body so much as the birth of your heart. We need to be on the right side of history (as I mentioned in the introduction) as we evolve into an increasingly gender-fluid society, and that means being on the side of a human being's right to declare the birth of their heart rather than have it projected it upon them.

There are often heated arguments over how much of this gendering is imposed on children and how much we have innate gender affiliations, but there are as many studies demonstrating one as the other and no one really knows. We don't have to know its origins to observe its effects.

There's an old experiment, which might be apocryphal but which rings very true, about monkeys who try to get bananas off the top of a ladder. They're always sprayed with a hose, so they discourage new monkeys from going up there. Over time you can replace every monkey who's been soaked but the legend will still exist within the tribe and new monkeys will still be dragged away from the ladder.[5] There's only tenuous evidence showing that such an experiment happened, but the reason this story went viral is there's an anecdotal truth to it.

Tribal confidence, the confidence that we will be included because the group trusts us, is in short supply for women, for very good reasons. If you're a woman and feel certain that you or at least representatives of your tribe will be included in rooms of influence and trusted to act in those rooms, you're not paying attention.

It wasn't very long ago that women were actively and brutally excluded from medical degrees, law firms, parliaments and space programmes, as we've explored in previous chapters. Our tribe is used to being excluded. It is a tradition, like Christmas or morris dancing.

There are a few common responses to being routinely excluded. The first is to self-exclude. Most people who are routinely excluded learn to exclude themselves before anyone else can do it. Do you remember as a teenager assuming you were included in a group of cool teens, only to find that they did not agree? It's the worst feeling in the world. It feels like you've lost something. If you self-exclude, you no longer need confidence and you don't feel you've lost anything the way you

---

5 This is one explanation for how religions evolve.

do when the tribe excludes you. 'Male-dominated professions' are often those where women are actively excluded or where inclusion is made difficult for them. If you keep excluding people, they'll start to do your work for you. In other words, most of the time all you have to do is say 'men only' and most women won't want to be there.

A second common response to exclusion is anger. A small but chunky percentage of a tribe that is routinely excluded starts to demand inclusion. This is where the stereotype of the angry black woman or the humourless, furious lesbian comes from. Anger is a natural residue of exclusion. If you think men don't get angry when they're excluded, try starting up a new women's network in your industry. Hold a women-only *Wonder Woman* movie screening they didn't want to go to in the first place. White men are often angriest at these suggestions, simply because they are not used to exclusion. If every room you've entered has a welcome sign on the door, the first one that reads 'Not For You' is likely to provoke a horrified reaction. Likewise, if you're sure you're the excluded one, it's easy to think you're the *most* excluded and that isn't always true. Straight, white, cis women often get defensive when told their spaces aren't inclusive because we only notice the doors that are closed to us and not the ones that are open to us or the ones we barricade to others.

A third common response to exclusion is persuasion. If you have a particular personality and probably a little privilege in the form of social status, mentoring, education and some book smarts or other talent, you may become skilled at persuasively charming your way past bouncers whose job it is to exclude people like you. Michelle Obama is an expert at this. It's much harder for a white, straight man to develop Michelle-like powers of persuasive influence because it's a muscle he doesn't have to work out.

Let me be clear: self-exclusion and anger are both highly justifiable responses to being ritually excluded, and it's valid to choose either and sometimes we all do. Some days we can't put the extra effort in and bother to show up to that city-of-the-damned industry networking event so that men can talk over the top of us or assume we're the waiter and give us their empty glass. Other days we snap and say, 'Why is there not one woman of colour on this panel when I said I was available?' or, 'You knew I was coming, and yet the room is not wheelchair-accessible! For god's sake!'

There's a time for going home and there's a place for anger, but most of us can do those on our own. To self-include through persuasion, smarts and the deft use of strength and empathy is much more difficult and really worth learning if we want to change the world, especially if we want to create a fairer world for women in general.

As Sheryl Sandberg points out, if a man gets angry and dismissive in a meeting, it's seen as assertive but if a woman does it, it's described as aggressive. I was once asked by an HR exec to coach a man to be more assertive and a woman to be warmer and 'less aggressive' in the same meeting. I responded, 'Well, you have one assertive one and one warm one, what's the problem?' The problem, we both knew, was their styles were not conforming to gendered expectations. We're not on a level playing field but we still need to win the game or at least stay on the board. Not everyone has the energy or desire to become persuasive and influential but if you have a measure of privilege (and you probably do because you're reading a book about feminism), then you might want to pick up the influence and confidence slack for others who can't. To do this, it's useful to know how you operate when you get a creeping sense that the room doesn't not trust *you* so much as it doesn't trust *women*.

Knowing when to hold 'em and knowing when to fold 'em

I was performing at a month-long fringe festival in Australia in 2011 and spent the evenings drinking in the bar with comedians after our shows were done. One night my friend Phillip slipped off early without explanation and turned up again later being vague about his secret midnight rendezvous. The next night, Phillip and Martin disappeared together and two nights after, Bradley vanished too.

I started to feel like I was in some kind of biblical comedy rapture, so I demanded to know what was going on. Phillip caved and said there was an all-night poker game that some of the techs were running. I love Texas Hold 'Em and told the boys I wanted in. It was then I was told it was a men-only game. As discussed, this is the trigger that usually causes self-exclusion, but this time it inflamed my sense of injustice more than it did my fears. I insisted I was a pretty good player and the guys said they believed me but that it wasn't their gig. They were the metrosexual performers on a table of 'real men', and the last thing they could do was turn up with a woman when they'd only just managed to blag invitations for themselves. In other words, they doubted they'd be trusted, so they couldn't turn up with someone who would definitely be deemed untrustworthy on sight, based on gender.

After I'd gone on and on about what kind of sexist poker game these guys wanted to go to anyway, Martin agreed to try to get me in. It was 1 a.m. We walked to a small circus tent in a pitch-dark park where the shows were held in the evenings. Martin told me to wait outside. After a few minutes of fast talking he returned and said, 'All right, you're in.' His look said, 'Do not embarrass me.'

I entered the tent and made eye contact with a man who

was shuffling cards at the end of a long trestle table. He looked like a pirate in a children's book. His face was twice the size of mine and his beard was twice the size of his face. 'This is Digger,' said Martin nervously. 'It's his game.'

'Thanks for having me, Digger,' I said, as loudly as I could manage, trying to demonstrate how much I trusted myself to fit in and play an awesome game of cards. Digger nodded, without a smile. 'Your money's as good as anyone else's,' he said, as if he were already spending it in his head.

More men who looked like Digger came into the room. They knew each other and joshed around, offering each other beers and joints. I took a seat, feeling highly conspicuous in my show clothes – a very femme dress, gold heels and a bowler hat. The game began. I counted twelve men around the table. Nine techs with proper muscles and tattoos, three male performers . . . and me.

I knew I was a pretty good poker player, but the room reeked of suspicion about my girly capabilities. I was determined to play extra well. There was no way I was going to bet like an amateur and confirm their idea that 'women couldn't play'. I had to know when to hold 'em and know when to fold 'em. My heart was beating under my dress. I only drank water because I needed to focus.

Normally I'm an intuitive player. I don't fold my cards early unless they're hopeless. I have fun bluffing. I play with flashes of brilliance and crash and burn as often as I win the pot. I chat, drink and play from the gut. Overall this gives me as good a return as a more cautious player and a lot of fun. But I knew being true to my style was too big a risk at this table. What if I had a bad night and it looked as if I couldn't play? Not only would I not be invited back, but the next woman who tried to get in on this game would be turned away. I was playing for my whole gender. The most important thing to demonstrate here was not brilliance, but competence, because competence was what was in question. A flashy game with some big losses might mean my wins were put down to beginner's luck or 'having the cards'.

I decided to play not my game, but my husband's. Not for reasons of gender but for reasons of caution! Tom is a much more process-driven player who plays it safe and folds unless he has the cards. He wins steadily and loses the same way. No one could play with him and think he didn't know what he was doing. I looked at my first hand and folded immediately. Played with my second and won. I raised at the right time and didn't bluff unless it was necessary. I won pot after pot, and soon had the biggest pile of chips at the table. I could see a surprised sort of respect flickering in some of the men's eyes. Digger kept his poker face, reserving judgement. Man after man blew his chips and went home. The other performers were wiped out too.

Now the only people left were the regular travelling techs who played this game night after night . . . and me. The game was a tournament, which meant cash prizes for the first-, second- and third-place players. There were only four of us left. Digger looked across the table, pushed his chips into the middle of the table and said, 'I'm going all in.' I had the best part of a straight but he didn't know that. I saw the look in his eyes. 'Are you going to play, or are you going to fold like a girl?' I pushed my chips forward, hoping like hell an ace or a ten would come down. I was riding the river. (If you don't know poker terms, this means I had a heavy menstrual flow. Joke! It means everything was riding on the last card for me. If it went my way, I was quids in; if it didn't, I was wiped out.)

It was a three. Wipeout. And here's the thing: I was glad. I had done something better than win. I had shown these men what I was made of without taking their money. So they respected me but they still liked me. I would definitely be invited back.

I got up to leave, and Digger stood and offered his hand. He smiled for the first time and said, 'You're welcome at my table any time.' I had to stop myself punching the air in triumph. I had done it for the girls. I had shown them that a woman can play poker as well as any man and better than most. I had ended the regime of the all-male game.

I walked out the door, triumphant. Digger followed me, saying the gardens were locked and he'd have to let me out. As we crossed the park he said, 'Run when I tell you, or you'll be caught by the sprinklers. They're on a timer. Three, two, one, go!' I ran into a freezing shower of hose water as he roared with laughter. He had deliberately soaked me at 3 a.m. to show me I was accepted as 'one of the boys'. I laughed and was pretty pleased with myself for being so in the gang I was hazed, as I walked home shivering with the cold. I knew I had a story to tell the guys in the morning, and that seemed worth freezing over.

Before I pull this apart, let me say I liked Digger and his card-playing mates. Looking back, I have no idea how big a deal it was for them to have a woman at the table. I brought a lot of angst and attitude when I'd heard it was a men-only game and I'd reinforced those feelings when I walked through the door, because I made assumptions based on the men's physical appearance. Are big men less likely to be feminists? Do men with tattoos and bushy beards respect women less than less physically imposing comedians do? (If you've dated both you'll know they don't.) This week I phoned one of the comedians who'd told me it was a men-only game and asked him how he'd known that. He said, 'I don't really know. I think it's because we'd never seen a woman there before and we felt as effete artists we were essentially outsiders ourselves.'[6]

It's likely the vibe I sensed did reflect a suspicion about my gender, but I'm sure I exaggerated its importance to them. They were playing their own game, relaxing after work and having some fun. I doubt any of those men remember that night, with the exception of the sprinkler prank. I'm convinced Digger still chuckles to himself about that. Also, it's only poker. It was a fun night. I was in no actual danger. I lost a little cash. The stakes were low.

Caveats done with, I think this story exemplifies how women often respond in environments that overtly or covertly exclude women.

I'd been told that this game was men-only. As soon as I heard that, I thought, 'We'll see about that.' It's one of the classic responses – second only to 'Not for me then.' I wouldn't have been anywhere near so focused on getting in if they hadn't told me that my gender was a bar to entry. Where a fun night out, a job interview or a place on a panel can be just that for a man, for a woman it's often a mental fight before we've walked through the door.

I wasn't going to angrily storm the tent and demand a place at the table, because that makes a fun game impossible, so I needed an ally to get me in. I leaned on Martin's conscience and frankly, wouldn't shut up till I got what I wanted. Often women have to be highly persistent and make emotionally exhausting arguments for our inclusion before we're allowed to start the actual work.

The ally got me through the door and sent me signals that

---

6 Please note if your conference room, writers' room or political cabinet doesn't have any visible women in it *people will assume it's a men-only game*! One woman will be seen as the exception that proves the rule.

I was riding on his coat-tails and if I screwed up, he'd be out along with me. This meant I had twice the responsibility the other players did. Women often carry this burden of a boss, mentor or advocate and their 'Don't let me down,' rhetoric. 'I've gone to bat for you, so screw up and you'll damage my reputation,' is a genuine stress we live with.

I was also playing for half the population of the globe. Potentially excluded for my gender, I knew others would be judged on my abilities. That's a lot of responsibility that women take into staffrooms, courtrooms, surgeries, cockpits and onto TV shows. When a new young man has a quiet night on a comedy panel show, people blame his greenness and his youth. When a new young woman does the same, they blame her femaleness. Don't believe me? Check the internet.

I had a physical response to being in a foreign tribe. Being surrounded by extreme manifestations of traditional male behaviour activated my amygdala, putting me into the fight-or-flight/freeze-and-friend response. I'm not a nervous, sweaty person. I do stand-up comedy for fun. However, that night I was aware that I'd talked my way into a tribe that had, at least allegedly, expressed a specific desire not to have my kind around for this activity. Sometimes women are accused of looking nervous in male-dominated environments and it can be a biochemical response that comes from an anthropological need to survive.

I felt my competence was in question because of my gender, so it became more important for me to prove myself capable than brilliant. When our right to be in the room is questioned, we can't risk trusting our intuition and talent the way men can. Men are assumed to be fit for the gig. Crashes and burns aren't anticipated, so they're more readily accepted. Sometimes it'll be written off as 'bad luck'. Other times someone will come out and say, 'The President is new at this.' Their gender will never be blamed. At worst, it'll be seen as the failure of an individual.

Fireworks and genius are celebrated if they are male. I believe many women sacrifice their talent to safely demonstrate core competencies, because failure will reinforce the gendered expectations of their bosses and peers. I sacrificed authenticity for safety and it worked. I was rewarded and admired for coming fourth, when their expectation (at least in my mind) was that I'd be bottom of the pack. If I'd gone back to that game, that might have become my regular strategy. I'd probably have retrained myself to play it safe, rather than play it my way.

When I came fourth, I was thrilled to have won their respect but not their money. I knew my success would be at the risk of their egos. I have no evidence that those particular men would have been anything but delighted for me, but I was basing that hunch on experience. When someone expects you to come last, they can high-five you getting runner-up but they rarely like you taking their trophy. 2018 me is a little shocked that 2011 me considered fourth place a better option than number one. I'm a feminist but I was glad to lose and told my friends how clever I'd been to not win and how much more likeable that made me! Now I would see that as the ultimate guilty feminist act.

While remaining likeable by not taking the pot, I had still shown I could play and won respect, which was my chief aim. Sometimes we're so busy chasing what's automatically gifted to our brothers and fathers, we don't think to gun for the pot of gold as well. Winning big is a risk for a woman. Sometimes a woman can't win the prize unless she's prepared to lose allies. I'm not saying that's never true for a man, I'm saying men are expected to win and are often celebrated when they do.

Finally, when I was soaked, I was pleased because they were treating me like 'one of the boys'. I'm a feminist but I was flattered by this pretty childish behaviour because it was a sign of acceptance. In this case, the guy was being playful and I really did laugh and don't remember feeling in any way upset by it – but sometimes, humiliations that men dish out to test each other's manliness are about playing with the very status society gives them for being blokes in the first place. If women arrive with less privilege and then even the little status we manage to carve out for ourselves is taken away, ostensibly in jest, it can cause us to withdraw further. The message is often, 'If you really want to be one of the boys, you have to accept that this is how we deal with each other', forgetting that a) men's mental health is daily eroded by that kind of undermining behaviour, and b) it is not a level playing field for women.

When Als lock other Als outside in the snow, it's a status game because the real-life status is even. That's why it feels like a joke. When Als lock Bobs out in the snow, it's a tangible demonstration of the real-life status gap that exists in the world, disadvantaging Bob and fuelling Al's privilege every day. That's why it doesn't feel funny and isn't 'just a joke'.

Some men struggle with these kind of 'jokes' too. That is usually because there are signals from their male tribe that they are a Bob among Als. Not all Bobs are female and not all Als are male.

Stepping back to look at the big picture of that card game in 2011, my usual (personal) confidence in my ability to play poker was tested by my confidence in my ability to be included in the game at all. Sometimes women need to prove ourselves in ways men have never imagined. Conversely, if you are assumed to be competent and included (if your tribal confidence is high) you can risk being brilliant. If you have entry level trust because you 'look like the right sort of chap', you've got some time so you can play with panache.

I've changed a lot since 2011. Doing the podcast, and having to challenge myself to more powerful behaviours and report back to my audience, has fundamentally altered how I see the world and my place in it. 2018 me will not be intimidated into playing my husband's game. His game isn't better. It's just different. What if I did crash and burn? So what? I'd do it with style.

It's not my job to demonstrate to men that women can play competent poker. I'd rather show them that they're missing out by excluding women from the game. That can be done any number of ways, and it can certainly be done by playing my own fabulous game. If that game involves taking home the pot and they don't like it, whose problem is that? I'm all right with men having a problem when a woman beats them at a game they assumed she couldn't play. I'm more than all right. I'm delighted. I'll be there to celebrate with a woman who can do that, any day.

But it's in industry, politics, academia and medicine where feminism needs us the most to say, 'I can. I want to. I'd be brilliant'.

If you are persuading, you're leading the room. You're not alienating, fighting or going it alone. You're taking people with you. A manager is someone you don't want watching you. A leader is someone you want to look at and follow. Great leaders persuade you to follow them. Feminism needs leaders. We must start to lead for each other and demonstrate our trust in ourselves. Male and female feminists need to be clear that they trust women to contribute and act. People often say that we need to treat everyone the same. I disagree. We need to treat everyone in the context of history. You do not need to patronise anyone to make overt and covert signals that you trust a woman who you are aware may have lived a life without tribal confidence. If you have no evidence that this particular woman can do what she needs to do, assume that she can and treat her with trust and she will most likely meet or exceed your expectations. You know the ripple of distrust that goes around a plane when the pilot's voice is female? Yes, you do. Even if you deny it. Those vibrations are everywhere, not just on planes. We need to start reversing that trend by displaying trust even when we've been trained to doubt that a woman can fly, drive fast cars, be CEO or the President of the United States.

Society needs women who trust themselves to lead and can communicate that trust to others. In the next chapter, we'll look at how anyone can learn to adopt more of these leadership behaviours, even if they feel they're starting from behind the eight ball.

Finding Your Inner Obama
(Michelle, of course)

I'm a feminist but I negotiated a half-price kitchen by studying the men's team on The Apprentice.

Stand-up comedy and why I do it for fun

I'm aware I'm someone who, to other people, seems magically confident. I get on stage regularly to do *The Guilty Feminist* podcast with little written down. Mostly the stand-up comedy is brand new and I just have a few notes on the back of my hand. I trust that if I open my mouth and confidently start a sentence, my brain will finish it. I know that if I start a sentence tentatively, my mind might offer me nothing because I've convinced it I don't know where I'm going. That's why I act confidently on stage. Most of the time it works.

When I was at high school in an Australian beach town, sporting prowess was the way to get kudos. I couldn't run fast or jump high, so I joined the debating team. I know what you're thinking: 'You're running in the opposite direction of cool there, Deborah.' But I worked out that if we could beat rival sporting schools and be funny at the same time, then that would bring us glory. I took the role of third speaker, who has to make up rebuttal on the fly, and trained my brain to get fast and funny. Soon our interschool debates started to draw a crowd. Talking fast and riffing jokes was as good as running fast, after all.

After my family joined the Jehovah's Witnesses, I had to quit performing because it was 'worldly'. I tried to find outlets for my need to be on stage. At the Kingdom Hall, where we had our church meetings, women weren't allowed to teach or preach from the stage but we were permitted to do short plays that demonstrated knocking on doors to improve our evangelising technique. 'Sisters', as women were called, were often too nervous to perform on the night and phoned in sick. I volunteered to understudy every time. Ever hungry for laughs, I discovered the Jehovah's Witnesses found nothing funnier than taking the piss out of the Born Again Christians and I wrote sketches in which I would meet an evangelical Christian and paint her into a theological corner using only questions and scriptures from the Bible. These were so popular, the elders asked me to write and perform them for the Jehovah's Witness stadium conventions: they went down a storm because everything else was pretty damn dull. I had to wait to be asked, and these performances were only a few minutes long, but it was something.

When comedy improv became popular in Australia, I got a few young JW friends together and started a secret improv group: a kind of *Whose Eternal Life Is It Anyway?* gang of four. When the elders found out we were mixing with 'worldly' people, they banned us from going, but for a while I'd found a play space outside the cult. I kept a copy by my bed of Keith Johnstone's *Impro*, an inspirational manual for those who were interested in performing improvisation on stage, that I used to let my mind run free and invent fanciful scenarios if only in my own head.

After some truly oppressive experiences in this fundamental religion, I moved to London. Though I was still attending meetings, I started to wake up and realise that this wasn't a sustainable way of thinking or living. Eventually I made the decision never to go to the Kingdom Hall out of guilt again, and within days I knew I'd gone for the last time. The first thing I did was sign up for improvisation classes. It was a place of being in the moment, not second-guessing your instincts, and of saying 'yes, and' rather than 'no, but': the opposite of high-control group-thinking.

The trouble was, I had lost my confidence. Years in a patriarchal cult meant I no longer trusted my own ideas, and believed that everyone else had more experience on stage and had overtaken me, like it was some kind of race. Being on stage wasn't something fun that I looked forward to any more. It was scary and crippling. An improviser called Patti Stiles arrived in London from Canada to teach a master class and she had been trained by Keith Johnstone, who'd written my favourite, secret book that would certainly have been banned if the elders had known I'd had it.[1] After that first class, I abandoned my car to get on the underground with Patti so I could talk to her. She agreed to teach me twice a week if I could find three others who would join us and a living room where we could work. It took me twenty-four hours to meet her requirements and we began.

Patti taught me that the way to find confidence on stage is to stop trying so hard to be good. She demonstrated that failure, in this context, has no consequences. 'What's the worst-case

---

1 Keith's whole philosophy would have been seen by the Watchtower Society as 'worldly' and 'independent thinking'. His book would have been banned because it had a chapter on wearing theatrical masks and allowing the characters they generated to overtake you in a way that would have been seen by the elders as 'allowing demonic forces to enter your body'.

scenario?' she used to say. 'So, you bore the audience for a few minutes? No one's going to get hurt.' She taught us a game called Seen Enough. One person comes out onto the stage and starts improvising. When the other people at the workshop are bored, they walk out of the room. When everyone has left and the performer is on stage alone, the scene is over.

That sounds awful, doesn't it? The first time it can be. But if you keep playing, you start to see it as a process to find out what will keep an audience happy. 'They stayed a bit longer this time. Why?' If the group gives each other feedback about why they stayed or why they left, everyone learns what keeps an audience interested. People say, 'You looked like you didn't want to be there,' or 'You did the same thing again and I didn't think I'd see anything new, so I went.' And then, 'I wanted to know what was in the box, so I couldn't look away until that was solved,' or, 'You seemed like you knew exactly what you were doing, so I stayed.'

The group can develop an extraordinary confidence playing this game together, as long as the feedback is honest and no one stays 'to be kind'. I've had the audience leave seconds into my 'great idea' precisely because I thought it was a great idea – and I found their immediate departure hysterically funny. This is because, in that moment, I'd managed to separate the ego from the work. Much of confidence is recognising times when there is nothing truly at stake and that failure can be seen as 'gathering data' rather than evidence that we as individuals are 'no good' at something.

I understand that if you work in a science lab or on a construction site, failure can have a much heftier price tag, but a job interview for that position, a meeting where you have to present your ideas, a conversation with someone new in the breakroom or a networking event for your industry, doesn't.

It's perfectly okay to line up six interviews and use the first three as 'data-gathering exercises' for interview technique.

Actually, if you do that you'll probably be offered at least one of the jobs because you won't seem anxious like the other candidates; rather, someone who's curious about the process and truly interested in the role and the company. I'm aware that many people who are in industries or locations where job-seeking is soul-destroyingly competitive and poverty is real may not feel this way, and I don't want to minimise those struggles in any way. I do want to point out that the best process possible is to mentally lower the stakes and have as many turns as you can without attaching an 'end of the world' mental consequence to any one of them.

I am aware that I speak from a place of privilege here, and that for some people not getting a job is the end of their world. When I was knocking on doors with *The Watchtower* full-time, I did seasonal casual work to survive and there were times when I had no money for food. I remember going to a job interview sure that I wouldn't get the job and being offered it. I think I accidentally radiated a 'lots of goes' energy because I was so past believing it would happen. Others tell me this is a common experience.

I think for that reason I knew this intuitively, but I vividly remember my first big success using this way of thinking. I'd travelled to Canada to work with Keith Johnstone, the author of the book himself, and I was cast in an elimination-format improv show at his theatre, the Loose Moose in Calgary. The audience scored each scene and the improvisers with lower scores had to leave the stage after each round until one improviser was crowned 'the Maestro'.

After I surprised myself by surviving a few rounds, my anxiety tapped me on the shoulder: 'Now you've come this far, you're in with a shot at winning this thing. Do your best. Don't look down. You'll fall.' I heard Patti's voice in my head, 'Trying your hardest is not your best strategy. Just be in the moment and have fun. There's nothing at stake here. Being eliminated is part of the show. The audience will enjoy it if you crash and burn as long as you stay good-natured and you enjoy failing!' I walked out with that attitude every round and I was Last Improviser Standing. I won.

I've had to learn that same lesson many times in my career. Television auditions. Network heads coming to my show. Going into stand-up comedy. I've run back into the comforting arms of anxiety many, many times. When I try to be better than I am, it does not work. When I come to play, not to work, I can be better than I was last time.

Piloting the plane

Willingness to lead others is the ultimate manifestation of personal confidence. It tells others that you are assuming you have tribal confidence. You trust yourself so acutely and you assume the trust of the tribe so obviously, you are not waiting for anyone to validate you. In fact, you are taking responsibility for the confidence of others. You shouldn't feel obliged to, but if you want it for yourself and as a tool for feminism, you absolutely can.

As far as individual career development goes, there's nothing like leading with confidence. Whenever you advance in the workplace, whether it's a supermarket or No. 10 Downing Street, you're generally asked to manage or lead others. Giving status from a place of status is the most obvious manifestation of confidence in the world and the most powerful leadership and communication style there is, because it makes you magnetic and likeable.

Most women are not nurtured in an environment with this kind of powerful and positive leadership. Women like Elizabeth Garrett Anderson, the first British female doctor; Charlotte E. Ray, the first woman in Washington DC called to the bar; and Jerrie Cobb, who was almost the first woman in space well before her time, are the breakout Bobs who buck the trend with sheer force of will due to their personality, opportunities and superhuman persistence, while most Als undermine them with jealous sibling rivalry. Some Als act as Al-lies. We need allies, and we can create more with persuasion and influence.

Great leadership comes down to two things: the ability to self-include and the ability to include others. To do this you need to trust yourself, signal that self-trust to the tribe and, crucially, show the tribe that *you trust them*.

Donald Trump ran his 2016 election campaign on a platform of exclusion: 'I'll build a wall. I'll keep them out. America First.' He chiefly includes himself: 'I'll make America great again.' All he could promise was that Middle America would be on the right side of his wall, that they would be included by default. The big exclusion happens first, and those who are left are treated to the inclusion that's left over. Trump always looks included because he was born included. Almost all rooms of influence have people inside of them who look like him: white men who went to a school like his, had a rich father like his and have bank accounts like his. All he had to do was convince America that there was an imminent danger and that their best bet was to be under the protection of his privilege.

Hillary tried to run a campaign of inclusion. However, she never really looked fully included herself. She told the photo-blog *Humans of New York* in September 2016, 'I know that I can be perceived as aloof or cold or unemotional. But I had to learn as a young woman to control my emotions. And that's a hard path to walk. Because you need to protect yourself, you need to keep steady, but at the same time, you don't want to seem "walled off".' She said,

I was taking a law school admissions test in a big classroom at Harvard. My friend and I were some of the only women in the room. I was feeling nervous. I was a senior in college. I wasn't sure how well I'd do. And while we're waiting for the exam to start, a group of men began to yell things like: 'You don't need to be here.' And, 'There's plenty else you can do.' It turned into a real 'pile on'. One of them even said: 'If you take my spot, I'll get drafted, and I'll go to Vietnam, and I'll die.' And they weren't kidding around. It was intense. It got very personal. But I couldn't respond. I couldn't afford to get distracted because I didn't want to mess up the test.

On the campaign trail, Hillary looked like she trusted herself but never looked as if she believed the tribe would trust her. There were any number of systemic, corrupt and political reasons she lost, but the leader of the tribe has to be certain of their own inclusion and Hillary always looked like she was expecting the kind of abuse she experienced back at Harvard in that exam room when those men shouted at her, 'You're taking my place! You don't deserve to be included here. Your inclusion could mean my death.'

Her campaign slogan was 'I'm With Her'. That slogan put the onus for inclusion in the wrong place. It should have been 'She's With Us'. You can't make every voter say, 'I'm with Spartacus!' especially when those same citizens have unanswered questions about some of your decisions and mistakes.[2]

I'm amazed Bill Clinton didn't spot that the campaign slogan was wrong. He's the master of inclusion. People who meet him almost always say the same thing: 'I felt like I was the only person in the room.' At times he has misused that

---

2 Her official slogan was 'Stronger Together', but 'I'm With Her' was the one most used on social media. The *New York Times* 19 October 2016 reported all the slogans her team considered which they had found in her famously leaked emails. Of the ones they abandoned, I wish they'd gone with 'Your Family, Her Fight', or 'She's Got Your Back'.

charisma.[3] His own first presidential campaign slogan was 'For People, For a Change'. It wasn't 'Bill's the Best and I Can Definitely Personally Vouch for That'.

Obama's 2008 campaign logline was brilliant: 'Yes We Can'. It united the voters with the candidate and made him central and them necessary. Everything about Obama says, 'I'm included and so are you.' When an angry Tea Party protester disrupted a rally he was speaking at in 2016, Obama told the crowd, 'He's just supporting his candidate ... We have a country that supports free speech.' He included the Trump supporter who'd crashed the Democrats' party and found specific reasons to do so: 'He's a senior and we need to respect that ... He looks like he's served in our military and we need to respect that.' That kind of inclusion is powerful because it seems like you are entirely unthreatened by the presence of others.

Michelle Obama has a laid-back sense of self-inclusion. She signals that she knows you trust her in her walk, stance, laugh and pace. There must be days when she doesn't really but she can message that she does and that's just as good. When she comes out on stage, you don't doubt for a second that she's central to proceedings. She never signals in her voice or physical bearing that she's unsure you'll like her. She never opens with, 'Hope the PowerPoint holds up. Bear with us,' in her words or manner. When you listen to her, you feel like she thinks you're clever and important too.

In her famous campaign speech for Hillary in New Hampshire, she told the listeners how necessary they are and made them feel so included they found themselves in a call-and-response situation.

---

3 In a series of affairs that he lied about, most famously with Monica Lewinsky who was young, single, in his charisma grip and blamed because the world is a sexist place.

Michelle: We need you to roll up your sleeves. We need to
    get to work. Because remember this: when they go low,
    we go . . .
Audience: High!

In that same interview, Hillary said, 'I'm not Barack
Obama. I'm not Bill Clinton. Both of them carry themselves
with a naturalness that is very appealing to audiences. But I'm
married to one and I've worked for the other, so I know how
hard they work at being natural. It's not something they just
dial in. They work and they practise what they're going to say.'
Hillary did not manage to work on this so well that it became
convincing. This is probably due to a combination of her personality and the extraordinary sexism she'd experienced: she is
a generation older than Michelle and has been in the public eye
for most of her life. It's hard to change the public's perception
of you, so it's best to grow into yourself first and get famous
second. (Personally, I've always made it a policy to bide my
time.) Whatever the reasons, 'being a natural, confident leader'
is something she's seen Obama and Bill Clinton work at until
it looks natural. It's like CGI in movies. People say you can
tell when someone's faking it, but you can only tell if it's bad.

Charisma is a sort of visceral persuasion. Charismatic people
are confident enough to draw people to them or lead them
somewhere and make them want to come or follow. People
always think that people are born with charisma, but they're
not. Everyone works at it. Some people learn their confidence
and influence intuitively in secondary school in order to get
boys or girls to like them or to get bullies to leave them alone.
Some people, like singers, actors or politicians, get a coach.
Comedians find it on the job, through trial and painful error.
Everyone learns it. No one's born with it. When I returned to
performance as a shell-shocked grown-up I used to ball my fists

up on stage, but now it's the place where I feel most at home. I look forward to performing the podcast and love spending time with my audience. It's not innate talent. It's learned behaviour.

We can use these role models, like Michelle Obama or your favourite stand-up comedian (doesn't have to be me!) as a way of beginning to answer the question: 'How could I learn to behave in a more charismatic way?' Because charisma is just behaviour, I believe anyone can develop their own brand of charismatic behaviour, even if your experiences to date have been bruising, made you feel excluded and sapped what confidence you had.

People can't see how you're feeling, they can only see what you're doing

I work with women and men in business and at *Guilty Feminist* events to break down what I do when I perform stand-up comedy and how I see charismatic leaders and communicators acting. People think their anxiety is visible but no one knows how you're feeling: they can only make guesses about how you're feeling based on what you're doing. They say, 'She seems confident,' and 'I felt nervous.' They know how they feel; they can only make assumptions about you based on what you do with your body.

I am endlessly fascinated by this, and have made a big part of my living from analysing social cues and breaking them down so that people (especially women and other marginalised groups) can learn to include themselves and even lead. When you decide to lead, you become more visible. Giving a presentation is a good example of leading a room. What I find fascinating is that what you do with your body changes your biochemistry: you start to feel more powerful or more anxious depending on your physical choices. Your body sends messages to the brain, like 'Get ready to run', or 'I'm in charge here'. Your brain in turn tells your body to sweat or shorten its breath or calm its heartbeat.

Here are some physical choices you can make if you want to look more powerful.[4] You only need to choose one or two of these behaviours. Those will trigger the rest. Don't try to do them all at once. You'll look like The Terminator.

Put your weight on your front foot. It's hard to look scared of people you're coming towards.

Take up space. Make yourself a little taller and stand like a cowboy with your feet further apart than normal.

Be comfortable with stillness. Practise it when you order coffee. Allow your head to be still like a pond, not still like a rock. (Don't overdo it, unless you want to look intimidating!)

When you move, move with purpose. Allow your movements to have beginnings and ends.

Take up time. Pause before you speak. You don't need to fill the silence with 'er's that tell us you don't want to waste our time.

If you're the centre of attention – on stage, in a meeting, on a conference call or in a staffroom – it's easy to feel like prey. This is because historically (and even prehistorically) if you saw twelve pairs of eyes looking at you, bad things were probably about to happen. You were about to be eaten or beaten, so it's

---

4 Although not exactly the same, these tips may remind some readers of Amy Cuddy's famous TED Talk on Power Poses: https://www.ted.com/talks/amy_cuddy_your_body_language_shapes_who_you_are. This has been enthusiastically debunked recently: http://fortune.com/2016/10/02/power-poses-research-false/ and I'm all for scientific rigour, but I think the debunkers have largely missed the point. If audiences respond differently, and people report that they feel different when they adopt these techniques, then they 'work' in any and all interesting senses of that term, regardless of what happens under MRI machines in carefully controlled laboratory settings.

easy to feel edible, like a gazelle in front of a pride of lions. The more you twitch like a gazelle, back away and make indecisive movements, the more you'll send a message to your brain, 'Release the adrenaline! I need to get ready to run!' and the sweatier and shakier you'll become.

If all eyes are on you and you lean towards those watching in a purposeful manner and you're happy to be still, then you must be the lion in charge of the pride. They'll see you as Henry V, leading his troops to glory. Your brain will also receive this message from your body and your adrenaline will subside. You'll start to feel more powerful, like you're captaining a ship. You can instigate biochemical and mental confidence by taking strong, lion-like physical decisions.

Our verbal cues are an extension of this. How we speak also tells the room and our brain how confident or anxious we are about the situation. Most people have been sitting in a meeting thinking, 'I haven't said anything yet ... Is it too late to say anything now? Will it just point out that I haven't said anything yet?'

Rather than worrying about what you're going to say, divide up the time available by the number of people present. Sixty minutes. Six people. How many minutes do you need to speak for? Ten for you. Two extra for the history of the patriarchy. Keep an eye on the clock. Fill your airtime. Note on a piece of paper how often the confident people speak and what they say. You don't have to have something brilliant to say before you speak! Often people are just chiming in to reinforce and share their airtime. Agree with others: 'That's an interesting point, Geoff. Could you unpack that a bit?' Geoff loves you now, and will encourage you to speak again. (Obviously wait till Geoff says something interesting. Don't give him positive reinforcement when he's being dull!) 'I like that idea, Julie. I think it could really work.

I'd love to have a brainstorm with you about whether that could work for my team.' (Now Julie loves you too, and will encourage you to speak more, which will help to fill your twelve minutes.)

I'm not suggesting you become a giant sycophant to make others feel included. I'm saying that if you find speaking in groups daunting, reinforcing ideas you like is a great place to start because too few people are prepared to be a cheer squad for others and everyone needs validation. Once you get used to speaking out and hearing your own voice, you'll find more things come out of your mouth unbidden. The more you contribute, the more your confidence will grow.

Amplifying others can be a great tribal strategy for feminists. Obama's female staffers famously reinforced each other's ideas to stop their male co-workers stealing the credit for those ideas. They called it the Shine Theory, and made a pact that they'd repeat the origin of the idea until it became cast iron in everyone's mind and couldn't be pilfered. You don't need a formal agreement to do this. Start doing it for others, and odds are they'll feel so safe with you they'll return the favour. This is a simple way to put feminism into action.

Self-undermining

When working in the corporate world, I often ask the audience to guess whether it was a man or a woman who said the following: 'You're in a meeting and someone says, "Well it's obvious, isn't it? We've got to expand into Singapore."'

The audience will guess it's a man.

What about these words? 'You're in a meeting and someone says, "I just had a thought, I don't know if it's worth mentioning . . . I just had a thought about Singapore on this one, and

I know it might not be the right time to pop it on the table, but I just thought I'd mention it in case it's useful." Is that a man or a woman?'

The audience will guess it's a woman.

Both female and male audiences make that assumption.

If we don't know if it's worth mentioning, then why are we mentioning it? When we speak like that we are undermining our own story, our own research, our own ideas and our own brilliance. We are saying, 'It's all right if you don't agree with me, because it was only an idea. There's no need for a confrontation because I will withdraw rather than fight.'

Historically, there is a good reason why our tribe has used this strategy. Our upper-body strength wasn't going to win us many fist fights, so we avoided confrontation in order to survive. People do things for good reasons.

In staffrooms, classrooms, doctor's waiting rooms and cocktail bars, most of the time, if we live in a country where women have civil liberties, we are not in physical danger and we can afford to tell our story, share our views and present our findings as if they are worth hearing.[5] We can retrain ourselves to begin, 'I'm very interested in Singapore. This project would work brilliantly there. Here's why.' If you're making a phone call, try cutting out most of the qualifiers. Instead of saying, 'I wondered if you might have ten minutes to have a coffee with me, but I totally understand if not. I just have a few ideas you might be interested in if you have time.' You can just say, 'Andrew, I've got something I want to run by you. Are you in town this week? It's one for a coffee.'

---

5 The recent uncovering of years of institutional sexual harassment and assault in the workplace demonstrates that sometimes we are in physical danger and women often favour a freeze-and-friend rather than a fight-or-flight strategy, as is explored further in Chapter 5: The Power of Yes.

I noticed when I watched *The Apprentice* in the UK that when the women's team had to haggle in shops they'd say, 'You couldn't do anything on the price, could you?' The seller would inevitably say no because they had literally told them that they couldn't. The men's team would say, 'Mate, I've got a hundred quid cash. It's all I've got.' They'd put the cash on the counter and go for the handshake. The seller would find themselves completing that transaction because when someone offers their hand you've got to have a great reason not to shake it. I started bargaining like this. That's how I got my kitchen. I notice the current British *Apprentice* teams make more authoritative negotiations regardless of gender, and I wonder if they've watched and learned too. To be clear, I don't think men are better at this stuff. I think many are given Al-style trust by the structures around them and that cockiness leaks out. Bobs have to break it down.

If someone objects or finds fault, a confrontation is not inevitable. If we're curious and excited to hear their objections and can make the objector feel included or at least heard, we can use the Obamas' strategy of including others, not just ourselves.

There are many different ways to demonstrate confidence, but including others is the most powerful, confident thing a person can do. Listening to others and bringing them into the tribe is a far more powerful act than excluding them. The good news for women? It is easier for Bobs to do this than Als, because Bobs know who's being excluded, when and how. Bobs know how it feels. Bobs know the signs of exclusion. They're knowledgeable. Als often don't notice it's happening because it's outside of their experience.

Bobs can even include Als who are dealing with a changing world in which they're used to singular inclusion and don't know how to share. Bobs don't always want to do this or feel they should have to, but it can be powerful.

You will seem at your most radiantly confident when you learn how to make others feel as if they belong in your meeting, at your school gate, in your carpool, on your conference call and at your poker game. One reason you will seem so confident is that an includer is a leader. Another reason is that as soon as you become conscious of others you will lose your self-consciousness. This is the bedrock of feminism. It's a demand for inclusion made by a collective of excluded individuals. It's an invoice for inclusion by the most-included members of our tribe on behalf of the least-included.

The turn of phrase 'I'm a feminist but . . . ' encourages us to include each other's failings as well as our triumphs and that's why, I believe, it is valuable. It's a manifestation of confidence without perfection. I think the reason guilty feminism (due to the podcast) has caught on is that it allows us to include our whole selves, even the parts of us that want to watch terrible romantic comedies and blow off our friends who are going to watch a feminist documentary. It allows us to show our whole selves to our sisters and say, 'I just texted the toxic ex again, but I still believe I can be a better feminist tomorrow, with your help.'

True confidence isn't conditional on full marks and doesn't require a hundred per cent attendance. When I returned to comedy, newly out of a patriarchal cult, I felt like a nervous wreck but looking back I clearly had enough confidence to leave the house and turn up at an improv class. Today I have more confidence than I did then. Wherever I go, it's my aim to take other women with me and amplify their voices because it's a wonderful thing to do, because most people we include include us back, and because we recognise real confidence when someone who is sure they're included, includes.

Later tonight, on Dave

Doing stand-up comedy, I've shared the stage with a lot of other performers, none more confident in her persona than Zoe Coombs Marr, and not just when she was appearing on stage as a man.

Zoe, could you tell me a little about who you are? Just some context for readers who don't know your work – the philistines.
Hi! Why don't you know who I am, you bastards?! You know today I got recognised at the dentist. By the dentist. In the chair. He had his hands in my mouth and he goes, 'Oh! That's where I know your face from! You're a comedian, aren't you?' So there. I mean, it did take him a while . . . he had actually been looking at my face undisturbed for half an hour.

So you're a dentist-goer, and a comedian, is that right?
Correct. I am a comedian. I started when I was a teenager and have been doing it on and off since, but for the last five years or so I've been performing as a parody of a male comedian, named Dave, with hair glued on my neck and my breasts bound down. Dave is a kind of amalgam of every sexist male comic ever. People seem to like him.

God, I'd be tempted to do that just so journalists would stop asking me 'What's it like being a woman in comedy?'
All women in comedy get asked that all the time. Men never get asked that. Like, why is the onus never on the person with the privilege? And after being annoyed about that for ages, it occurred to me that I was in a position

of privilege too. Duh! Because, while being a woman in comedy is tricky, being a white person in comedy has benefited me in countless ways. So that's how I answer that question now. I say, 'Well, it's hard to say what it's like being a woman in comedy, but being white's given me lots of opportunities.'

That's genius! Because it acknowledges that it's easier to be a man in comedy without saying it but it also owns your privilege and points out that it's harder still for women of colour. You've come up with a perfect way for women who can identify a privilege they have to answer that question, which is the bane of our lives.
So, it's looking broader than just 'Women should be equal to men,' and asking, 'Which women? Which men? How? In what ways?' To me, intersectional feminism is about a) looking beyond myself and my own limited experience, and b) acknowledging the complexity of things. Which can be kind of tricky. Things are complex.

Annoyingly so.
And there are lots of different levels to feminism and lots of ways of engaging in it. Like you can say 'cats are felines', and that's scientific, but science is also, you know, molecular biology and stuff. The fancy-pants molecular biology statement doesn't make the 'cats are felines' not true, it's just taking a few more things into account. (And just because molecular biology seems a bit much, that doesn't negate it either. We don't all have to be highfa-lutin scientists, but we can still pay attention and try a little harder.)

You do a character, Dave, who you talked about, who is a parody of a super-confident male stand-up comedian. How does gender fluidity play into queer politics now, do you think?

I think the conversation around gender has changed massively in the last few years, and it's really exciting. When I was a little baby queer, lugging my bindle from the country to the big city streets of gay old Sydney Towne, there wasn't much discussion of gender or gender identity in the circles I was moving in, and there certainly wasn't much discussion of it in the mainstream. I mean, when I was a kid there weren't even gay people on network television.

And when there were, they were usually stereotypes.

Right, but as we've progressed, and more people have come out, and there are more visible trans people, that conversation has shifted towards gender. And now there's this really exciting swathe of young people who are thinking about gender in a whole different way. They're gaining confidence and I love it.

And you see all these people who are so terrified of it. Like, gender-neutral bathrooms and, god forbid, boys in dresses, does their head in. I find it kind of amazing and baffling. Like, what are people so afraid of? I suppose they feel like something important is being taken away from them. But what? Like, what even is gender?! Gender is bogus, really, isn't it?

It is an odd construct because so much of it is performative.

I mean, biology certainly exists, but what that determines about who a person is and how they should behave, is pretty much made up. I know I've never felt any real connection to the signifiers of my gender. Like 'girliness' or whatever always felt totally made up to me. My experience, though, has been shaped in very real ways by the fact that I inhabit a female body, and the perceptions that come with that have shaped my life. So I identify with that experience. And that's how I define myself. I'm a woman because I'm perceived that way. And that is still a very real and defining factor for a lot of people. So I think we're in this transitional time, no pun intended!

I feel like that pun should be intended.
Either way, it's a time where we are gaining the confidence to push the feminist cause forward for women, while also challenging the idea of gender itself. Both are important, and I hope that we move towards the abolition of gender altogether. Maybe we should just all give gender up for Lent and see if we miss it. The fact that that veil is being lifted on a large scale is pretty exciting. Bring it on, I say.

How much of the 'performance' of gender has been revealed to you by the fact that you are a performer, which gives you confidence in the first place?
A lot of my experience of that veil being lifted was through stand-up comedy. I felt like I was seeing all of these guys get up in the same outfit and do pretty much the same act, and the audience would receive them in this particular way and that would gift them confidence. And for me, I would go on stage, and before I'd even opened my mouth the audience had made a judgement just by virtue of my gender. And that happens all the time. In comedy, it's very pronounced. It affects your confidence, of course.

Yes, when you see people in the front row comment on the fact that you're a woman as you're getting the mic out of the stand, saying, 'I don't find women funny,' or MCs who say, 'The next act is a woman, but don't worry – she's funny.'

Yes, for a long time I thought I was just crazy, and that I was just crap. To be fair, for a long time I was pretty crap, too.

It takes a while to find your confidence on stage because of your own skills, but also because of what the audience often project onto a woman.

But after doing it for years and years, I just became more and more aware of it. It's not a level playing field. There's a silent understanding between audience and performer, and audiences just intrinsically and immediately trust a man more. And I love the audience. It's pathetic, but I'm basically in love with the audience, so I was actually just really jealous of the blokes' relationship with them! I wanted it.

I actually considered transitioning. I mean, I've never really felt that tied to a gender, and it all feels made up, but like I say, my experience has really been shaped by inhabiting this female body. And that's okay. I'd rather stay in my lane, as my own version of a 'woman', whatever that means, really, and support the gender-fluid and trans people around me. And I would like to be clear that that's not a choice available to everyone, obviously – some people really do need to transition. So anyway, transitioning wasn't for me. Short of that, I glued some hair on my face and bound my breasts down, and just did what the guys were doing. It is a parody, but there is a weird thing I've noticed: that even as a fake man I get more respect than as a real woman. It's just different. You're imbued with the confidence of the audience.

Wow. That is astounding.
I've always maintained that when I am performing Dave, even though I've got a costume on, it's no more of a performance than when any other actually male comic does it. They are performing masculinity as much as I am. People often think I'm joking when I say that, but I'm not. It doesn't really feel that crazy to me that I would dress and act like that – at least, not any crazier than all the guys who do. It's like, sure, I'm dressed as a man ... but so's that man! It's all just made up.

To me, being queer is an experience of otherness, of being on the outside looking in, your whole life. Because we live in a straight world, we see straight culture, we're fluent in it. But straight people don't quite understand us. Why would they need to? But things that a straight person would never question seem absurd to me. I think there's a particular queer experience of being in the world, but also observing it and questioning it, that's hard to articulate. It's like a kind of second sight almost. Basically what I'm saying is, queers are magic.

Hah! It's like a gay Hogwarts straight people can never visit. How can straight feminists be better allies to the queer community and particularly to queer feminists? Where do we sap confidence when we should empower?
Hmm. Not really sure it's about straight feminists needing to be better allies to queers, but about being better allies to each other. I think the male gaze and the need for the approval of men is a really strong driving force for a lot of straight women.

It can be. We're taught to crave it, I think.
I couldn't care less what men think. Even if I wanted
to! I can't even really tell them apart. Honestly – even
movie stars.

**I get it. I honestly couldn't tell the difference between
Jimmy Fallon and Jimmy Kimmel until Kimmel got
political. How do you see queer feminism intersecting
with race, class and disability? Is there anything useful
we can learn about the crossovers there?**
If you're anything but white and straight, you are going to
be looking at the world from a different perspective. Those
different perspectives are valid, and powerful, and magic!
Our differences are our superpowers. Those perspectives
are different from each other, but their difference from
the norm is a common factor. There's a fine line, though,
between understanding someone's experience and taking
it on as your own. But I do think there is a commonality
in otherness that can help us understand each other's
experiences and empathise. And I think empathy is key.
Let's all just listen to each other, okay?!

Zoe puts her finger on something here. When we listen we give
the speaker confidence that they are being heard. We build
trust. We need to take time to listen, hear and contemplate for
our whole tribe to learn to trust ourselves and each other. Once
we feel safe in our tribe, then we need to be able to be ourselves
within it and not feel the need to conform all the time. For this,
we will need to understand 'the power of yes'.

The Power of Yes

I'm a feminist but sometimes if I'm talking to another feminist I agree with her, even if I don't think she's right, because I want her to like me.

Call me Tallulah, dahling . . .

In 1962, when the actress and wit Tallulah Bankhead was sixty years old, she felt like singing 'Bye Bye Blackbird' to an audience, so she threw a spontaneous party to make that happen.[1] She was, of course, very wealthy by then, but she had always behaved this way. In 1923, at the age of twenty-one, she was an aspiring actress who'd had no particular success in New York. She was cast in a London play called *The Dancers*, based solely on her photograph and a recommendation. The producer got cold feet and sent her a telegram telling her not to come. She ignored it, borrowed money for the fare, got on the boat and talked her way past customs, who told her she had to report to the police station in the morning as she had no visa, money or evidence of an employer in Britain. She arrived in the West End ready for work. 'Didn't you get my cable telling you not

---

1 http://www.robert-temple.com/nostalgia/tallulah.html.

to come?' said the producer. 'What cable?' said Tallulah. Since she'd come all that way, he gave her the job.

Tallulah's father was a respectable American senator who had warned her of the dangers of men and alcohol but, as Tallulah often observed, 'Never said a word about women and cocaine.' Tallulah was a proud, adventurous, queer woman and identified as 'ambisextrous'. She often opened the door dressed only in pearls and said at parties, 'What's the matter, darling? Don't you recognise me with my clothes on?' She was the orgasmic embodiment of sex positivity.

She was a big hit in *The Dancers* and soon became a West End star with a huge following of young, working-class and queer women who'd often queue overnight to get penny tickets. Her fans were called the Gallery Girls. Some of them worked as her personal assistants and became close friends. She was a forerunner to Lady Gaga.

Tallulah Bankhead is my favourite guilty feminist from history. She was fierce, independent and ran every room she was in. She was also superficial, vain and hedonistic. She often remarked that she had no idea where her next magnum of champagne was coming from. She loved to drive (which was the exciting new technology) but was very bad at directions, so would hail a taxi and ask the driver if she could follow behind. Her legendary parties were attended by people of different races, classes, gender expressions and sexual orientations. She once said, 'If I had to live my life again, I'd make all the same mistakes, only sooner.' Tallulah lived her life as one big 'yes'.[2]

Not everyone has the freedom from responsibility or the access to cash that allows them Tallulah's lifestyle. No one can

---

2 Anecdotes taken from *Tallulah: My Autobiography* (first published by Dell, New York, 1952).

talk their way past border control any more. But the spirit with which she lived, the desire to see and be seen without apology or embarrassment, is something we could all borrow. She had no shame about her sexuality, which was extraordinary for a woman in the 1920s and is fairly rare now.

Think about how many things you'd like to say and do, how much self-expression you're hiding because of what other people might think. Think about the boldness with which you could live if you talked, walked, danced and dressed like the bravest part of you. Sometimes when we stop caring what other people think, other people think we're wonderful. I am not just talking about confidence to do things well and be included, as I was in the last chapter. We can have plenty of confidence to do the things society approves of competently and be happy to be centre stage – as long as we are con-forming. I am talking about having the freedom to live large without validation, to try new things that seem dangerous in some way and to swim against the stream just because it makes us feel whole.

Most of us are scared of ourselves. That's the biggest win the patriarchy has made through undermining generations of women, keeping their top-class brains away from books, their wit under house arrest and their intentions in the dark. Consequently, we, the great-granddaughters of anxious women, can be fearful of the voice inside of us that does not wish to conform and play nice, and so we mostly keep it in check. Many of us are living at half-mast. We are quieter than we want to be. We carry tension in our body because we swallow our opinions. We hunch to make ourselves smaller. We laugh less than we could. We make funny faces in photos to hide our true selves. We pretend we are happy when we are not. We have inadequate sex. We lie about who we are and what we want.

Only part of us is sane

British author, journalist and wordsmith Rebecca West once said, 'People call me a feminist whenever I express sentiments that differentiate me from a doormat.' She also wrote:

> Only part of us is sane: only part of us loves pleasure and the longer day of happiness, wants to live to our nineties and die in peace, in a house that we built, that shall shelter those who come after us. The other half of us is nearly mad. It prefers the disagreeable to the agreeable, loves pain and its darker night despair, and wants to die in a catastrophe that will set back life to its beginnings and leave nothing of our house save its blackened foundations.[3]

We pretend all the time that we are content with the longer day of happiness and deny that sometimes we love pain and to scream at the sky and take up space and demand attention and request affection.

This is true for men as well as women, but men are socialised to live larger and to more often say yes to things they're only half-convinced they can do. Many generations of even relatively privileged women could only look forward to living in corners of rooms with their hands folded and ankles crossed. Needlepoint and pianoforte were two of the most extreme sports available to them (heavy on the piano, light on the forte). Words like 'demure', 'well behaved' and 'submissive' were compliments. When I interviewed the authors of books about the suffragettes engaging in civil disobedience[4] and

---

3 *Black Lamb and Grey Falcon: A Journey Through Yugoslavia* by Rebecca West (first published by Macmillan, London in 1941).
4 *A Petrol Scented Spring* by Ajay Close (Sandstone Press Ltd, 2015).

the Special Operations Executive women who acted as spies during the second world war[5] for the podcast, a theme that came up again and again was that life was boring for women in the first half of the twentieth century. Their willingness to fight for these excellent causes – which seems extraordinarily brave to us now – was, at least in part, motivated by a desire to make some noise, blow stuff up and refuse to be told what to do. They were rare opportunities for women to say, 'Yes! God, yes! A thousand times yes!'

Twenty-first-century women who live in democracies clearly have more options than our foremothers and great-aunts, but saying yes and opening doors with brand new keys that don't turn easily in the lock is scary. What if you say, 'Yes, I speak French! I studied it for four years and lived for a year in Montreal,' and then it turns out you've forgotten half of what you knew? What if the language they're asking you to translate is too technical? What if you don't know absolutely everything in front of absolutely everyone? It's really easy to let an opportunity go to a man who's half as good at speaking French but twice as fluent in blagging as you are.

What if you say, 'Yes – I am going to ask you out on a date because I feel like you might never get around to doing it, and I suspect you desire me madly and are too nervous of my potent sexuality and our quivering chemistry to do anything about it'? What if she doesn't say, 'Thank you for finally asking, you divine creature,' but stamps your library book, a little confused – clearly uncertain about who you are? What if he says, 'Thank god you asked,' and then doesn't turn up at the midnight train to Paris like he promised and instead ghosts you for ever? What if they say, 'That would be very nice,' and do turn up at the Hitchcock marathon and then spend New Year's Eve with you, marry you,

---

5 *Lonely Courage* by Rick Stroud (Simon & Schuster, 2017).

get bored of you, cheat on you and leave you alone on your deathbed telling you they've never really loved you?

What if you say, 'Yes – I'm going on a Tampon Tax sit-in this weekend. It's time I got political and kicked off with my sisters and demanded more'? What if you got there and couldn't find the people who promised to meet you and you were all alone and you didn't know how to make friends at a protest and it was too crowded and you felt claustrophobic and you couldn't get out and you fainted and everyone thought you were a terrible feminist?

Yes is dangerous. No keeps you safe. No is *Friends* reruns and thinking about writing a blog and staying in a relationship with insidiously sexist Sam who won't commit, or boring Samantha you don't really love in a part of the world you don't really like because it's where she wants to live. No is not putting yourself forward for a new role because you're not sure you're good enough at the old job yet. No is easy. 'Not yet' is a cakewalk. 'Maybe but probably not' is our delicious bread and butter. Yes makes us vulnerable because it means we've brought on the consequences ourselves – whether sad, embarrassing, challenging or exciting. Yes means self-directed change. Nothing is scarier than change.

Many men will relate to this fear, too, but when they watch movies or the actual news they see people who look like them in drivers' seats all the time. Men walking on the moon. Men down on one knee proposing marriage. Men releasing new iPhones. Men leading revolutions. They're supposed to step up to the plate. They get depressed if they don't – but at least they have societal permission.

Authenticity is overrated

A friend of mine was asked to host a panel at a television festival. All the professionals put forward for the panel were men.

She kicked off and said she was sick of seeing all-male panels and would refuse to host it unless it was gender-balanced. Her boss agreed and told her to invite any women she liked. She'd been in the industry for fifteen years and knew everyone, so she picked up the phone, excited to get some more interesting voices on her high-profile conference session which was going to be different from all of the others. She couldn't find one woman who'd say yes. They all said 'I'm not qualified,' or 'I don't know enough about it.'

She countered that the men angling to get up there knew just as much jack-shit as the women did, because the panel was about programme piracy, and the whole point of discussing it was that no one knew how to deal with it and whether it was actually a free marketing opportunity or a financial drain that was threatening the future of the media. Woman after woman said no, while man after man put himself forward without even being asked. She was furious. She'd always assumed women were being excluded, but it turned out they were being asked, but they were just avoiding the exposure. To be fair, the men were more confident because they were more experienced and they were more experienced because they had been included more often, but even so that didn't totally account for her having to eventually strong-arm one solitary woman onto the stage.

This is clearly not always the case. Some women are desperate to get on panels and stages and volunteer all the time, but the fact that it's *ever* the case (and we all know that this is not an isolated anecdote) is something we have to change. We need to say yes to being the representation we want to see in the world. This is urgent work. There are not enough women anywhere. It starts from birth. *Paw Patrol* is a current animated dog-based television phenomenon captivating toddlers globally. It features six male characters and one female one – a tiny cockapoo, dressed in pink with her head tilted coquettishly to the side.[6] We've got to do better than this for the next generation! How do we break through and say yes to things that scare us?

The answer is that your first six yeses will be scary and your seventh will be normal. No is a habit and yes is a habit. Some people worry about authenticity. 'If I'm not a panel person and it's not true to me, I won't do well.' 'If I'm not the kind of person who asks someone out or who speaks at my kids' school, I won't be any good at it anyway. I need to be authentic.' Authenticity has become a real twenty-first-century watchword, and while it is important to be who you are and say what you mean, authenticity is very ... limiting, isn't it?

My authentic self likes to sleep late and watch movies. My best self likes to get out of bed and make movies. I find if I just do the things my best self would do for six weeks or so, that becomes my habitual self. Your authentic self is simply your habitual self. If you want to be someone bold, brave, rhythmical, regal, defiant, deviant, loud, loving, energised, ebullient, fearless and full of yes – you just have to do the sorts of things that someone like that would do. If you appear on five panels in a year, that becomes something you do. No matter what anyone says, you are 'that kind of person'. We are what we do regularly. Habits are hard to break, but my big revelation of the last few years is that once we've replaced old habits that are holding us back with new habits that are propelling us forward, those new routines are equally as difficult to shift.

'No, I couldn't possibly.' 'No, I'm not sure I'd be any good at it.' 'No, what if it doesn't work?' is a habit. 'Yes, I'll give it a go.' 'Yes, I'm good at that sort of thing.' 'Yes, I've got a good feeling about it,' is a habit too.

The way to get good at yes is to challenge yourself to new

---

6 A couple more female characters have been added, in response to complaints, but they're just as pink.

behaviours in safe environments. The most obvious reason that doing *The Guilty Feminist* podcast has changed my life so dramatically is that I've been required by the format of the show to challenge myself to new behaviours most weeks. I'm used to challenging myself now. It's normal for me to look for opportunities to try new things. I often see an advertisement, hear a story or find out about a new class and think, 'Oh, that sounds scary. That'd be a good *Guilty Feminist* challenge.' I swerve to collide with my fears and inexperience, not to avoid them.

Two years ago, if you'd asked me to jump out of a plane, I'd have said you were crazy. I don't like flume rides because I don't like the feeling of dropping straight down. Not only did I skydive recently, I filmed it, I was exhilarated by it and can't wait to do it again. My twelve-year-old goddaughter saw the video and asked me to take her for her birthday. I couldn't wait to say yes (after parental permission was granted by text with an unnecessary number of emoticons). Did jumping out of a plane make me a better feminist? Not directly. But it did make me feel more invincible, larger, more adventurous and less frightened of other things. The way it affects my feminism is this – if I say yes to doing something scary, then it is easier to say yes to doing something important.

Right after I jumped out of a plane, I heard an influential man teasing a teenage girl about eating too much and telling her she'd get fat. I didn't hesitate. I took him aside and said, 'Don't say that to a teenage girl. Comments like that contribute to girls developing eating disorders.' He was a nice guy who clearly hadn't meant any harm. I think, ironically, he'd meant to josh with her to make her feel in the gang. We had the conversation and I'm fairly convinced he won't do that again. A friend who overheard me said, 'I'm so impressed that you said something. I thought it, but I'd find it hard to stand up to someone like that. What if it went wrong?' Honestly, I didn't think. How can I jump out of a plane and not into a difficult conversation? I've got used to saying yes.

I know not everyone has the budget, freedom, ability or time to jump out of a plane but there are a million things you can do every day to live larger, go for it and see life as an opportunity for yes. Each of those can make you a bolder, more present, more dynamic feminist who asks for what she wants for herself and others. Singing in a choir, posing for a life drawing class, talking to teenagers about feminism, volunteering for a charity, doing karaoke sober, speaking at your children's school or even taking up more space as you walk down the street or gliding into rooms as if you're Bette Midler appearing on stage at Carnegie Hall, are all brilliant ways of feeling and seeming freer, larger and more emboldened. No one is born full-Bette, not even Midler herself. It takes practice.

Sex and sexuality

I want to talk about the issue of 'consent' in the chapter titled 'The Power of Yes' and not in the one titled 'The Power of No' because it is a concept that is inherently flawed. Consent implies that one party is doing something to a second party who is capitulating. Consent, in law, implies that the state of mind of the victim is what determines guilt rather than the actions of the perpetrator. As Catharine A. MacKinnon points out in her article 'Rape Redefined'[7], in the Akayesu decision of the International Criminal Tribunal for Rwanda, rape was defined internationally for the first time as 'a physical invasion of a sexual nature, committed on a person under circumstances which are coercive'. She goes on to argue, 'Non-consent is absent from the definition because it is redundant: coercion

---

7 *Harvard Law & Policy Review* (2016).

is present because consent is absent. Coercion can be circum-
stantial as well as physical: "Threats, intimidation, extortion
and other forms of duress which prey on fear or desperation
may constitute coercion, and coercion may be inherent in
certain circumstances".[8] She points out that no one in real life
says, 'We had a great, hot night – she (or I or we) consented.'
Enthusiasm – or I would suggest engagement, because good
sex doesn't always feel rabble-rousing – should be standard for
a sexual encounter.

While we continue to talk about sexual consent as if we are
reluctantly allowing a neighbour to build a fence on our land,
against our wishes but not our will, we play into the idea that
the power imbalance expressed in the boardrooms, businesses
and backrooms of society will naturally be extended to the
bedroom. Do we consent to earning 75 pence on the pound?
Do we consent to 78 per cent of our elected officials being men?
Do we consent to the films we watch not passing the Bechdel
Test? We live in a society rife with inequality, so some women
do not know any different and feel safer with the status quo;
others freeze-and-friend because fight-or-flight is a far more
risky strategy. Some women are resigned to that which they feel
they cannot change and so they protect themselves by zoning
out. Other women fight, struggle and scream but are unable to
get any distance from oppressive forces. Does anyone consent
to a power imbalance?

We need to start talking about coercion. Men have been
trained through books, films and societal assumptions that
women and their bodies are there to be colonised. Our bodies
are not something to be conquered. Our genitals are not a place
to plant a flag. While we speak about consent so often, we may

---

8 To be clear, I really don't agree with Catharine MacKinnon on everything
but her logic in this article is hard to fault.

be co-creating a culture in which some men are looking for signs of acquiescence, giving in and resigned permission rather than arousal, invitation and initiation.

Women have been trained throughout history to please others, not make a fuss and be polite and well behaved. We've also been taught that our virginity is a prize to protect and our virtue is to be guarded. These contrary instructions mean young women often have very little experience of saying no, as elsewhere it means they're branded as difficult and punished for it. We cannot expect young women to do as they're asked and make no trouble until they're alone with a man and then expect them to be brilliant at clear, decisive, loud boundary-setting. Girls are trained to turn down things we really don't want, politely. It is the backbone of tribal female etiquette.

'Would you like some cake?'

'Thanks so much, I'm not really hungry right now but it looks delicious and I'd love to have some later,' is more polite than 'No, thank you.' It is even more polite to ask for a small piece of cake, take one tiny bite, play with it a bit and leave it on your plate.

'Would you like a lift home?'

'That's so kind of you, but my dad is picking me up.'

'Well, I can drop you to the end of the street and he can collect you from there, because that'll be on his way home.'

'Oh, okay ... I'll let him know ... thanks ...'

And *getting into a car you do not want to be in* is more polite than, 'No thank you. I really don't want to do that.'

When women are in a sexual situation we often use the same non-verbal cues and the same soft language and pleasing tone because we've been trained to since childhood!

'Is it okay if we stop for a while? Maybe later? Could we do more another time? Would the next date be okay?' 'I feel hot. I'm just going to get some water. Would you like anything?

Do you want to watch some TV?' These are not signs that a woman is hoping a white knight will impose his will on her. These are the softly, softly signals that we want to stop without being rude. Sometimes we are with someone we trust and we don't want to hurt his feelings. Other times experience and relative upper-body strength tells us that under no circumstances should we blame, rile or provoke because we may be in danger.

Something that many straight, cis men may not understand is the vast difference between penetrating and being penetrated. Having someone enter your body is intrusive and invasive in a way that is impossible to describe, if it is not something you welcome and are excited by. Consent is not enough if someone wants to insert themselves inside your person because consent implies permission rather than invitation. You may give someone permission to borrow your jacket, but you must *invite* them into your home and *desire* them to be in your bed. Now think about how much enthusiasm you'd truly need to welcome someone into your orifice.

Straight, cis men need to make *sure* that their partner hasn't checked out and glazed over because her mind is escaping where her body feels it can't.

This is not to say women are not up for sex. When we're up all night to get some, we're up all night to get lucky. Women are conditioned to feel embarrassed about being sexually voracious. I saw a TED Talk recently from a sex therapist who jokingly said, 'Married people prefer doggy style. He's on all fours, begging, and she's playing dead.' This stereotype of women not wanting sex is everywhere. Women who like or want sex are often described as 'nymphos'. Satyriasis is 'male nymphomania'. There's a reason you've probably never heard of it. Men are expected to have sexual appetites.

So many women I know want more sex than their male partners. It's such a common lunch topic. The women I discuss this with never ever talk about how to get a man to give in or put out. They talk about how and when to truly arouse their partners or to find more exciting ways to fly solo or end the relationship and find someone whose sexual appetites are as large as their own.

It is difficult to communicate what we want and what excites our imagination. What if we found a language to talk about it, that didn't kill it? What if we could say yes to the things that made us feel desirable? The truth is that sometimes both men and women want to be objectified. For a moment, an hour, an afternoon, we don't want to be respected for implementing sustainability policies, we just want to be physically admired. We want to be seen, wanted and taken. Some feminists want to be dominated. It can be hard to reconcile this with our feminism, but sex isn't an intellectual pursuit, so wanting to feel small or chastised or overpowered isn't just okay, it's sometimes necessary to feel whole and powerful and life-affirmed. This has to be communicated to our partners incredibly clearly because of the issues with engagement and coercion already discussed.

Sometimes feminists want to debate fiercely in the restaurant and then be handcuffed and ravished in the hotel room. Sometimes they want to dominate and talk dirty and watch porn and role-play sexual harassment. Many men struggle with these ideas, especially right now as feminism and sexual power imbalance seem to be twenty-four-hour rolling news. Lots of younger men have been raised by feminists and ritually schooled that no means no (rightly!), and they find it difficult to role-play it meaning anything else. Even if it has been clearly agreed that 'no' on this occasion means 'yes' and 'Cosby' is the safe word which kills all passion. It is completely understandable that this can be anxiety-inducing territory for men, but it shouldn't shame us. Asking for what we want and not being embarrassed about wanting to dominate or be dominated is a noble goal. Sometimes we don't let go because we are fearful. What if he hurts me? What if he doesn't respect me? What if it's embarrassing? What if I feel stupid? It is hard to say yes, especially if we've had bad experiences.

Working towards mutual sexual fulfilment doesn't sound very sexy. We are often told to work at our relationships but sexual attraction is constructed almost entirely of play. Flirtation is play. A first date that's described as 'hard work' doesn't lead to a second one. Working at a sexual relationship is like using a pick axe to repair a cobweb. Try playing at it instead. Find ways of saying 'yes' to your sexual self and making yourself whole. It will seep into your gait, your posture, your voice and your defiance. All the magic lassoes and bullet-proof shields of feminism.

Living at full mast

I sometimes wonder if the reason transgender women who are out incur so much opprobrium from society is because they are living wholly as themselves without apology, despite what it costs them. Even transgender women who pass, at some point have not. Transgender women are confronting to society because they risk both physical and structural violence to live as their most magnificent selves, and they do it anyway. For trans women to live their truth they have to go the full hokey-cokey and put their whole selves in because society leaves no option to put just one arm in and shake it all about.

This is true, in a way, of the whole queer community. If you're going to be hated for something you are, something essential to you that you can't change, you might as well stick some sequins on it, turn up the Kylie and go into the street and dance. Gay Pride celebrates the realisation that there is no point conforming because conformity won't get you validation. That's why there's no need for 'Straight Pride'. Straight people already have societal approval for their congenital condition.

The closer we are to societal norms, the more rewards there are for playing the game and saying 'Yes, sir' rather than yes to our best selves. The truth is there's no real benefit to women conforming to the status quo because it doesn't serve us. As Margaret Atwood rightly tells us in *The Handmaid's Tale*, 'Normal is only what we're used to,' and we're used to second place, poor representation and a life in the margins – some, of course, much further into the margins than others. We want to conform because we want to be liked and be good and get points, but we have to ask, if the fascist regime takes hold and *The Handmaid's Tale*'s Gilead becomes a reality, how likely are we to be shoved into a green, brown or red dress and forced into some kind of menial, demoralising or oppressive role? For women, the prize for conformity is almost always more conformity. That's not true for some men in Gilead who get to make and break the rules.

There are garments in all of our wardrobes we don't wear because we don't dare. We bought the jumpsuit for when we were feeling brave and it turns out we never are. A friend of mine had a party and asked us to wear that thing we already own that we never dare wear and it was the most wonderful night. One woman wore her bridal gown. Others wore more cleavage than clothes. Some wore glam rock shoes and velvet capes. Others, tight jeans and crop tops. Some, cosplay costumes. We were all given permission to say yes to our most daring selves. The one we leave hanging up at home. You don't have to be queer to leave the best part of yourself in the closet. Most of us are doing it all the time.

Tallulah Bankhead only left her most beautiful dress in the wardrobe when she came to the party naked. One day I hope to be brave enough to throw a spontaneous celebration because I feel like singing 'Bye Bye Blackbird'.

We need to practise leaving the house in the piece of (perhaps metaphorical) clothing that is most us until it's all we know to wear, or at least until we know how to shake it when we want to. We need to say yes to being on panels and speaking on topics on which we are not experts but about which we can make educated guesses until that becomes fun for us. We need to be and invent the change we wish to see in the world because we are sure we are the best women to do that. Ask people out and get used to them saying no – and even more scarily, yes. We need to invite people round for feminist choir practice and do a spontaneous photo shoot with a dressing-up box when they're there. We need to learn from the queer community, if we are not already in it, to get our glitter on and turn the tunes up. Let's tell the world we never received the cable that said, 'Don't come' and turn up anyway, shameless and ready for work. What cable?

Microclimates of yes

So far, I have been talking about saying yes in resistant environments. Now I want to look at structures that give permission to men where they deny entry to women. I want to look at the architectures of support.

Comedian Louis CK recently admitted, in the wake of some accusations that were part of the #MeToo movement, that he had exposed himself to, and masturbated in front of, women. These women were in his industry and the settings were often work-related – either offices or hotel rooms after the gig was finished and the bars were shut. There had been rumours for years. I don't know Louis CK or anyone who knows him, but I had heard about what he had done through the comedy grapevine. Almost everyone in the industry knew.

Obviously what he did was horrible and abusive, but that has been deconstructed at length already by many voices in the media and the Twittersphere. What I am interested in is the climate that allowed and enabled this behaviour and the effect this permissiveness has on powerful men.

Louis CK developed his comedy in an environment designed for and by men like him. When he first entered a comedy club, a white guy in t-shirt and jeans probably had the mic. Everything about the architecture told Louis that this was a place for people like him. Did he have to work hard? Of course. Did he have to die on his arse and hustle for gigs? Definitely. Was he broke and uncertain at times? For sure. But nothing about the environment told him that anything inherent to his identity was unwelcome or foreign in the space. Comedy isn't like a running race with an outright winner. Much of it is about trusting your random associations and comic observations and delivering them as if they're funny. Louis worked hard at his craft and colleagues and bookers started to notice that he was good, and that validation turned into confidence. Self-trust. After this virtuous circle had expanded over a long period of time, people started to say that Louis was the best. A genius, even. Tribal confidence.

Louis heard that. Now how does a genius write and perform comedy? What kind of confidence does that inject into his observations, routines and shows? His shows get even better. Comedy is subjective but many, many people agree that he's a genuinely excellent comedian and almost all high-profile comedians and well-respected comedy critics think so too.

One night at a comedy festival, during this rise to genius status, Louis CK offers two young women in a double act a beer in his room after the bars are shut. This is an ordinary offer for comedians who clock off after midnight. When the door is closed, he asks them if he can masturbate in front of them. Nothing about the context indicates that this is a sexual moment for them. He is not confused. They've not been kissing. He says, 'Can I jerk off?' They assume he is joking. He is not. He whips it out and begins. They don't know what to do. Their biochemical response tells them 'fight or flight' isn't their safest strategy because their predator can outpunch and outrun them and is closer to the door – so they do what most women do in situations like this. They 'freeze and friend' and leave as quickly as they can. They are confused and feel humiliated and abused.

When they get out of the room, they tell other comedians and producers what has happened. They are shut down. They are told that Louis is a genius and a gentleman and that he wouldn't do that. They are told that maybe they sent out the wrong signals and led him on. They are told that this is what happens in comedy and that if they don't like it they should get out. They are told that they'd better shut up or they won't be invited to the right parties or booked for the right gigs because 'it'll be awkward'. They are told they're lucky that Louis likes them because he is influential.

So now Louis's colleagues, friends and employers *know* that he is doing illegal, abusive and degrading things to women. And what's more – Louis knows they know. Everyone knows. And *still* he is encouraged to work, given budgets to make television programmes, invited on chat shows and hailed as a genius. *Now* what kind of a genius does Louis CK believe himself to be? A genius whose peers believe he must not be silenced at any cost. A genius worth any number of women who share his art form. That's not just enabling. That's emboldening. How exciting is his next gig? And how intoxicating is his next abuse of power?

I'm not surprised his shows were brilliant. I'm amazed they weren't twice as insightful and delivered with four times the panache. He must have thought he was one of the greatest comedy gods to walk the earth.

What about the women? The double act invited to his hotel room, for example? What signal does the industry send them about their worth in the world and their creative contributions? They are treated like comedy cannon fodder. They are not booked for shows because it is 'awkward'. They have never felt less like geniuses. No one values their work or even their person-hood enough to put their safety before a man's opportunities. I'm sure their work is wonderful, but I am not surprised they are not more famous. Nothing about the architecture of their busi-ness makes it possible or sends them a signal that it is desirable.

Look at the movies Harvey Weinstein made and the careers it turned out he killed. Women who had worked incredibly hard at their craft and slogged their way up in an industry of crushing and constant rejection, sexually rejected just one producer – and barely worked again. Other producers were told that certain actresses were difficult and that they should avoid casting them. The whole industry supported Weinstein in a move that said, 'The value of the films you produce is worth the cost of these replaceable actresses.' The message was clear – these women were pretty faces and there were plenty more where they came from. Almost everyone knew something wasn't right. He had non-disclosure clauses in his contracts. I'm surprised he didn't win twice the number of Oscars he did. His tribe was sending him a message that he could do no wrong – even when what he was doing was a despicable, illegal 'open secret'. Imagine Weinstein's thrill in knowing that almost everyone knew and no one cared. Think of his arrogance in knowing that the world was happy to pay a human sacrifice for his great art. The misuse of power isn't a regrettable side order for these men, it's the very fuel that feeds the ego that drives the work. It is a giant throbbing 'yes' to whatever pleases them.

And that 'yes' is powerful. Some say these abuses of power are isolated, but we know that's not true because of the use of the term 'casting couch'.[9] If you have a piece of furniture named after your entitled abuses of power, the establishment has been supporting your bad deeds for too long. I suggest we institute the 'don't you fucking dare divan' and challenge the system that tells men that being good at their jobs might get them hired again. It doesn't mean they can touch women or touch themselves while they make women watch.

Not all men respond that way. There's a story in Michael J. Fox's autobiography about a time in the 1980s when he was at the height of his fame and was caught speeding recklessly in his sports car. He remembers being terrified, thinking he'd ruined his career and would be sent to jail because he'd been going so fast – but far from arresting him, the policeman was excited to meet him. The officer told the young star to slow down because his family loved watching his sitcom so much. At that point, he recounts being even more frightened, because he realised he was above the law and that he'd have to restrain and control himself.[10] Some men – too many men, as it turns out – respond to this realisation with delight that they're now above democracy and so behave like potentates.

Sexual assault isn't the only way high-powered men abuse or flaunt their status to fuel their narcissism. The documentary *Jim and Andy* is a behind-the-scenes look at Jim Carrey's portrayal of the avant-garde comedian Andy Kaufman in the film *Man on the Moon*. Kaufman was a provocateur lauded

9 'The casting couch' refers to coercive, exploitative sexual advances made in show business with the promise of work (usually from producers or directors to actresses). I explain that only because some young people tell me they don't know this term. I hope that indicates it's on its way out.

10 Anecdote taken from Fox's autobiography *Lucky Man: A Memoir* (Hyperion Books, 2002).

as a genius, mostly for making others deeply socially uncomfortable. Some people adore his stuff, and again, comedy is subjective and many people loved him (though his comedy was divisive) but for me, this emperor of comedy is very lightly dressed. When Kaufman joined the cast of the hit American sitcom *Taxi*, he turned up late, caused endless delays on shoots and generally made life difficult and embarrassing for the other actors. He started wrestling women and provoked them into fighting him by shouting that they should be in the kitchen and were not men's equals. His alter ego, a character he performed called Tony Clifton, was an even bigger jerk, horrible to women and generally abusive.

This is a man who wanted to 'shake up the system'. A system that had been created for and by men like him. A system that allowed him to do and say whatever he wanted and worshipped him for his most anarchic acts. This is a man who thought misogyny was a subversive act. He probably didn't really believe the sexist things he shouted. He was playing the contrarian. But he didn't care what impact that had on the society that women were living in either. He didn't care that it emboldened sexism in the street, their homes and their workplaces. I am not suggesting that Andy Kaufman should have been censored, but I am noting how many high-profile outfits gave him the brightest, loudest possible platform while making little to no room for female voices. I am also observing what a remarkable impact that had on his confidence to embarrass, agitate and aggressively bait others – especially women. He heard a lot of powerful yeses in his career, no matter the impact on those around him.

When Carrey came to play Kaufman in his biopic, he decided to embody the man day and night and make the film set as disruptive and nightmarish as he believed Andy would have. Watching one influential man who is never told no play another worse offender is something to behold. I am not commenting on the artistic merit of the piece. I am rather in some wonderment at men's ability to make life so unnecessarily difficult for others in order that their own self-proclaimed 'genius' can flourish. I am in awe of it.

There is a reason you have never heard of a female Andy Kaufman. She wouldn't have lasted twenty minutes on a sitcom set. She'd have been fired for being difficult.[11] Even Marilyn Monroe, one of the biggest box office draws in cinema history, was eventually fired for bad behaviour. I am not claiming that women are never badly behaved or that stardom doesn't go to women's heads. I am pointing out the obvious fact that women are not routinely structurally supported in illegal behaviours, sexual assault, sexual harassment and antisocial, disruptive actions that shut down film sets, cost money and distress other people. If a woman has power and influence she can behave like a 'diva' but only if she's emotional and seems slightly out of control and needs to be helped. She can be cut-throat and mean for her own ends, but she can't be intentionally, provocatively and whimsically destructive for fun. It won't be tolerated.

There isn't a culture that supports 'genius at any price' for women. In turn, women rarely tell the story, 'my genius is invaluable'. There is no architecture to support us if we do. That particular yes is reserved for men.

The Petri dish – how to make a microclimate

Television and radio shows are generally thrust upon us. They are what is available at the time we most want to watch or

---

11 Sam Simon claimed on Marc Maron's podcast in 2013 that it was a fiction that Andy Kaufman disrupted the *Taxi* set, but when Jim Carrey was recreating the mayhem in *Man on the Moon*, the rest of the *Taxi* cast (who'd come to recreate the events) were very clear in the attendant documentary that this was 'exactly like Andy'.

listen to something. Podcasts are an underground club. People recommend them to each other. 'You'd love this podcast' is invariably a compliment that implies you're a person of great taste and rare critical faculties.

When we began *The Guilty Feminist* podcast, it was a play space and discussion house for women. About thirty people attended the first recording. Our live audience built very quickly. I'm not implying it is because we were so amazing, rather it is because the people who wanted to hear what we had to say knew where we were. In the last few months I've noticed that it has grown its own culture apart from me and, frankly, beyond my conscious ambition or intentions.

I have realised that it has become a microclimate where women are expected to do well and where the audience have come to celebrate women and treat them the way men are treated in other places. It is not an environment that will automatically reward Louis CK before he has opened his mouth. He would not be assumed to be a genius on our stage. *Now* it's fair to say that he'd be booed off our stage. But I mean a Louis CK-type who hasn't made the news (yet).

We've had a few men on as guests, and lately I've seen something interesting happen. The (always female) guest co-host and I are having a terrific time doing one-liners, chat and stand-up comedy and the audience are absolutely with us. Then I introduce the male guest and I see them lean forward slightly in their seats and raise their eyebrows as if to say, 'All right . . . we'll hear you out, white man.' Those guests shrink a little and behave like the lone woman on a panel of men. They get nervous, take up less space, try harder than they need to. (This doesn't apply to all the men we've had on, and if you're one of our previous male guests reading this, I'm definitely not talking about you.)

Every time without fail, the audience have warmed to the

male guests we've had, and they've relaxed in turn and the show has been terrific. I am trying to create a comfortable space for all my guests and I wouldn't have booked the men if I didn't think they had something valuable to contribute, but the microclimate that we've inadvertently created gives more power, space and assumption of brilliance to women. Women who come on regularly start to shine more each time and take power from the audience they know is excited to see them. Fans tweet about comedians they've heard on the show, copying them in and telling them how much a particular joke, story or revelation meant to them. *Guilty Feminist* podcast listeners go to see their favourite comedians' solo shows and other gigs. In this environment, a woman is far more likely to start to believe her ideas to be genius and present them as such than a man is.

I'm not claiming our podcast is unique. There are many spaces like this and there are more growing all the time. I've just been able to observe this one grow and thrive and it has been a remarkable experience and a true privilege. It is simply an environment where the tribe trusts women by default. We create our own tribal confidence.

Women being celebrated and imbued with a structural yes on my show, or others like it, is not the same as the whole comedy circuit or society at large determining how they are treated. But I believe this microclimate can turn into a culture as more spaces service women and celebrate them. The same effect is happening with our audience, in a different way. Listeners look forward to the show because it is for and about them. It makes them central. When people who work in the entertainment industry ask me about the success of the podcast as if it is a mystery, I reply, 'Women are thirsty. There isn't much directed at us.'

Reese Witherspoon has also created a microclimate with her production company Hello Sunshine. She delivered a speech at the Glamour Women of the Year Awards in 2015, which you may have seen online because it went viral. In it she said she had started a self-funded company 'with a mission to tell stories about women' and was told that she would go out of business in a year or two and lose her very expensive shirt because 'there wasn't a market for female-driven material'. The people who told her that were wrong. She went on to make *Wild*, *Gone Girl* and *Big Little Lies* among others and has over twenty-five films and TV shows in development all with complex female leads. Reese says that 'films with women at the centre are not a public service project. They are a big-time, bottom-line-enhancing, money-making commodity,' and points to many contemporary examples of the industry waking up to this, including the *Hunger Games* franchise which has made $2.2 billion worldwide. I think what she is saying is that women are thirsty and that female stories are human stories. She goes on to invite women in tech, business, healthcare, construction, politics and other areas of business and public life to be ambitious and assertive about closing the gap in representation and pay in their patch of the world. It is easy to think that all of those arenas are more important than film and television, but I am not sure that's true.

The world has been done a great disservice by Hollywood because for a hundred years most of the stories we've consumed have been delivered from this portal (or another more local one imitating it), and that means for a century everyone in the world has almost exclusively been invited to empathise with white men. The result is the Trump administration. The President of the United States can refer to human beings from 'shit-hole' countries and the media can report that this 'resonates with his base'. He can be caught talking about 'grabbing pussy' and yet (mostly white) women will vote for him.

A story is a chance to look out of a different window and

see life through someone else's eyes. If the only window we are asked to look out of is a white man's over and over and over again, we breed a population of white male supremacists who subliminally think white and male is the norm, even if that results in their own self-deprecation or self-loathing.

Imagine you're in a tall building with a hundred windows and you see a parade in the street. It looks like it's all men dressed as footballers and gamers and superheroes. You are convinced the parade is 100 per cent male because you cannot see out of any of the other windows. If you wanted more information you'd need to look out of the window below, the one in the room to the right and left of you. Then you'd know if it were all male or if there were other people there. Maybe through one window you can see women on a float and through another you can see an LGBT brass band. It's fine to look out of the window that shows only men sometimes but if you only ever look out of one window you get a distorted view. Most of the time, most of us, no matter who we are, look out of the same window featuring white men, over and over.

Stories about black women are funded and marketed as if they are niche. Executives assume only black women will want to see them. But black women watch stories about white men all the time. They have to empathise with white men or they can't enjoy *Breaking Bad*, *Mad Men*, *Superman*, *Casablanca*, *The Big Bang Theory* or *Doctor Who*.[12] Want to watch a Christmas movie that'll make you cry? *It's a Wonderful Life* makes me weep every time. It's about a person who ... It's about a straight, white man who realises the world would be a worse place if he'd never been born. Asian women, black men, queer teens, transgender women in wheelchairs, biracial

---

12 Now with a woman in the lead role after over fifty years of white male actors – a change that was the cause of some outrage to men.

bisexual people all weep along to that. It's normal for us to do the work to filter our experiences through the same window.

Stories matter. It can be argued that Dickens did more for social healthcare and housing in Britain than Marx because Dickens told the story of a little orphan boy who fell into poverty and was criminalised. He made people feel and understand and want to make a change. He made people look at real-life orphans on the street and see them differently. Obviously Oliver Twist was a white male child, but you see my point. The hero of your story is a vehicle for empathy. This is urgent. 'Sassy' black female best friends are funny and lovable but you're not asked to imagine yourself in their shoes the way you are the hero. It's always the hero's window you're seeing the world through.

We need to start creating more microclimates in which female talent can flourish and female stories of all kinds can be told. I am not talking about individuals doing feminist or egalitarian shows, as wonderful as that is. I am talking about structures and networks which centre women and have high expectations of them. I am talking about places where female work, skills and ways of operating are rewarded in the ways that have traditionally been reserved for their male counterparts. I am talking about inventing our own tribal confidence.

If we can get enough microclimates operating, and we can join them up to form circuits, then potentially women can operate so often in spaces which reward them for their talent and hard work that when they need to do deals, demand space and be heard in patriarchal spaces they'll take their swagger with them. They'll question disrespect. They won't be spoken over. They'll see that the guys in these spaces claiming genius are not all that – because they'll be used to being seen, heard and appreciated. Microclimates give Bobs a chance to feel like Als and Als a chance to experience what it is like to be a Bob.

How can you create a microclimate? Create a space that is led but collaborative. Invent and originate. Shine a light on people who are not already being regularly platformed.

When women are mentored, we're often treated as remedial. We're given a scheme, a tiny pot of money and someone to guide us and a Noblesse Oblige scholarship for Best Female Woman. When men are mentored, they get a *Top Gun* approach: 'You're the best of the best. We're going to make you better.' Notice that men are allowed to boldly fail over and over again until they get it right. (That is literally the plot of *Top Gun*.) Women are traditionally given one shot. Even if they succeed they're often not funded again because then they're not seen as remedial any more and told they should be able to make it on their own now – as if the landscape has magically changed to allow that. Let's start to create Top Gun Academies in all our industries and make the gender split around 60/40 female and non-binary people to male (to rebalance historical bias) and see how all of us thrive over the next five years. The work will be better, more diverse, more exciting and your whole population will start to fire on all cylinders. We'll double our Als and halve our Bobs.

If you're doing this grassroots-style, don't only stand in opposition to something – stand *for* something. Find your tribe using the internet. Experiment. Sometimes you need luck.

Here's one I made earlier with a little design and some happy accidents. As a *Guilty Feminist* challenge on representation I started a traditional British comedy panel show called *Global Pillage*.[13] I did it because, to paraphrase Gandhi, I decided to

---

13 If you're not familiar with a traditional British comedy panel show, it's one in which two teams of (two or three) comedians compete in a quiz. There's usually a host, in this case, me, and sometimes a scorekeeper/fact clarifier, in this case Ned Sedgwick.

be the change I wanted to see in light entertainment. My brief was clear: to make the format one in which traditionally marginalised people could not be seen as token, by baking diversity into the show. The questions are all about cultural diversity and the audience get to answer playing for 'the hive mind'. And, because diversity works, they almost always win.

Several interesting things have happened in the *Global Pillage* Petri dish. One is that the live audiences have become more and more diverse. So many more people of colour come to *Global Pillage* than any other show I've done or been involved with. Recently, as the audience filed in, I saw two Somalian women in hijabs and abayas come through the door. I said to my friend (and regular *Guilty Feminist* guest co-host) Bisha K. Ali, who was one of the comedians on the panel, 'You don't normally see women dressed like that at comedy shows like this, do you?' And she replied, 'They feel safe here. They feel welcome. They've listened at home and they feel sure they're included.' If you are white, it may be hard to understand how daunting it can be to be the only non-white person attending a show, much less the only person wearing a hijab.

There are a number of factors at play here. It is not extraordinary for all four available seats on the panel to be taken by women of colour, so an Asian or African woman is likely to recommend the show to her friends and family. And the audience get to speak up, so women hear female audience members contributing questions such as, 'My family is from Iraq and there we have a saying – *I will eat your liver.* What does that mean?' (It actually means I love you. As in, 'I love you so much, I could eat you up'.) A woman listening at home now knows she is not just represented on stage, but also that she will not stand out in the audience.

We decided to stage these shows as weekend matinees because venues and comedians are more available then. We did that for our own convenience, but what we hadn't realised was that it is also easier for some women to come in the day. They feel safer, can get childcare more easily and generally are less daunted and less likely to find themselves up a dark alley or in a drunken pub. We accidentally made our show more accessible, and I notice that we get more parents, elderly people, people in wheelchairs (because the building has ramps and lifts), unaccompanied women and women from different backgrounds than I see at other comedy shows.

The other thing that happens at *Global Pillage* is that comedians with sharp elbows, those who play the competitive panel show way, don't really have an easy time of it. The very act of putting a female-heavy, diverse group of comedians together over time has created its own culture – over and above my expectations. If someone else took over hosting *Global Pillage* now, it would have its own life without me and, I am certain, would continue with the same energy. The audience don't respond to blokey, winner-takes-all-style jokes and are much more likely to laugh at the comebacks from the comedians who are playing to have a fun time and make others feel good. We put some ingredients into a Petri dish and the rest happened on its own.

Questioning strategies and refusing to copy patriarchal architecture is a great way to build your own microclimate, build tribal confidence and find some happy accidents. In 2005 Franklin Leonard, a Hollywood script development exec, sent an email out to almost a hundred of his industry colleagues and asked them to name their favourite scripts from that year that had not been made as feature films. In return for revealing this information, he told them he would supply them with the complete list.

The same screenplays were mentioned by many people. One was *Juno*, a film written by a young woman called Diablo

Cody. You probably know the story because the film was an indie hit. It is about a flawed, complicated, funny teenage girl who gets pregnant, considers an abortion and then favours adoption. Turned out almost everyone in the industry loved the script but no one dared make it because the material was too edgy, too female and too out there. No one wanted to take the risk. When the script topped Franklin's list, suddenly it didn't look like a risk any more. If so many tastemakers in Hollywood loved it, there must be an audience for it. Now it was a hot property. The Black List (as Franklin named it) adds the tent pole of credibility to outliers and alternative windows for narrative.

Franklin decided to make the list annual. It has completely changed the landscape of independent and even mainstream film-making. Franklin chose the name The Black List because, as an African American man, he hated the shorthand of the 'black-hatted cowboy' being bad. He wanted to create a black-list everyone wanted to be on. Over three hundred Black List screenplays have been made as feature films. Those films have earned over $26 billion in worldwide box office, have been nominated for 264 Academy Awards and have won 48. Ten of the last twenty Oscars for Best Screenplay have been won by screenplays from the Black List.

I heard Franklin speak recently and he said that a working parent in Idaho can't and shouldn't throw it all in to write screenplays in Santa Monica coffee shops until they're discovered, so he's gone on to create extra scaffolding for the voices of Hollywood outliers. He has developed The Black List into an online forum where unrepresented or developing writers can be read and rated by professionals. He's changed the architecture that favours certain sorts of storytellers and has removed barriers to entry for others.

Your microclimate doesn't have to stay micro for long. It

can smash the patriarchy like a strong, green, healthy plant breaking through the foundations of an old house.

Me Too is a piece of global architecture that empowers women to speak out about their sexual harassment. Individual women have complained for years, and almost invariably those women have been accused of wanting publicity or money. Others have feared for their safety and careers and said nothing. Now there's a structure, a place to credibly submit your story and it has humbled the establishment (and not the kind of 'humbled' people claim to be at awards ceremonies when receiving trophies). Jon Stewart admitted on the American chat show *Today* that his response to accusations about Louis CK on *The Axe Files* podcast a year before had been flippant. He said his response was first, 'What?!' Then to make some jokes and say, 'I know Louis. He's always been a gentleman. *To me.*' He followed up on *Today* by admitting, 'It speaks to the blindness that a man has: *Hey – he's a good guy – what are you talking about?* It's an endemic, systemic, complex problem that we all haven't had the urgency for. Certainly, myself included.'

In the same interview he talks about the broader climate for women: 'Comedy on its best day is not a great environment for women ... to do it was an act of bravery in and of itself. The idea that there was this added layer of pressure and manipulation and fear and humiliation ... It's endemic ... I think it's a question of men are used to being in charge and I think if you talk to women they're in a very difficult position. And you get mad at yourself too for laughing it off or thinking: *that didn't happen.*'[14] The reason this acknowledgement is important is that the culture is now validating men for speaking this way

14 *Today*: https://www.youtube.com/watch?v=AGVW9Z4RcUc.
Podcast: https://www.youtube.com/watch?v=Da5VYSPsoEO.

and making it impossible for them to continue to ignore what they previously felt embarrassed to voice or just didn't really see. His two responses, a year apart, are so vastly different in tone and humility, demonstrating how much a systemic change alerts individuals to their own blinkered thinking.

In December 2017, John Oliver challenged Dustin Hoffman about sexual harassment allegations in an interview at a Tribeca Film Festival panel.[15] Oliver has made his reputation as a principled stand-up guy who pulls no punches, so this isn't entirely surprising, but I'm not sure he'd have raised it two years ago in a friendly interview at a film festival when it could, potentially, have been career-damaging for himself. Maybe he would have, but what I do know is that now he can do it sure that even if there's a certain amount of blowback, there'll be some solid support and appreciation too. Some people may see that as unnecessary 'cookies for allies'[16] – but it's exactly the kind of structural reform that's critical for lasting change. Men are rewarded for all sorts of good, bad and random behaviours. Society works on validation and opprobrium. We need to start collectively rewarding the right things and letting them feel the trust of the tribe when they act as allies.

Some people, including some feminists, have asked whether everyone sharing their #MeToo stories on Twitter is just a trend. What does it really do? I believe it's already irreversibly changed the culture. A friend of mine was in a show eighteen months ago and suffered nightly groping from a famous actor. We discussed her best strategies but, ultimately, she felt she couldn't afford to complain because when the play went on tour, if there was any awkwardness they'd make an excuse to

---

15 *Washington Post*: https://www.youtube.com/watch?v=bZNuhoxxKis.
16 An internet expression that refers to people wanting praise for doing the decent thing: 'So you spoke out against racism. Do you want a cookie?'

recast her part, but his box office would outweigh his assault. Post #MeToo, the show is heading off to a series of glamorous venues and I asked her if she'd consider putting up with his behaviour again. 'God, no,' she said. 'I wouldn't dream of tolerating it now. I'll go straight to the producers and tell them it isn't to happen again if it does – but to be honest, I don't think he'd dare now.' She and he both know that the broader societal structure and awareness won't support his sexual harassment any more. Obviously I'm not saying sexual harassment is at an end. There are many abuses of power across multiple industries and locations, happening right now. I'm saying that some of the scaffolding that supported flagrant, well-known perpetrators to the extent that they felt entitled is being dismantled, and while it hasn't smashed the patriarchy exactly, it's hobbled it. It's certainly looking over its shoulder in a way it hasn't needed to before now.

Personally, I feel emboldened. Some years ago, at a comedy festival, a well-known comedian's assistant texted me at night summoning me to her boss's hotel room. I had had no sexual contact with the man before but he'd made it plain he was attracted to me. I politely declined and I was summoned again. First by her and then by him. I did not go. If he had come to my door, my natural politeness and fear of turning him away would have made me invite him in. I wouldn't have known how to shut the door in his face. Now I would. Me too. Time's up. This new climate doesn't make a 'yes' to women being heard easy, but it makes it possible.

Create book clubs, activist groups, choirs, discussion panels, comedy groups, podcasts and play spaces that say yes to women, non-binary and femme people. Put things you suspect might work into Petri dishes. If they don't, it's an experiment! Have another go. Some of the happy accidents like putting a show on in the daytime, or letting your audience speak up, might be the very ingredient that creates the architecture that supports those you wish most to amplify. The more environments that say yes to feminist, female and other marginalised voices, the bolder those voices will become and the louder and clearer they will ring out into the wider world. Be ambitious. Have a go at creating a tribe that has confidence in you and people like you. If we all make microclimates, it won't take long for our collective efforts to simply be 'the climate'. Not just 'the current climate', but a climate for permanent change. A climate for the power of the female yes.

Cool Black Friend™

Susan Wokoma is a wonderful actress, a trusted friend and a black woman who has taught me much about the intersection between gender and race in her role as regular guest co-host of *The Guilty Feminist* podcast. She says 'yes' to life and 'yes' to feminism in a way that I find magnetic and contagious. I can think of no one better to talk to us about the power of yes and give us a broader perspective.

> **Susie, you're much loved on the podcast and a favourite *Guilty Feminist* voice. Could you give us your favourite 'I'm a feminist but ... '?**
> I'm a feminist but the character I relate to most is Muriel from *Muriel's Wedding*. It's not to do with getting married, it's to do with having a wedding ... and ABBA ...
>
> **You radiate 'yes' in your attitude to life. Where did that come from and how do you practise that positive energy, and is it just the way you came into the world?**
> I think it's the way that I came into the world because

there wasn't much to be positive about for a long while. Childhood was basically me slowly collating a list of hurdles I'd have to come up against. Oh, I'm poor – some people don't like that. Oh shit, I'm black – some people really don't like that. Oh, I'm dark-skinned, oh, I'm not skinny, oh, I'm not beautiful like the girls in *Shout* magazine, oh, I can't sing and everyone here really expects me to be able to.

I've had amazing friends and mentors in my life. They're the reason. That, and I cherish humour.

I know you sometimes say yes to things that are out of your comfort zone because you agreed to jump out of a plane with me as a challenge for the show. Why did you say yes to that?
Because opportunities do not come flying at me (pun intended) to jump out of planes. That's what white people do. So I thought, 'Fuck it, I'll jump out of that plane with my great white ally friend.'

Honest answer? I hate regrets. I'd rather do something and hate it and receive my 'L' than not do it at all.

How do you think saying yes to new things and things that scare us is related to feminism or important to feminists?
I dunno if it's related because to me it's quite fucking obvious that everyone should be saying yes to anything related to feminism. But yes, realising the world as we know it is designed to scare, suppress, even kill over half its population is a pretty depressing thing to confront, and so saying 'yes' to the movement by maybe joining it, or something, can be scary.

I'm not suggesting you speak for all black women – but you've taught me a lot about how especially dark-skinned black women are marginalised and demoralised by society. Do you ever feel or observe that there are times when it is more dangerous for black women to put their heads above the parapet and choose to be visible or take a leadership role because there is a higher cost to them failing or a higher barrier to entry?

Absolutely. For a couple of reasons. Black women are not supported by white women when we do. Not in quite the same way that white women support each other. I get it – it's about empathy and seeing yourself within things. It's thoroughly human. However, yes, it makes me think twice about adding my voice to an already full choir. A choir who wouldn't be interested in shouting about women's issues because it's regarding some 'far-flung' land.

Too many times have I received a much harsher tongue for knowing my worth and using my voice. It doesn't always stop me but sure, it's exhausting.

The last reason is that black women have been shouting this shit for years. Ask your girl Gloria Steinem – she gets it. Now it's fashionable and 'in' to be a feminist. Sweet. Great. Whatever propels the movement. But I know a lot of black women who are like, 'Cool – you lot handle it, then. I'm gonna have a piña colada.' Black women for so long have not been afforded individualism or the time for self-care or self-love. One of my dear black girlfriends uses the term 'Protect Your Neck'. Look after yourself. Just like Audre Lorde says, 'Self-care is a revolutionary act', which I believe a hundred per cent regarding black women. So much of black female history and narratives have been self-sacrifice and servitude and suppressing and suffering. I was happy to be a guest at the Women's

March but I did absolutely feel like a lot of people's Cool Black Friend™.

Do you ever feel personally that there are fewer opportunities to say 'yes' to – for example, as a black actress – and so are you more likely to say 'yes' bravely to those that come your way?
Yeah, I do. Which is why so many black women are creating their own stuff (I'm talking about my career mainly, here). I remember talking to my US manager about going over to LA and auditioning for pilot season (a month in which lots of television pilots get made) – I was nervous about it. Unsure how a size 14, dark-skinned, quite plain-looking girl would fit into LA.

You are definitely not plain but carry on . . .
She totally understood my reservations but said, 'Suz, in just one month you'll audition for more things in LA pilot season than you would a whole year in the UK' – bang on. I work a lot but that's because I get a lot of jobs that I go up for. And I've only had one lead role in the UK.

So yes, I've learned to be brave – and actually recently I was given, straight-out offered, a lead role in a movie out in Nigeria. The shoot was to start in exactly seven days and I was a post-New Year's Eve/birthday party mess of a woman. I was in no state to star in a film. The part is an all-out drama about a young mother who loses her daughter. I didn't feel healthy enough or talented enough. So I said yes. 'Cos fuck it. And also I have amazing friends who see me and my capabilities when I can't see them or myself.

I think *The Guilty Feminist* is a microclimate for women to shine. Do you feel that, and if so, are there other places where you feel that way? What environments allow you to be your best self and say 'yes' to your whole self, as it were?

I absolutely feel that about the podcast. Case in point – I had never ever attempted stand-up comedy before co-hosting *The Guilty Feminist* with you. And days before my first go at it, I was sick with fear. I remember I took myself off to Brighton for a couple of days to eat saveloys, get my tarot read by some dude on the beach and write stand-up. But that crowd are so supportive and open and proud of you that you just burst with it. It's not quite admiration because it includes them. It's just a lovely harmony, I guess.

An environment that mirrors this is my WhatsApp group called The Boardroom. Its members are five other black women in the arts and it was set up as a self-care hub away from the onslaught of online racism and explaining your existence to sceptical white people all the time. Being an educator. And it's honestly my happy place. We mainly joke and laugh and share memes and give each other support and advice and we meet for dinner all together once a year. Even though the origin of it came from pain, The Boardroom reminds me every day how funny, witty and sharp as fuck these black women are. How I am, when I feel safe and happy and valued.

What was that like, doing stand-up for the first time? It's many people's worst nightmare – what made you think you could do it?

Yeah, it was terrifying. Also because if I were a stand-up comedian, my set would just consist of very dirty, very embarrassing, very real stories that happened to me. I can spin a good yarn but I don't want the world to know about that one time a guy tried to put his willy in my belly button. I didn't need it and the *Guilty Feminist* audience don't need it.

Again, I only thought I could do it because a) friends were encouraging me, and b) fear of regret. I would have stayed up, awake, for months thinking about it if I didn't try.

I think it comes from something my drama teacher at RADA said to us: 'Follow the path of most resistance.' If something scares you/makes you nervous/makes you doubt your tenacity, strength, courage, talent, then you should probably be doing that very thing.

How can we create microclimates in theatre, film, academia, feminist spaces and across industries to celebrate and endorse women of colour and particularly black women? What things help? Especially if it's a space curated by white women? What are we getting wrong? Have black friends. I'm not saying collect ethnics like they're stamps, but get to know people outside of your race. See, I tell you what I used to do before I got a life and before Twitter became the cesspit of hate that it is now – if someone white followed me, I'd check who they followed. So many people solely followed accounts run by white people. I didn't follow many people back based on this research. What is the news you're getting? The jokes? The stories? If your sources are solely white and you're a feminist, 'ave a word.

I had a dear white girl friend once – we were tight for years. We talked every single day. But there was one thing I eventually noticed. On social media, her accounts were like a whitewash. I was nowhere to be seen. She always went to events and posted pictures with her white, petite girlfriends. This was actually pointed out to me by someone white. So basically what I'm saying is this – get to know people outside of your own experience. Too many well-meaning white feminists only know other well-meaning white feminists. Travel outside yourself.

Just like I fully allied up during the Women's March and countless other White Feminism™ events and talks – ally the fuck up, too. This creates understanding, empathy and the fact you'll miss us if we are not invited into your rooms. And on the other hand, if, like my now ex-mate, you like to keep your black friends a secret, just don't bother. Don't try. Just do you. Do the full white thing. Be honest. Live your truth. Do a Series One of *Girls* (which I loved, by the way) and stick to it. There's nothing worse when you're invited into a room or space and you know your only function is to alleviate guilt or to quietly be appreciative.

What does intersectionality mean to you? How important is it for feminism?

If I was to be super-fricking-wry I'd say intersectionality is about understanding that not wearing high heels on a red carpet really is neither here nor there, and that women are dying as a result of misogyny so let's talk about that. Like I said – wry.

Intersectionality is understanding that there are different kinds of women. And it's integral because we make a bigger noise, together.

I also interviewed the woman who introduced me to the wonderful Susan Wokoma – the astoundingly talented Phoebe Waller-Bridge. Phoebe has created and brought to life characters who embody 'the power of yes' in her hit theatre and television show *Fleabag* and television show *Killing Eve*. The characters in these shows don't conform to patriarchal norms for women, while remaining gloriously, wholly female. Phoebe is widely thought to have moved the bar for the sort of transgressive women who can appear on screen and find a large, excited audience. In doing this, she has provided much needed representation for women who want to live at full mast, flying their own colours. To do this she needed her creative partner, Vicky Jones, who directed and developed the live show *Fleabag* and script-edited the television version. Phoebe and Vicky had to create a microclimate for success and put a lot of different ingredients into the Petri dish that is their company, DryWrite. To know Phoebe is to know the power of yes in human form. She offers her insights here.

Phoebe, when I met you, you seemed to be bursting with a desire to live at full mast and tell stories to the world, but the power structures (in this case the entertainment industry) were rarely responding to women as writers with voices or directors with vision at that time. What made you think you could do it and approach it with the confidence you did?

I just loved doing it so much that I couldn't stop trying. It's a compulsion more than a confidence. I was so excited at the prospect of making an audience laugh and cry that I wanted to be a part of making that happen. I also had a great creative partner in Vicky Jones. She made me think I could do anything. I did feel I had something to offer. Mainly the comedy. I knew I could land a joke and I knew I had an instinct for telling stories. Outside of that I was totally in the dark until we set up DryWrite. Producing those nights became the training ground for bringing those instincts together and giving them purpose. As an actress I hardly came across any roles for my age that felt real or relatable to me. I just wanted to play someone who wasn't either a victim or a ball-breaker. When you asked me to write for the storytelling festival, I'd written a bunch of short plays for DryWrite, but I'd never written anything just for me solo. Most people I knew would roll their eyes at the idea of a 'one-woman play', which made me want to do it even more. It was my chance to put my 'interesting, funny, complicated, female character' where my mouth was. There was something so raw and pure about simply sitting on that stool, looking directly into the eyes of the audience, with nothing to distract us other than the words, jokes, twists and turns of a story.

It might be worth saying that the one good thing about being another twentysomething out-of-work actress was that no one cared what I said or did – no one was expecting anything – so I was in the perfect position to surprise people and I had nothing to lose. I stopped trying to write like other people or act like other people. I just thought, I'm gonna do this how I've always *secretly* wanted to do it, and let's see if it makes Vicky laugh. Once I took the pressure off myself to please everyone and just wrote things that Vicky and I would guffaw and cry at, I felt incredibly liberated, and sort of ... dangerous.

How did you create your own model or microclimate for success in DryWrite? What did you and your co-creator Vicky Jones do differently? Lots of people start their own projects or companies but yours seemed to be magnetic? Do you (consciously) know what the ingredients in your Petri dish were?
I think, most importantly, we just made it really *fun*. Most of the free nights of short plays – the one place new actors

and writers can flex their muscles when out of work – were writers testing scenes from plays they were working on and their friends and family coming to see it. Although that was useful to the writers, it wasn't attracting a huge audience – which is exactly what new writers need more than anything. So we created DryWrite and put on monthly shows, each with eleven or so writers that put the focus on the audience. Each month writers were challenged to inspire a specific reaction out of the crowd: make an audience forgive a character of a heinous crime, fall in love with a character in under five minutes, heckle without them knowing that's the goal. Giving the audience a role i.e. voting or heckling meant they were engaged in a new way, and giving the writers a specific challenge freed them from just having to write 'the best thing ever', which we're all trying to do the rest of the time. Each piece of work was presented anonymously so writers could be really outrageous with the risks they took and the audience got a kick out of guessing who had written what. But at the heart of all that, Jones and I were putting on theatre that we were personally intrigued and excited by . . . That's what kept it fresh, I think. We wouldn't put on an event unless we had an idea that made us both buzz.

The lead character you created in your live show and television comedy *Fleabag* lives life at full mast in a way that we rarely get to see represented. She is bold, transgressive, badly behaved, unapologetically sexual and she enjoys her own misdemeanours and adventures so much – winking at the audience and allowing us in on the fun. They say you've got to see it to be it but she seems like a genuinely new creation. What gave you permission to do this? Where did you find the

fearlessness to write and perform her? And do you think it's an important step for feminism that women are represented as flawed and at times unempathetic and not always as care givers but takers too?

Those words you mentioned were often used against female characters to describe them as 'unlikeable' ... and the ingredients I found most exciting about the character. I think people are unnerved by 'unlikeable' women because we're brought up to believe that women are supposed to care deeply about what you think of them. That it is, in some way, possible to 'fail' at being a woman. Men have their own version of that of course – society is a bitch to everyone – but ambition, cut-throatiness, confidence, sexual voraciousness, rebelliousness is behaviour often admired in men, and punished in women. If a woman displays qualities that aren't people-pleasing, she isn't playing the game. If she's not playing the game, how do we control her? Fleabag, Villanelle and Eve in some way are all women who *appear* to play the game – lipstick, eyelash-batting, apologising for everything in Eve's case, but scratch the surface and there is a whole load of other complicated glory going on underneath ... but to look at and speak to in the real world they do not stand out as anything other than Nice Functioning Women. I feel like that comes part and parcel with being a woman ... the presentation of an NFW is pretty homogenised. I mean ... a woman who grows her underarm hair is still edgy as hell in most places. We're brought up with media messages like: 'Be unique, but don't be too edgy', 'Be natural, but don't be undesirable', 'Be YOU, but for god's sake shave it off. SHAVE IT ALL OFF'. I don't actually think many men care that much about that stuff, but men and women alike are trained to believe it matters so we buy more things to SHAVE IT OFF. All of that hypocrisy drives me mad. I also felt that what I was saying could have power because, even though it was truthful, it felt unsayable at the time. Now, thank god, the conversation has since exploded.

Let me also be clear that there are also just basic, boring, horrible, unlikeable female characters. Every character should have an element of them that charms an audience or we won't watch or care. It's just interesting that what is considered unlikeable in a female character can be so forgivable in a male character. But the more women writing out there the more this is challenged.

In _Killing Eve_ you explore work-obsessed (at the expense of romantic relationships), violent and psychopathic women. It was a big hit, in part perhaps because it's done with a lot of playfulness and in part because it's a side to women we hardly ever get to see explored. If we are writers and creators and we want to fully delve into our gender on the page or the stage, how do we portray women who have these qualities without just writing men? I so often see films where, for example, women just punch their way out of trouble now. They answer problems in a traditionally masculine way while happening to be a woman. Your characters seem to remain authentically female – while being single-minded workaholics or violent and sociopathic. Do you know how you do that? How can artists explore these sides of women which allow us to acknowledge our darker urges and selfish selves so that we can see ourselves and be seen as fully human and not just saints and cyphers?

Jones and I talked a lot about the 'glory of being a woman', but by that we mean the mess of it all and how we can laugh at it. I love being a woman. I mine the glorious, goriest details of it for these characters. Tapping into female idiosyncrasies through these characters has made me treasure them even more. It feels like a celebration, but overall it's always about the level of psychological detail you bestow on your character and constantly checking in on what feels real and truthful, rather than what seems badass or whatever. There are some women who *would* punch their way out of a situation, there are some who wouldn't, but either way they are both likely to struggle finding jeans that fit perfectly, whether they want to care about that or not. It's the little things like that which unite us.

In episode one of *Killing Eve*, while Eve is waiting for the microwave to ping, she stands, deep in thought, fiddling with a little hair on her chin. I LOVE THAT. I HAVE DONE THAT. It makes me laugh and it makes me relax to see little details like that. My advice would be to create a character who has a real heart, a real dilemma and a real contradiction then honour her with the details of her womanhood, however trivial they may seem in the moment, because up there on a screen they will sing.

Phoebe dares to express herself boldly and often, and has found huge success in doing so. Her vision for the ways women can be fully human has liberated her audience to not just sit with the part of themselves that is sane but the other half of us that, as Rebecca West says, 'wants to . . . leave nothing of our house save its blackened foundations.'[17] I can think of no better segue to take us to the next chapter, in which we will explore finding our most truthful voices and using them fully.

---

17   *Black Lamb and Grey Falcon: A Journey Through Yugoslavia* by Rebecca West (first published by Macmillan, London in 1941).

Hear Us Roar

I'm a feminist but I used to think that The
Feminine Mystique *was a classic perfume, like
Chanel Number Five, not an important feminist
text by Betty Friedan, and I only discovered
it wasn't when my university tutor asked me
about how I felt it related to Sylvia Plath – and
I replied that I didn't know she wore it.*

Aemilia Lanyer, who lived from 1569 to 1645, was the first
woman in England to publish poetry and be paid for it. She
is the answer to Virginia Woolf's famous question, 'What would
have happened to Shakespeare's sister?' Woolf was wrong. She
didn't die young of syphilis in a ditch. The answer is she actually
did lots of amazing things, but you've never heard of her because
when women kick ass, history rarely bothers to write it down.

Some people have suggested that Shakespeare and Lanyer
were lovers and that she was his 'dark lady'. I don't care if they
were or they weren't. Why do women always have to be defined
by the most famous person they went to bed with? I don't want
to be defined by Jon Hamm or Justin Trudeau (two men I
think we all assume I'll have a memorable sexual relationship
with before I die).

Lanyer's most famous poem is a proto-feminist work called *Salve Deus Rex Judaeorum*[2] in which she defends women from the then commonly held belief that Eve was responsible for the 'fall of man' and humanity's eviction from the Garden of Eden. She argues that if Adam was created first and was supposedly wiser than Eve and meant to be in charge, then he should take the rap. He did what he did deliberately – as opposed to Eve, who was tricked by the talking snake. Then Lanyer throws down: 'Anyway, even if a woman did get us kicked out of paradise, you men killed Jesus.' I'm paraphrasing, but that's the gist.

> Then let us [women] have our liberty again,
> And challenge to yourselves [men] no sovereignty.
> You came not in the world without our pain,
> Make that a bar against your cruelty;
> Your fault being greater, why should you disdain
> Our being your equals, free from tyranny?

She made a public case for gender equality in 1611 and what's more, she charged people to read it.

She points out in the preface to that same poem that Jesus was

> begotten of a woman, born of a woman, nourished of a woman, obedient to a woman and that he healed women, pardoned women, comforted women, yea, even when he was in his greatest agony ... took care to dispose of a woman, after his resurrection appeared first to a woman, sent a woman to declare his more glorious resurrection to the rest of his disciples ... All of which is sufficient to enforce all good Christians and honourable-minded men to speak reverently of our sex.

---

2 'Hail, God, King of the Jews'.

I have no idea how she got away with that at a time when being the wrong religion was one of the leading causes of death. I assume it was because she was funny, and the piece was seen as clever satire. There's a long tradition of women claiming that they'd had a message from God in a dream in order to get away with having and sharing ideas. No one wanted to mess with the divine in those days, so it was the safest way for a woman with attitude not to find her head on the chopping block. Lanyer, however, claimed God only gave her the title. The poem was all her, and she wasn't giving the Lord above or anyone else the credit for that. That's the cheekiest use of the female divine dream in recorded history.

Lanyer is another one of my favourite historical guilty feminists. She was born a working-class girl and managed to get an education through an enlightened female aristocrat she was working for, who believed girls should be allowed to learn. She was an It Girl in Elizabeth I's court, dating the much older Lord Hunsdon (who was effectively Shakespeare's boss, being the patron of his theatre company). When she got knocked up and was no longer welcome at court, she married an Elizabethan rock star – okay, he was a recorder player, but that was basically the electric guitar back then. He played at Elizabeth I's funeral. After he spent all her money, she became a businesswoman and was extremely litigious with men who tried to rip her off. She opened a day school at a time when lots of children couldn't get an education. As a final act of defiance, she outlived Shakespeare. She was seventy-six (an enormous achievement for someone who started out working class and participated in childbirth), whereas Will died at fifty-two.

We know quite a lot about her because she regularly visited a creepy therapist/astrologer called Simon Forman, who specialised in female patients and hit on all of them, keeping a comprehensively nasty journal of his conquests. Where historians failed, a sex diarist saved the day. Forman referred to shagging as 'haleking' (his own slang) and after a long time trying (including one night with some wine and a little over-the-bodice action) he complained that Lanyer 'would not halek!' After that he called her a lesbian and a succubus (nympho demon). You read that right. She suffered from Jacobean trolling. The more things change for women, the more they stay horribly sexist. Her self-expression, powers of persuasion, bravery and well-directed defiance are something to behold. When she took a man to court, which she did regularly (lawsuits with landlords and business partners), she always won. She referred to herself as an 'oratrix'. I think that might be the title of my next show.

Words have always been the tools, the weapons of feminists. Some golden examples ...

From Gloria Steinem: 'A feminist is anyone who recognises the equality and full humanity of women and men.'

To Erin McKean: 'Prettiness is not a rent you pay for occupying a space marked "female".'[3]

From Maya Angelou: 'You may write me down in history/ With your bitter, twisted lies/You may trod me in the very dirt/ But still, like dust, I'll rise.'[4]

To Roxane Gay: 'When you can't find someone to follow, you have to find a way to lead by example.'[5]

Feminists need to be able to package their feelings into words, find places to publish and platforms to stand on. Emmeline Pankhurst famously said 'Deeds not words', but she also said, 'We have to free half of the human race, the women,

---

3 *A Dress A Day* blog by Erin McKean: https://dressaday.com/2006/10/20/ you-dont-have-to-be-pretty

4 'Still I Rise', *The Complete Poetry* by Maya Angelou (Virago Press, 2015).

5 *Bad Feminist* by Roxane Gay (Corsair, 2014).

so that they can help free the other half', so I am going to suggest she knew the power of words very well.

If you want what you say to be heard and put a dent in the universe, you have to determine two things: how you feel and how you express that feeling. It is clear that some feminists on the internet think that if they feel outrage, then outrage in its most explosive, unfettered form is the only expression available to them. That isn't true.

Sometimes a joke is a Trojan Horse that will make your idea travel faster and hit its target harder. When people laugh, their defences come down. I think that is much of the success of the podcast: because it's mostly comedy, it doesn't feel like homework.

There are times when a story, a vulnerable plea, a clever metaphor or a new idea will gather a crowd of new listeners to your tribe when a furious display of outrage will alienate.

Sometimes outrage is all that is available to you, in which case, be furious and express that fury in 280 characters or a YouTube video or on a soapbox. But I would suggest the more privilege you have, the more obligation you have to persuade rather than just vent. Becca Bunce, the activist for women's rights who I interviewed for Chapter 9: There is No 'Try', taught me that unfettered anger without strategy rarely changes anything. You need influence. You need a plan. She taught me that a simple expression of anger might be art but it would rarely lead to actual change. Of course, riots and violent protests have changed history, but generally as part of a wider strategic movement. I feel it's my job, as a privileged woman who is not suffering under the most oppressive forces, to do more than let my anger out in random, undirected bursts. I need to turn my anger into influential words and persuasive ideas wherever possible.

The brilliant feminist comedian Bridget Christie told me

that I wouldn't really find my audience until I expressed what I wanted to say but feared voicing the most. She explained she only found her success when she risked alienating her audience by saying what she was pretty sure would be unpalatable to many. That's when her people came in droves. It took me ages to get up the courage, especially because part of what I wanted to say was, 'I don't really know what I'm doing, gang,' but she was dead right. Sometimes I discover something about my voice because the obligation to invent some stand-up or do a challenge forces me into a corner. Creating deadlines or creative constraints for yourself helps. Stop saying what you think others want to hear. Say what you're too scared to say and use what means you have to publish. I caveat that by adding, make sure the thing you want to say doesn't erode any marginalised group's humanity or identity.

Speeches

The podcast is weekly now, so I make fifty-two episodes a year. It's become the main way I use my voice, so it's the best example I have to work through how you might use yours. Most of the content is ad-libbed. I am trying to be bolder and more inclusive in my topics – both things requested by many of the listeners. Every week we are flirting furiously with disaster. I know I will definitely screw up and upset a bunch of people three or four times a year, and all I can do is listen, understand, apologise and learn for next time. I've come to the conclusion that me accidentally stepping on a landmine, apologising and surviving encourages other people to find their voice and see that getting stuff wrong is survivable. I also have to accept that sometimes an individual will take me to task for something that I then re-examine and decide to stand by. It's my voice and I don't have to capitulate to another's belief every time.

Here are some pieces I wrote for the podcast that had a

particular impact on listeners. Some listeners requested written copies of these pieces, so I'm cataloguing them here. More importantly, I want to unpack how I wrote and delivered them because listening for your own voice and then giving it volume in the world is probably the single most empowering thing a woman can do for herself and her people. Maya Angelou lost her voice for many years as a child, due to deep trauma. In that time, she read voraciously. When she found her voice again, it had developed into one of the most potent, eloquent and sonorous in history. As another extraordinary African American writer, Zora Neale Hurston, wrote, 'There is no agony like bearing an untold story inside you.'[6] You need to find a valve for yourself.

The process and end result of you finding your voice probably won't be anything like the results reproduced here, which is a good thing because everyone's ideas, experience and expression are different. But I hope telling you a little of the story of how I found my voice in writing these pieces is useful in further finding yours.

When the Leave campaign won the Brexit referendum, I wrote this quickly to channel my anger. I asked myself who I was really angry with and did not allow myself to censor any of the answers. I had to include myself and my middle-class friends in the answer. I would have overlooked this or edited it out if I hadn't challenged myself to be rigorously honest. I had to confess as well as accuse. I recommend this way of writing for expressing your most powerful, personal feelings on social issues.

---

6 From her book *Dust Tracks on a Road* (first published in 1942 by J. B. Lippincott), often misattributed to Maya Angelou's *I Know Why the Caged Bird Sings* (first published in 1969 by Random House).

When I feel angry inside, it often comes out in the form of tears, which makes me sound upset and like someone who needs to be comforted. I do not wish to seem vulnerable when my anger is justified. I want to seem proud and strong and like someone who needs to be listened to, not looked after. I am never ashamed of tears, and don't think 'female emotions' are less valid than 'male emotions', but society often excuses tearful women while disliking angry ones and my body has responded to this by weeping when it wants to be powerful, calm and direct. I rarely admit that I'm angry. I do not like confrontation. I'm much more likely to say, 'I'm a bit upset by that', or 'I was quite surprised to hear . . . ', so I gave myself the challenge of opening with 'I am angry'. I got through most of it without breaking when I stood and delivered it to the audience. I was a little tearful at the end but fought it and managed to give the rage the voice it deserved instead (mostly).

So here is my speech delivered on the *Guilty Feminist* podcast soon after the nation's decision on Brexit. It's expressed as clearly and cathartically as possible. I still feel angry and confounded every single day that we voted to leave the European Union. I was worried it would become normal and my anger would dissipate. It hasn't.

Brexit

I am angry about Brexit.

I am angry that entitled, smug, privileged, powerful men got in a big red bus and told poor people lies so that they could have even more entitled, smug, privileged power. Even though they knew it would make those poor people poorer.

I am angry at those men. I am angry at myself that I was complacent. That I knew the inequality of wealth and property and opportunity was getting worse and I didn't do anything about it. Not just because I didn't know what to do but because I benefited from it.

I am angry at myself that in truth, my own most immediate and fearful reaction is – what does this mean for me? What will my flat be worth? Will there still be fun and easy, high-paid work for me?

I am angry that most of my middle-class friends are angry with the poor, disenfranchised people who were told lies. I am angry that British citizens and residents are being shouted at on buses because they look and sound different. I am angry that racism and fear of human beings who are from somewhere else is the outlet for those who have been fed on a diet of Rupert Murdoch's poison for too long.

I am angry at Rupert Murdoch, who knew he would have more influence on Number Ten Downing Street than Brussels and so incited racial hatred in his tabloids to split us up. I am angry that today I watched the President of the European Commission in the European Parliament shout at Nigel Farage, 'Why are you here? Why are you here?' in exactly the same way Polish people are being shouted at at British bus stops.

I am angry not because he was shouted at – I want to shout at him too – but because it was virtually the first time in my life I felt unwelcome somewhere because of my nationality. It made me realise I may not be welcome in Europe for a while because of my accent. That people might shout, 'Why are you here?' at me in Paris or Frankfurt or Madrid.

I am angry that it has taken feeling like this for us to do more than post stuff on Facebook.

I am angry that most of us will continue just to post stuff on Facebook.

I am angry that there is not more room for women in our

society, that diversity of thought and emotional intelligence and biochemistry is not deemed necessary, or in some cases desirable, because women are deemed an unknown quantity in leadership; and that we continue to trust straight, white men with almost all the decisions and influence, even though they have shown us time and time again that as a homogenised, unsupervised group they make terrible, unsustainable decisions which tank the economy and the environment and everything for everyone.

I am angry. I am angry. And if I feel this anger and bring it out into the light, maybe I can turn it into action and hope and power.

Not long after the Brexit referendum, even more implausibly Donald Trump was voted in as the forty-fifth President of the United States of America. If Brexit hasn't got any more normal, the decision to elect Trump gets more incomprehensible every day. I stayed up all night to watch the election and cried all morning. I felt like there was no point in doing anything any more. I wanted someone else to take charge and tell me what to do.

At about 4 p.m., it dawned on me that other people must feel like that and that I could arrange a place for people to assemble and create the hub I was hoping someone else would arrange. I didn't have any answers but I could provide a starting place. I went on social media and asked how the podcast listeners would feel about us doing an emergency episode the very next night. The response was overwhelming. A venue was donated and the show booked out in minutes. It was like we all needed to be together and process it. The aptly named Hospital Club was heaving and grieving with shell-shocked feminists. I wrote this speech because I'd invited people there and then felt I had to say something with an element of battle cry to it. We wanted focus. A plan. I wrote this by asking myself: 'What do I need to hear right now? Because I'm guessing that's what other people want to hear too.' I also tried to focus on the groups of women who would be most affected by the election and would feel the most hurt by the large quantities of white women who'd voted for Trump. There's nothing like feeling that your people are part of the problem for motivating you to be part of the solution.

On the night, I tried to create the platform I aspired to by inviting the most diverse panel I could muster from the marginalised groups who'd have the most to lose from a Trump presidency, both in America and, through the cultural zeitgeist, around the world.

If you're not sure what to say in a time of crisis (which is all the time these days), create the event you want to go to and then write the speech you want to hear. Write the blog you wish someone else would write. Compose the tweet that would get you to wake up and do something, rather than keep scrolling. Look at your favourite feminist authors. What inspires or enlightens you when you read Angelou, Gay or Atwood? Deconstruct what they're doing. Are they calling you to arms? Pointing out your hidden powers? Identifying what we should be fighting for? I'm not saying you should plagiarise their thoughts or replicate their style, more that you can learn from the mechanics of their writing.

Here's my horror at Trump, written with as much get-up-and-go as I could dredge up, the morning after the night before.

Trump

I am devastated by the result of the US election and what it will mean for women, people of colour and people who are lesbian, gay, bisexual and transgender and people who are disabled.

I am frightened not just about what it will mean for America, but what it will mean for the mood of the world, and the direction and speed our globe is hurtling towards selfishness, greed, fear and self-destruction.

Last night I could not stop crying because I felt there was no point trying any more. But today I realise that one of the factors of Hillary Clinton's defeat was that women are simply not included enough at any level of society. People could imagine a white man in a grey suit in the Oval Office because that is what a person of power and influence looks like.

We – all of us – are not used to seeing women in influential roles. Women are still an aberration on an average television or even conference panel. We are told nightly, shown nightly, that one woman on a comedy show or political panel sufficiently includes our gender. We do not see our reflection very often. We do not imagine ourselves being seen or heard.

We see that a woman in the public eye is an exception and therefore we quietly infer that only exceptional women should be given a voice. We fear we are unexceptional, so we exclude ourselves before we can be excluded.

Donald Trump is rich, white and male and as such was born included.

He has only ever known inclusion in every room he's ever been in. He's the judge at the beauty panel, he's the one who says who's fired. He decides who is included and who is excluded. And that was the platform on which he ran, that clearly comforted too many people. He has become so entitled to inclusion that he has manspread his way into the White House without preparation or humility.

Women. We need to get better at including ourselves. We need to get comfortable with being seen and being heard.

So comfortable we start to enjoy it. Women, if you are in a meeting for one hour with six people, you need to speak for ten minutes over that period. I do not care what you are saying. Practise being heard.

If you are interrupted, keep talking. Or interrupt the interrupter. Women speaking when men are present needs to be normal. They need to think it's normal and so do we.

Women, if you are asked to do a presentation or appear on a panel or speak at a conference – say yes. If you are not asked, and you even suspect you have the expertise, include yourself. Tell them why you need to appear. Do this even if it scares you. Be visible. Assume inclusion. Expect inclusion. Like money, inclusion is rarely given until it is applied for.

If you have been routinely excluded, this may cause you some anxiety. Do it anyway. Do it for women who can't. Do it until it is normal for them and normal for you. Until we include ourselves, we can't include others. You can't get someone into a party you're not invited to.

And women, we need to include others. White, straight, cisgendered women, I'm talking to us. We drive white, cisgendered bodies. We are included more frequently than other sorts of women. We can deny it and focus on our own exclusion, but then we are on Team Trump.

White people are especially included. We don't notice our extra right to inclusion because it's all we've known.

Many white women in America voted for their white tribe over their female tribe this election. They chose exclusion for others, even over inclusion for themselves. They chose to exclude people of colour even if it meant voting for a president who saw them as a number on a scale of one to supermodel. Even though he saw them as a pussy to be grabbed and a pair of lips to be kissed against their will.

They made the choice to dehumanise others out of fear, snobbery and misplaced self-interest, rather than fully include themselves in a society led by a president who would respect, say, their right to autonomy over their own reproductive system.

White women who find that a disgrace – it is not enough for us to tut. We must include women of colour. We must find room, wherever we have influence, to listen to their voices and provide platforms for their fears and complaints – even when sometimes those fears and complaints include us.

We must make women of colour on the agenda normal. It is not enough to embrace Michelle Obama. She's an exceptional woman with an exceptional platform. We must provide voice and visibility for the women around us to find their exceptional voices until that act itself becomes ordinary.

We must over-include and repeatedly include women of colour, queer women and disabled women until they feel included. Until they self-include. Telling those women that there is a seat at your table is not always enough. We need to make them feel like they belong and prove that we mean it.

Men. You have a big opportunity to exclude us now. The world just got more toxically masculine. I would ask you if that feels like the right thing to do, or just easy and normal and safe to create your boardrooms, panels and line-ups without us.

You can play along with Trump's agenda and leave us outside the rooms where decisions are made, or you can put one huge middle finger up to Donald Trump and include us in whatever you're doing. And we promise to show up. And be seen. And be heard. Until it feels normal.

That night, I spoke out of necessity, but the overwhelmingly positive response from the audience made me braver about giving speeches. Oratory went out of fashion, but now that our politicians are serving up such classics as 'Brexit means Brexit' and 'Why would Kim Jong-un insult me by calling me "old", when I would NEVER call him "short and fat"?' it feels like it's time for a comeback.

I went to see a brilliant gender-blind production of Shakespeare's *Henry V* at the Regent's Park Theatre. My great friend Jessica Regan played the French duke, Montjoy, and I remarked afterwards that I'd never seen her appear so high-status, sweeping around the stage in coat-tails and boots, declaring and persuading. She responded, 'I normally play low-status characters,' and I replied, 'Well, you've never played a man before.' That week I decided to rewrite the famous 'Once more unto the breach' speech as a feminist call to arms, keeping the rhythm but re-gendering the language. It got a great response from the live audience, and the podcast listeners and I felt high for days afterwards. It was much more of a buzz than I thought it was going to be. Jessica came on the podcast later and explained that most of Shakespeare's female soliloquys are about feelings, whereas the male ones are about action.

We should recite this speech every morning. I defy you to say the words and remain apologetic or uncertain. The rhythm makes you mighty, changes your posture and dares you to imitate the action of the tiger. It's easy to sit around feeling less-than. Reading these words aloud – or even in your head if you're on public transport – will change how you walk down the street and into a meeting. It makes you write more direct emails. It will make you swipe left more readily on Tinder. It will propel you to train your daughters to take less crap. It will drive you to demand change and inspire others to come with you.

Jessica has since turned this into a brilliant workshop where women sample famous texts, write their own power speeches and deliver them to the audience, front-foot – like old-school orators. The participants are dared by the same rhythms and active verbs that have been in men's gift since Shakespeare was a boy.

For context, in case it's not familiar, *Henry V* is a play about the young English king who leads his troops into battle with the French during the Hundred Years War. This speech is his successful attempt to win over those of his men who suspect that the attempt to lay siege to the French town of Harfleur is unwise. It is a famous speech of leadership and motivation. The feminist flourishes are mine, I would say with apologies to Shakespeare, but Henry V wouldn't apologise so neither will I!

Henry V

Once more unto the breach, dear friends, once more;
Or close the wall up with our female dead.
In peace there's nothing so becomes a girl
As modest stillness and humility:
But when the blast of war blows in our ears,
Then imitate the action of the tiger;
Stiffen the sinews, summon up the blood,
Disguise fair nature with hard-favour'd rage;
Then lend the eye a terrible aspect;
Let pry through the portage of the head
Like the brass cannon; let the brow o'erwhelm it
As fearfully as doth a galled rock
O'erhang and jutty her confounded base,
Swill'd with the wild and wasteful ocean.
Now set the teeth and stretch the nostril wide,
Hold hard the breath and bend up every spirit

To her full height. On, on, you noblest women,
Whose blood is fet from mothers of war-proof!
Mothers that, like so many suffragettes,
Have in these parts from morn till even fought
And sheathed their swords for lack of argument:
Dishonour not your parents; now attest
That those whom you call'd mothers did beget you.
Be copy now to dames of grosser blood,
And teach them how to war. And you, good women,
Whose limbs were made in feminism, show us here
The mettle of your pasture; let us swear
That you are worth your breeding; which I
    doubt not;
For there is none of you so mean and base,
That hath not noble lustre in your eyes.
I see you stand like greyhounds in the slips,
Straining upon the start. The game's afoot:
Follow your spirit, and upon this charge
Cry 'God for Women, Feminism, and
    Saint Angelou!'

This next form of writing is more a kind of therapy to find out what you don't know you're thinking. It's called automatic writing, and I didn't invent it but I've found it one of the most useful ways of evading my feelings of guilt about what I should do, or must think, and finding out what I really feel. The rules are these: give yourself a topic, set your alarm for one minute and then keep your pen moving on the page or your hands skipping on the keyboard for the duration. You must write as quickly as possible. If nothing comes you write 'blah blah blah' until something does. If you keep practising, your brain will get used to spilling stuff.

  This method is a great way to establish your fears and low

self-esteem points, whether patriarchy-induced or not. Being a feminist involves building confidence and finding your voice. The scary thing about using this approach is that it may uncover your secret fears and insecurities. But while they stay hidden, you can never really confront them.

You have to do this regularly but everyone can find one minute every day. Go to bed one minute later or do it on your commute instead of all that urgent Facebooking you do. You will be amazed at what your unconscious knows that you don't and you might even write something you want to share.

Here are some good topics . . .

Confidence Builders:

- Good things people would say about me if I wasn't in the room
- Why people love me
- What I am better at than other people

Fear Busters:

- This is what I'd do if I weren't scared
- This is what scares me about myself
- I am weak/I am strong

Here's my 'I am weak/I am strong' – have fun writing yours. It'll only take a minute.

I wrote this piece backstage in the dressing room with a strict minute timer on. I cheated and let myself tweak it a little in the following minute, but I have an audience to entertain and the rules aren't the boss of me.

Please be aware I've been writing for years, so if I put a timer on, my writer self kicks in. If you're not used to writing, that doesn't mean you're not a writer. Everyone can write. You are whatever you do regularly. Write every day and then no one can say you're not a writer – even your inner critic. Your writing will become more fluent, articulate and honest all the time.

I just received an 'I am weak/I am strong' from a listener that included the line, 'I am strong because I was bullied but it did not teach me to hate.' Poetry. Trust parts of your brain that are under the ocean. That's where the treasure is.

I am weak / I am strong

I am weak because I am soft in the middle and nobody knows. I look sturdy and upright and full of life but sometimes I am an incapable lump of marshmallow and all that marshmallow is fabricated of is 'can't'. Can't move. Can't do it. Can't be good enough. Can't make it work. I am weaker than I look and can't open bottles. Slighter hands than mine have to work to open the resistance and let the fizz out into the daylight. It feels like an unfeminist act to ask a man to open a bottle of water but recently I almost cried I felt so tired and thirsty and sick – so I had to ask the cab driver to pull over onto the side of the road so he could open it for me. I felt weak and embarrassed and grateful for his help. Sometimes the bottle top of life resists my most determined grip. I muster my strength, then nothing gives but me.

I am strong because I find some things easier than other people. Things that make men, soldiers, kings weak at the knees – like standing on a stage and addressing an audience without much of a plan. The moment doesn't scare me. This moment now is in my gift and this next one too. What I know that most people don't is that one day I will die. This came at me sharply when I left a doomsday cult that had promised me eternal life on earth. On the way out the door, I looked my mortality in the eye and said, death is coming for me – but not yet. Of all the people who have ever lived and all the people who are going to live. It's my turn now. That's my strength. I'm acutely aware that it's my turn. And my power is in the awareness of my breath, my beating heart, my speed of thought and my understanding that there's nothing like being muzzled by men to make you appreciate the bellow of your voice when you're off the leash. My strength is one taught to me by Maya Angelou on YouTube. She told me, 'When you go into a room, a meeting, an interview – take everyone who loves you with you. Family, friends – they're all around you. See them there. Feel them there and they'll give you strength.'

That's the strength of feminism. The unseen army with sword half-drawn that emboldens me to ask for more and take my place. Maya Angelou and all her wisdom comes with me into the rawest rooms and roars. Sometimes using my lungs. I can pull the sisterhood over my head to protect me from the rain.

I was delighted to see protesters at the last, very wet, Women's March in London with rain hoods carrying signs that read 'The Sisterhood Protects Me from the Rain'. I learned a long time ago that trying my hardest is not my best strategy when it comes to creativity.[7] Turn off the censor and let your mind speak itself.

This next piece is some stand-up comedy I wrote as a parody of how we, as women, undermine ourselves. We talk to ourselves in a way that would be horrifying for anyone else to talk to us.

---

7 Keith Johnstone taught me this. His book *Impro, Improvisation and the Theatre* (Faber & Faber, 1979) has lots of other insights about accessing your creativity.

'Show not tell' is advice always given to screenwriters. How can you make the audience laugh about something by providing a parallel or metaphor that satirises the situation? I realised that if I had a flatmate who undermined me the way the voice in my head gaslights me, everyone would tell me to run a mile. The remove is the joke, that allows us to laugh at ourselves. If something is bugging you and you want an original, appealing way of presenting it, try finding a metaphor and see if that helps you demonstrate your point, rather than preach a sermon.

Judgement

If you had a friend who was like the inside of your own head, you'd be living in a thriller. That 'best friend' would be really evil and undermining. What if you came home from work and your best friend was there and you had a conversation like you have with your own brain? It'd go something like this:

You: So, I got asked to do a big presentation. For all the senior partners. At work, next week. Bit nervous.

Friend: You . . . ? You've been asked? What, to speak in front of other people? Is there any way you can get out of it?

You: Why do you think I should get out of it? Should I?

Friend: I think you should. You're just not good at things like that. Not if you get nervous. And you forget what you're meant to say. And your PowerPoint slides don't work. You don't improvise well, do you? Maybe you should ask – what's that guy at work, Jeff? He's good at presentations, isn't he? Maybe he should do it.

You: Jeff?

Friend: Yes. Jeff, the one you always tell me is so good. He's so much better than you at presentations. And in general. Why don't you ask him to do it? I think he'd be better than you. He'd never forget what he had to say. He's so dynamic and charismatic. Although . . . do you think they asked him first and he turned it down – and that's why they asked you?

You: Maybe. Do you think so . . . ? Probably. I should do it anyway though. My boss has been really encouraging me to go up for a new role, and I know if I do the presentation, it will be really good exposure.

Friend: A new role . . . ? What kind of new role?

You: Oh, it's just, you know, next level, it would be more money and more responsibility. I mean, it would be a challenge. It would be a stretch.

Friend: How many of the skills would you say, right now, you have? That were appropriate for a 'new role'? Because it doesn't seem to me that you can do this role. It feels to me like you're an impostor.

You: Oh god . . . Can everyone tell that? Does everyone know?

Friend: Would you like a gin and tonic? I'm having one. Maybe you should have a gin and tonic to settle your nerves. Because you have got nerves about all of this, haven't you? In a very real way.

You: Well, I, um, I don't know if I, um, have time for a drink right now. I'm going on a date with that guy I met last week.

Friend: Are you? Is there really any point going on a date?

You: Why do you say that?

Friend: Because the reality is, every relationship you've ever had has ended. Every. One. Not one of your boyfriends is here, now, in this kitchen. Because not one of them wants to be with you. And that pattern is going to go on again, and again, and again, and again.

Because you and I both know, fundamentally, you are unlovable. You are broken. You are two-dimensional. You are bad in bed. And you are as much an impostor in your last relationship with David as you are in the boardroom on Monday morning. And you're not fooling anyone. You're not fooling me. You won't change. You can't change. The last relationship broke up and so will this one.

You: I can change! I can change! I've given up smoking.

Friend: Have you . . . ?

The week that the news of Harvey Weinstein's house of horror broke I was in Australia. We had multiple shows to perform and I had to find a way to make the worst excesses of his regime funny because I'd promised a comedy show. Irony was the only way through. The men of Hollywood claiming they were shocked struck me as absurd. I'm sure many didn't know the extent of it, but to say they had no idea felt pretty disingenuous. I decided to write something from their point of view and make it arch. Writing for a different character than yourself can give you insight and can help you find the funny in something that doesn't have a lot of humour to mine. Here's my open letter from the Gentlemen of Hollywood.

Open Letter from the Gentlemen of Hollywood

Dear Women Everywhere,

This is an open letter to reassure you that we, the men of Hollywood, vigorously reject Harvey Weinstein and his reign of terror, and as a sign of our concern and respect are proceeding to take his name out of the Academy of Motion Picture Arts and Sciences' official sorting hat!

We are shocked – shocked, we tell you – to discover that men treat women the way we see them treat them every day. We are dismayed that women have been exploited the way they've been openly and consistently exploited since Hollywood was founded.

We are outraged that eight seasons of *Entourage* and a full-length motion picture of the same name accurately reflected the world we live in every single day and wasn't a complete fantasy in the manner of *The Lord of the Rings*, as we assumed. We, and the young women we are currently trying to coerce into a sexual relationship in exchange for the auditions they so desperately need to buy food to eat, are equally horrified by the abuses inherent in the system.

The women we are right this minute Skyping for a little sugar in exchange for a good word to the right agent – despite their protestations that they do not want us to do this – are as surprised as we are that we are doing this. They didn't think it would be like this when they moved from Missouri to follow the love of their craft, and neither did we. We just can't understand how it continues to happen while every day we do nothing to change it.

An influential group of us were only saying at a strip club last night, as we deliberately conspired to block a hard-working, talented woman from directing a feature film she's been developing for five years to give it to her less experienced male colleague, that it was appalling that Harvey Weinstein has been allowed to operate this completely out-of-character operation of power abuse within the context of an incredibly egalitarian culture that tells women that they can be whoever they want to be as long as they're under 26 or look as if they are – and are happy to work in an environment devoid of women and throbbing with men.

Harvey Weinstein is certainly not invited to our next official Hollywood orgy for men over 55 and women under 22, and will not be receiving an invitation to our next Pin the Tail on the Ingénue and jacuzzi-themed barbecue.

We are now fathers of daughters and so care about women, where once we just saw them as tits who could remember lines and hit marks. You may say that this is no argument as Harvey Weinstein himself has four daughters. To that we say: yes, well . . .

Can we ask for your help by encouraging you to join Donna Karan in considering what you wear when you meet with us professionally and socially? Look in your wardrobe and ask yourself – what blouse and skirt combination says 'Make me watch you jerk off into a pot plant,' and don't wear that. Throw out your 'ask me to watch you shower' jumpsuit, because we think that would be a big help.

We also wish to say while we have your attention that we mourn the loss of our dear friend and colleague Hugh Hefner, and his Memorial Misogyny Drinks and Plaque Unveiling will be held at Oppression, which is the nightclub on the corner of Hollywood and Patriarchy, at midnight. Ladies welcome. Miniskirts get in free.

With all our love,

The Horrified Men of Hollywoodn't You Like to Stay and Have a Drink?

Finally, this is a piece of writing that moved me and that exemplifies the power of making your voice heard. It is written by my great friend Hannah Gadsby. Long before her genre-shattering Netflix special, *Nanette*, when Australia was holding a referendum on equal marriage she articulated through extraordinary storytelling and personal revelation why asking the question of the public was in itself damaging.

I'd never have understood this if she hadn't written it. It is a persuasive piece of writing only someone of her background, experience and age (a gay Australian woman in her thirties) could author. This is a wonderful way to write. What experience is unique to you? Was your single working parent an inspiration to you? Are you brand new to activism? Are you currently travelling alone? Struggling with fertility or society's expectations of you? Are you a single woman in STEM? A woman of colour in the arts? A mother of boys? A daughter who is transitioning? Dating offline? A plus size woman shopping ethically? Experiencing the menopause with mobility issues? A Gen Z girl who writes code for video games?

Your personal story is powerful. Your observations might be obvious to you, but a revelation to others. Your failures are as encouraging to others as your successes. Your fears are as powerful as your bravest thoughts. Write them down. The internet means the artists have taken control of the means of production. Write poems, songs, sketches and blogs. Make YouTube videos, podcasts and animations. Find the medium that suits you, share what it's like to be a human like you and then, if people take notice, try inviting in people who rarely get a platform and ask what it's like to be them.

Plebiscite by Hannah Gadsby[1]

Oh, hey guys . . . this plebiscite thing is a very bad idea. The very idea of an ongoing debate around marriage equality makes my stomach turn. It's not a pleasant turn either.

Let me be clear. I don't care about marriage equality for

---

1 A plebiscite is another word for a referendum. It is commonly used in Australia. Too commonly!

myself because I do not have an aptitude for relationships. The reason I care about this is because I don't want young kids to hear the kind of horrific bile I was forced to listen to in the 1990s when Tasmania debated on whether to legalise homosexuality. For many, the debate was theatre. For me, it made me hate myself so deeply I have never been able to develop an aptitude for relationships.

In the mid-nineties, I was the age when I should have been learning how to be vulnerable, how to handle a broken heart, how to deal with rejection and how to deal with all the other great, silly things about young love which help pave the way to the more substantial adult version. But instead I learned how to close myself off and rot quietly in self-hatred. I learned this because I learned that I was subhuman during a debate where only the most horrible voices and ideas were amplified by the media. These voices also gave permission for others to tell me that I was less than them, with looks, words and on one occasion, violence.

Every day of my life I deal with the effects of anxiety and low self-esteem. It is not nearly as debilitating as it used to be, but I don't imagine I will ever be truly free of it. Just imagine how brilliant I could have been if I hadn't been given such a shit show at such a vulnerable time in my life.

I am very concerned that the plebiscite debate is going to be another open season for hate. I fear for those, particularly in regional Australia, who are isolated from positive voices.

If this plebiscite has to happen then let's try and drown out the hate-filled commentators. They might not have the numbers but they will no doubt be handed a megaphone in the name of entertainment. But this kind of entertainment will not only ruin young lives . . . it will end some of them. Speech is not free when it comes at such a cost. This plebiscite is *fucked*.

You have a voice. If you live in a democracy (or what passes for one these days) then you're in less danger than Aemilia Lanyer was for writing a proto-feminist poem. If you have access to the internet, you have a platform, even if you're housebound, have a full-time job and/or are in charge of a number of children. Find your medium. Play around with genres. Release your story. If they complain, tell them it was a divine dream.

I interviewed Hannah about how she found her voice and why living in the margins might give you a unique voice and help you use it.

Hannah, how did you find your voice?
I think most people who are not straight white men tend to find their voice via what they're not. So, it's always comparative to the dominant. When I first began comedy most of my material revolved around the ways in which I wasn't a straight white man. I never talked about race, 'cos I was white.

Like the dominant group – so it was unremarkable.
But I would always speak to my sexuality, and my gender . . . and to a certain extent, my low socio-economic background. My jokes would often be about how I didn't look like what was expected of my gender. So that put me even further into a sort of explanation or excuse for my existence – like my weight, my lack of enthusiasm and of course being gender non-conforming in the way I dressed, and then of course my sexuality, so my stories revolving around interpersonal relationships were all through that lens, and so my voice was found via what I'm not.

And in *Nanette*, you said that for a long time when you started comedy you'd used self-deprecation and then you got to a point when you didn't want to do that any more. Did you consciously know back then that's what you were doing? And what made you choose to stop doing that? What made you go, 'Fuck this. I'm not doing this any more'?

Yeah, I knew what I was doing, because it didn't start on the comedy stage. It was a lifelong thing. Nobody's born with a sense of humour. It's what we develop in order to diffuse tension. That's part of why we make each other laugh, and when you exist as a tension in and of itself, it becomes a very critical and fundamental part of the way that you communicate with others. It's like being a power bottom.

Hah! So it's a piece of armour. It's a strategy to survive in a room where your status may be lowered by others. You learn to lower it first and get the laugh, so the laughs are designed by you and not on you?

Yeah, but I guess after a certain amount of time and maturation I saw the limit to my own humanity in the way that was for me – the way that I saw myself.

That those sort of jokes were coming at the expense of you as a person? Getting in the way of what you really needed to say?

I think to a certain degree self-deprecation is a really delightful way to communicate. But it really would only be healthy, I think, if we lived in an equal world. We simply don't.

We don't.

I think the reason I wrote *Nanette* was because there was a dissonance between the complicated way that I understood myself and the simplified version I had to put on stage. You know, by the time I'd muddled through all this sort of bullshit, you know, I couldn't get to 'Here's what I really think'. I still haven't – that's to come.

Really?
You know, I think I've, I've found my voice but I haven't used it. Because even with *Nanette* you could say I've shown people what my voice was, but I was still talking about the same old shit… Which is, again, explaining my point of difference. But the thing was in Nanette, I was making no apology for it, and that's why it was not funny and why it was important not to be funny.

Well, a lot of it's funny, but the parts that aren't funny are really not funny. They're designed that way.
They're decisions as opposed to a lack of skill.

Exactly. You put a lot of the funny upfront to demonstrate that when you're not being funny, it's on purpose, which is clever.
Yeah, some people didn't get that memo though.

Hah! Yeah, I heard some male comedians didn't get that memo. So, you think you've found your voice but you haven't used it yet? When you use your voice, what will you say?
Well I've got a new tour coming up. You'll probably find out then. But I now believe that the next thing I do will be from my perspective. I can start with my perspective instead of holding people's hands and going, 'This is

where I come from.' I don't think I need to do that any more, so now I can say, 'You know where I come from. This is how I see the world.'

I'm really excited for you to show us how you see the world.
I think there's a certain amount of danger that comes with asking people to look through the prism of your identity. There's a certain amount of power that comes with that and if you have a certain amount of power you have a certain amount of privilege. So I find myself in a really interesting position where I now have to be very aware of a privilege I have never known before . . .

Which is what?
Visibility.

What is that like, to suddenly have this massive visibility, having felt as a teenager and someone in your twenties that you were less visible than other young women? How is it to come into a voice that's now causing you to be very visible?
I'm taking it really seriously. I'm taking it like it's a huge responsibility, because I think when you have a public platform it should come with a sense of responsibility, even if it is just comedy. I think it's a bit juvenile to think that an audience these days simply exists in the room that you're speaking to. I hear a lot of, particularly male, comedians going 'Aw, you know, there's no fun in comedy any more', but what you say goes out beyond what you can control, so I think it's really important if you're a fan of free speech, which is what a lot of these guys say they are, to realise that cuts both ways.

People have a right to reply.

Yes, when people criticise the humanity of their politics, they say, 'It's freedom of speech.' Yes, but the reason we want freedom of speech is because speech is important. It's powerful. And that's why we want it, and that's why we need it. So, I don't have a lot of time for people who complain about the infringement of freedom of speech that so-called political correctness has brought, because it's like, well – be better! Think about what you say, and the affect that it has on people you don't know. Because we don't live in a closed world any more. Borders are open.

And especially if you're being recorded now. As soon as something's recorded, everyone with access to the internet can access everything you've said. Even in a comedy club, you don't know who's recording you now, so it's a different time.

Yeah, that's annoying because it's our work, so please don't record it and disseminate it. That is an issue. But at the same time, I can understand it, when people are being constantly silenced, why they would record offensive material.

The gravity with which you now see the privilege of visibility, if you'd had it all your life, you probably wouldn't appreciate it in the same way?

You know, I jokingly think that perhaps there is a lid on how far you can go in comedy, and that you can only tell your story and then you have to fuck off and do something that's serious. People are always going to need to laugh, and they will laugh, but people can laugh without comedians. I think we need to step off our own pedestal. There are videos of cats and dogs on YouTube that are very funny! Comedians didn't invent laughter.

How are you so good at articulating your ideas? That's a big part of finding your voice.

I spent a lot of time in my head. A lot of time. I believe that it has something to do with my striving for connection. I have late-diagnosed autism. And that has given me the framework to not think of what's going on inside of my head as being alien. There has always been a lot going on in my mind and I've always been watching the world around me trying to understand, and I think when you're not speaking, you get a lot more work done in your head.

You have time to figure out your ideas if you're less visible.

Yes. I haven't spoken much, in the scheme of things, in my life.

And if somebody's reading this book and they're thinking, 'I don't know how to express myself. I've got these feelings and I want to speak up ...' and because of marginalisation and oppression they've felt locked, do you have any advice for how they can find their voice? Or learn to use it?

Yeah. I think the first way into finding your voice or finding how to express yourself is really drilling down on what you respond to. Often that's a key to, to how you express yourself. So I don't hang out at dinner parties owning the room, being funny. I find them completely overwhelming. I'm best one on one. And I find it easy to talk to a crowd because I'm not distracted with multiple individuals. It's dark so I don't get distracted by all the details of each human, so that's part of why my voice works on stage. I think finding your physical community – offline – is a very important part of finding your voice, because if you're with people who you are comfortable being with, then you're able to be seen and heard. I honestly think that understanding how you are best situated in the world yourself is a better way of finding your own voice than looking at how others use their voice in the world. Fun for me, isn't what I've been told fun is.

Find your people, and they'll listen to your voice and let it develop.
Yes. Another huge part of finding your voice is learning the art of listening. Active listening, in order to really understand what feels true. Like for years women have been told that certain things are just jokes, yet it felt like assault. And we're now able to express that clearly in this moment because we've spent enough time listening.

Yes. That's really insightful.
And that's why I think so many marginalised voices are so much clearer and more compassionate than a lot of men who are in a reactive state right now because they've only been taught to talk, and not listen.

So true. We were in a position where we *had* to listen a lot...
Yeah, and that's not biological, that's trained. Give us a thousand years of not listening ... We'll be shit too!

Hah! Thank you so much, Hannah.

Listen to the voice inside of you that's trying to speak. Give it some space to forms its ideas and then tell its story with boldness, fury, flair and wit. Express your anger at injustice.

Find your funny. Sharpen your satirical skills. Play in different spaces until you find your favourite medium. However you do it, let them hear you roar! And don't forget to toast Aemilia and all the other guilty feminists of history for leading the way.

Part 3

All Change!

The Power of No

*I'm **a feminist but** I once drove an hour and a half out of my way to drop someone at a train station because when I explained how far it was and how tired I was, I thought she'd tell me not to worry, but she said, 'It's fine!' and caught me off guard, so there was no way I could say no. I need time to plan a 'no'.*

Madam C. J. Walker

Sarah Breedlove was an African American born in 1867 and the first person in her living family to be born free from slavery. After being orphaned at the age of seven, she went to work in a cotton field and to live with her sister and abusive brother-in-law. She married at fourteen, had a baby at eighteen and was widowed at twenty. She started working as a laundress and cook and raised her daughter on $1.50 a day. At the age of thirty-five she was tired, overworked, had left her second unfaithful husband – and, to add to her troubles, she was losing her hair. Her great-granddaughter later wrote: 'During the early 1900s, when most Americans lacked indoor plumbing and electricity, bathing was a luxury. As a result, Sarah and many other women were going bald because they washed their hair so infrequently, leaving it vulnerable to environmental hazards such as pollution, bacteria and lice.'

In 1904, she discovered a product designed by another orphaned African American woman whose parents had been enslaved and whose father had fought for the Union in the Civil War. Annie Turnbo, who had studied chemistry at school, had created a product for hair, the 'Wonderful Hair Grower', which really worked, and Sarah began to market and sell it. She also started to develop her own hair products, working with her brothers who were barbers. Around this time, she married C. J. Walker and built her brand – Madam C. J. Walker. 'Madam' had a French cachet that was respected in the cosmetics industry. Taking her husband's first and last names boldly rejected the disrespectful convention of white people referring to black women by their first names or the dismissive and loaded term, 'Auntie'. The husband didn't last long but she kept the name. It was a courageous act of parasite feminism.

Madam C. J. Walker's critics complained that her hair-straightening products encouraged black women to aspire and conform to white beauty standards, which was a fair concern, but she countered that she'd had a divinely inspired dream featuring a black man who gifted her the formula and that some of the ingredients were from Africa. She maintained that her potions couldn't be less white. They were saving women from pain and baldness and they were from God and Africa. The divine dream defence! There for motivated, defiant women throughout the ages.

Madam C. J. Walker's opening investment was $1.25. She is said to be the first self-made female millionaire in the United States of America. Some people dispute this and say that it was in fact her original supplier and eventual business rival Annie

Turnbo. Either way, they got there before any white woman. It's probable that Walker's fortune didn't reach a million dollars but to paraphrase Oscar Wilde, to become a millionaire is nothing, but to make people think one has done it when one hasn't, is a triumph. In today's money, Walker's fortune probably amounted to about eight million dollars.

This was a virtually impossible achievement in a landscape in which African Americans couldn't get bank loans or join most trade unions. Most black people were stuck in menial jobs and poverty for life. One of the only ways out was to be an entrepreneur in a market that was segregated by the Jim Crow laws. White-owned corporations rarely catered to black people's needs. Haircare was the perfect way to create a flourishing business.

Madam C. J. Walker became a philanthropist in the African American community and contributed $1,000 to the YMCA, which was a very large donation at that time (about $24,000 today) and the largest ever from a black woman at that time. She was making waves and decided that she wanted to attend the National Negro Business League convention in 1912. She turned up ready to speak, but Booker T. Washington, the founder of the league and one of the most powerful black leaders of the era, was not interested. He didn't respect her or her products.

Her response to this was a hard no. No. She would not be silenced and excluded. She'd worked her way up to being one of the most successful entrepreneurs in America in a segregated, white-dominated world. She refused to be silenced within her own community because of misogynoir.[2]

---

2 Misogyny directed towards black women where race and gender both play roles in bias. It was coined by queer black feminist Moya Bailey, who created the term to address misogyny directed towards black women in American visual and popular culture.

On the last day of the conference, while Booker T. Washington was addressing the audience from the stage, she stood up and announced, 'Surely you are not going to shut the door in my face. I am a woman who came from the cotton fields of the South. I was promoted to the washtub. From there I was promoted to the kitchen. And from there I promoted myself into the business of manufacturing hair goods and preparations. I have built my own factory on my own ground!'

Washington was shocked and angered and refused to give Madam C. J. a platform, but she had got to him. She continued to do more for the YMCA. She also contributed to an institute of higher learning for African Americans, called the Tuskegee Institute, that Booker himself had established. In 1913, Booker could see she was not going to take no for an answer and invited her to the NNBL convention as a keynote speaker.

Madam C. J. Walker once said, 'America doesn't respect anything but money. What our people need is a few millionaires.' Her motives weren't personal. They were social, racial and feminist: 'I am not merely satisfied in making money for myself, for I am endeavouring to provide employment for hundreds of women of my race . . . I want to say to every Negro woman present, don't sit down and wait for the opportunities to come. Get up and make them! . . . I got my start by giving myself a start.'

Madam C. J. Walker is another one of my favourite guilty feminists from history. She made her money on hair products and makes my hair stand on end whenever I read about her. She was the first person to use 'before' and 'after' shots – which is definitely more guilty than feminist. She said no to society's view of who she was allowed to be based on her race, gender and economic start in life. She created her own boundaries and never allowed a man to impose his limitations on her, even when he had the microphone and she just had her voice. She is the human embodiment of the power of no.

I'm just a girl who can't …

It is received wisdom that women have a hard time saying no. A little light Googling will bring up endless articles counselling women about the big N. O.

> *Psychology Today*: Why Women
> Have a Hard Time Saying No[3]

> CNBC: Why Women Should Say No More Often[4]

> Forbes: The 'I Just Can't Say No Club' That
> Women Need to Advance in Their Careers[5]

There are multiple articles and books about how to say no without actually saying it. They frequently contain advice such as, 'Try replacing the word "no" with "unfortunately"' or, 'Say, "I don't lend money to friends because that's the way I was raised."'

What if we don't want to say 'unfortunately'? What if it's not unfortunate to you that you don't want another date, an extra mile on the school run or a week's unpaid work packaged as 'training' in a sandwich shop? What if you're experiencing sexual harassment? Are you supposed to shift the blame to yourself by saying, 'Unfortunately, I don't want to watch you shower because of the way I was raised'?

I tried searching for 'how men can say no' and the first article up for me was an advice column for women on the HuffPo site called 'How to Say No Like a Man'.

---

3 *Psychology Today*, 2 November 2013
4 CNBC, 4 September 2014
5 Forbes, 28 June 2016

I don't want to say no like a man. I want to say no like a woman and mean it. I want to be able to create great big boundaries. The reason it's hard for us to say no, I think, is that it means revealing dissatisfaction. 'No' implies everything isn't just as it should be, that the person you're saying no to is wrong or lecherous or about to be disappointed.

Yes controls your own narrative, but no changes someone else's. As difficult as yes can be, no can be twice as hard. No is in danger of inconveniencing, embarrassing or angering someone else.

Most women do many things each week we'd rather not do. That isn't necessarily a bad thing. We are in a 'self-care', 'you do you' culture that tells us we must come first. But there's no reason we should wake up every day and do and have everything we like. Maybe we'd rather not go to pick up some milk for our elderly neighbour, take over some admin for a feminist sister, listen to a sad friend talk about her love life or take a detour to collect our partner from a night shift.

Sometimes we're made to feel that saying yes to these things is tantamount to being put upon and not looking after ourselves. That isn't true. Doing things for other people can be anything from a real kindness to a meaningful respon-sibility to a feminist act. If your health isn't suffering and what you're doing is making a difference to other people, you do not have to say no to everything that isn't a personal indulgence.

What is important is that what we do is intentional. Are we making a decision that minding our friend's children is important, kind and feminist because she's suffering from mental health pressures, and therefore worth the cost of our own time and energy? Or are we sending signals that we're a bottomless resource because we can't get the word 'no' out of our mouths? Intention is everything. Some of the most meaningful, satisfying things you'll ever do will be for family members, friends and women you don't know.

You are never too busy or too successful to help others. Virginia Woolf wrote to suffragist Janet Case enquiring, 'Would it be any use if I spent an afternoon or two weekly in addressing envelopes for Adult Suffragists?'[6]

You never know how taking time out to do a kindness for someone else, especially someone vulnerable, might change the world.

Maya Angelou tells a story:

'It is amazing, for me, to have been taken to a library when I was eight. I had been abused and I returned to a little village in Arkansas. And a black lady . . . knew I wasn't speaking – I refused to speak – for six years I was a volunteer mute. She took me to the library in the black school.'[7]

She goes on to say that the library had about 300 books gifted from the white school, but only the old ones so most of them had no backs, so they were covered in pretty cloth to make them look beautiful. The woman showed these pretty covers to Maya and told her she wanted her to read every book in the library.

This is how Angelou found her voice and wrote the books that gave a voice to so many more women and especially women of colour. We can't all be Maya Angelou, but we can all be the lady who takes one hour out of our day to drive a little girl to the library.

If we do not choose what to do and when, we will not have time to do what is urgent, important, necessary, kind and

---

6 Letter from Virginia Woolf to Janet Case, 1 January 1910.
7 New York Public Library speech by Maya Angelou, autumn 2010.

feminist. If we say yes to everything, we cannot author our own life and take care of ourselves and make choices about who else we will care for.

Saying no starts with technology. If one close friend invited us into a contract where we agreed to look at all their holiday snaps, kids' pictures, political views and rants about putting the bins out each week with an agreement that we'd write back or give them a thumbs-up validation, we'd politely decline. We've got our own lives, and that sounds like an onerous task for no reward. The truth is, most of us have volunteered to do that for people we'd move pubs to avoid. In the words of Congresswoman Maxine Waters in the House of Representatives: 'Reclaiming my time!'

Women are trained to be nice and respectful and let everyone else down gently, if at all. We feel our no has power. If we refuse to give someone else a kiss, a second date, a shot of our breasts, our time, our expertise, an explanation for why we need feminism or anything another person wants any time they want it, we feel responsible for their disappointment. But they haven't lost anything. We haven't taken anything away. We haven't ruined the booty call they had in the bank. We didn't take and burn four pages of neatly typed notes about the first draft of their novel. We haven't robbed them of a two-hour gender debate on Facebook they've already paid us for. We do not need to feel guilty for any of this.

Unless you've got an arrangement with someone for reciprocal babysitting or they've already invoiced you for legal advice, you do not owe them. Your no has very little actual power. You need to train yourself to see a disappointed face and move on with your life, knowing they will go elsewhere to get what they need. If you stop being a bottomless source of favours, they'll find another one. Take control of your time and energy. Practise saying the word 'no' out loud. Rehearse it. You don't need to be rude.

'No, I can't this week. I'm swamped. I might be able to help you next week if you're still stuck,' is a nice thing to say *if you mean it*. If you don't want to help them next week or ever, then just say, 'No, this one's not for me, but good luck!'

'No thank you.' 'No, I can't. Have you tried Geoff? I think he's free at the moment.' 'No, it doesn't sound like a good fit for me.' 'No, I'd love to help but I can't take on any more right now.' 'Much appreciate your offer, but no.' You do not need to say, 'So sorry, but I can't afford to have the eight-course tasting menu and chip in for the twelve bottles of wine you and your mates will drink' – you can just say 'no'.

Once you get the hang of no, you'll get a bit addicted to it. It's the greatest feeling in the world to say no and find that nothing happens. Often the person who's asked says, 'Thanks for getting back so quickly and letting me know.' No is always better than silence. No means the other person can move on and get what they need somewhere else. People often appreciate your no rather than an overcommitted yes which means that your help will be delayed or half-baked.

Saying no to men who feel entitled to a yes

All of this presumes that you're saying no to someone who is asking, not someone who is assuming your consent or cooperation. If someone takes without asking because they assume they're entitled, your no can come as a surprise to them and it can feel like a confrontation.

Have you ever lived somewhere without running water? When I meet people who have lived for a few weeks or months in a part of the world where they had no water on tap, I always ask them the same question, 'How long did you appreciate it when you got it back?' They usually tell me they appreciated it for about a day if they lost it for a week and a week if they lost it for a month. One woman told me the part of Bolivia where she was staying had inconsistent running water. Sometimes she'd go to the tap and there'd be a strong flow, other times nothing, and if there was a little dribble she'd be excited.

If you've been raised with running water and had it every day of your life, you will feel entitled to it. Hot and cold water from a tap doesn't occur in nature, so this is a privilege you've always known that's come to feel like a right. If your water got turned off today, you'd phone the council. If it wasn't back on in forty-eight hours you'd be tweeting, and if it wasn't restored in a week you'd be writing angry letters. At no point would you think, 'Well, I guess we don't have running water any more. Where's the closest river? I guess I'll have to walk down there with a jug on my head.' Although many people around the world live like that every day, it would almost certainly never be acceptable to you because running water is your standard, your normal, your expectation. Entitlement is the residue of privilege.

The way we feel about water is the way many men feel about inclusion, influence and the ability to get other people to do things for them: they assume the answer to any request they make will be 'yes'. If you've been included and heard in every room you've ever walked into, it is your normal to assume that there will be hot and cold running inclusion in the next one you enter. I saw a man in the financial district walk into *the wrong room*, look around and think, 'Well, it's the right room now because I'm in it,' and start advising the people who were in a meeting on what they should be doing. If you can't even find the right room, then maybe don't tell other people how they've got everything wrong.

Men who have been included as often as we've thoughtlessly left a tap running to heat up a shower often assume a yes before it has been granted. They will speak to you as if you have already agreed to their request for a night in your bed or a weekend working unpaid overtime. This is when you need to identify that they have made an assumption and turn the tap of their entitlement off.

Do you work with someone who is not your boss and shoots you emails saying things like, 'The client isn't happy. This'll take the whole weekend to do right, and we need to deliver Monday without fail,' without ever asking, 'Can you work this weekend?' You won't lose your job if you don't do this. They're just pressuring you because they want your help and assume it'll be granted because they feel entitled.

You need to turn their assumption into a request. 'Hi Toby, I see this is urgent for you. What a nightmare. Are you asking me if I can work the weekend?' Make Toby write back and ask. He'll probably say something like, 'Yes, we really need all hands on deck this weekend, and I'd appreciate the whole team getting on board.'

The thing is, you know that Toby has brought this on himself by delivering substandard work at the last possible moment, so this isn't your problem. It's his. He's forgotten that because he sees other people as a resource he's entitled to. You need to put yourself outside his circle of entitlement by saying, 'I can't do this weekend, but I'm forwarding the suggestions I made last week in case any of them are useful. Good luck!'

He may be annoyed because no water is coming out of this tap. If there was one tap in your house that never worked and couldn't be fixed, you'd stop expecting anything and use another one by default. You can be that tap. Or at least, be the Bolivian tap that works sometimes and not others. That way, Toby will be grateful when you give him something and will learn to ask nicely. Most of us don't mind helping when we feel valued and our contribution is recognised.

Many privileged men will dispute this because human

beings tend to notice only what is difficult, not what comes as a matter of course. Their experience of the path to money or success is a long walk to the VIP suite with lots of steep staircases on the way. What they do not realise is that as they walked down the corridor of their career there were many sets of doors that they walked through without even seeing that they were there. This is because the bouncers saw the posh white men coming down the hall and opened the doors in anticipation. Those men have to get used to hearing no, so you may need to train them to understand that some doors have different bouncers now and you're better at coping with a no and influencing a yes than they are.

After the men swept through the doors for all those years, the bouncers closed them immediately in the face of a short Asian woman coming up behind them. She could give up and leave, get angry or charm her way past the bouncers. As I wrote in Chapter 3: I Just Had a Thought, most excluded people self-exclude and a few get angry. The ones who get good at persuasion build that muscle. Why are three of the most influential people in the world Michelle Obama, Oprah Winfrey and Ellen DeGeneres? It's no accident that two of those people are women of colour and one is gay. The more reasons you're excluded and the more often you're excluded, the better you get at talking your way past the bouncers. This is why Madam C. J. Walker got the keynote speaker gig and died rich.

Men who haven't heard no very often tend to be deaf to it. Turn your no all the way up to eleven. Never consent to anything you're not sure you want to do just because a man is acting like you owe it to him. You're not stealing anything from a man just because he has an erection. He's not owed an explicit video, a sexual favour or a threesome because he's a charming steamroller. Turn your phone off. Call a cab. Tell him you don't want to see him any more. Don't sit around in the void he's created with his stifling, controlling brand of charisma. Make something. Do something. Meet up with women. Laugh. Invent. Organise. Do something for feminism. March. Shout. Dance. Sing. Run. Say no, then fill your life with yes so you're not persuaded to be his hot and cold running entitlement.

Sometimes 'no' can save your life. When I left the Jehovah's Witnesses, I slipped out the back door politely so as not to ruffle feathers. I moved towns and made no trouble. This was a good strategy for a number of reasons. It is the least traumatic option and it means I can still talk to friends and family who are members of the organisation and they are still technically allowed to talk to me.

A few years ago I made a radio show about my experiences and I was contacted by a young man called Ryan in Canada who wanted to get out the way I had, without being disfellowshipped, which means formal excommunication and shunning. Something about him made me get on a plane and fly to Vancouver to help him extricate himself from the religion. While I was there I ended up being escorted into a windowless room at the back of a Kingdom Hall (church building) by two elders who did not introduce themselves and locked the door. I was pretending to be a Jehovah's Witness as part of my cover story. I used all the right language and did all the right things. My performance was flawless. They interrogated me for thirty minutes until eventually it became clear that they did not believe I was a 'sister'. They started asking for names and phone numbers in my congregation in London. Blindsided, I gave them what I had and then one of them sneered at me and said, 'We need to run a background check on you.' It's difficult to make the Canadian accent sound sinister but he managed it. I was instantly furious. I stood up and said, 'This is why Ryan doesn't want to speak to you. This is why nobody wants to speak to you. This is why you seem like the FBI. You are not loving. It is not okay for you to hold a woman you do not know in a locked room. Now unlock the door and let me go!' They became very flustered and opened the door immediately. I strode out of the room and out of the Kingdom Hall and it was as if I had left heavy luggage behind me. I had been carrying a weight for years.

I wondered how they had known I wasn't really a Jehovah's Witness when my performance was such a good replica. Then I realised: a sister would never look an elder in the eye and offer him advice. My language was perfect, but I hadn't looked submissive. I wasn't a plausible Jehovah's Witness any more because there was a 'no' in my heart and boundaries in my eyes.

Then I realised that I had given them the names of my last congregation and elders. In trying to save Ryan from being disfellowshipped, I had led them to a way of excommunicating me. And then I realised they'd forgotten to ask my name! I had outsmarted them.

My whole life has changed since that moment. For years I was convinced that I couldn't be further away from the Jehovah's Witnesses. I thought I was a completely independent woman. But something was holding me back. I had to say a big, solid, certain 'no' to their faces before I was able to say 'yes' to myself. Men like the ones who'd locked me in that room had made all my decisions. All my life I was susceptible to angry, high-status men. No more. I said 'Let me out' and I walked through the door like it was the last scene in a movie and the first scene in my life. I would never have had the confidence to do the podcast or write this book if I'd not done it. I did not know I was carrying that trauma, but all I can tell you is that three months after I released it I had started *The Guilty*

Feminist and I have not looked back. Those Canadian elders did me a huge favour. They pushed me so far, I had to say 'no' and that 'no' led to all the 'yes' I had in me.

Saying no to each other

Sometimes it is especially difficult to say no to people from your tribe. Their expectation of alliance is higher. They can feel angrier that you're not capitulating because they feel you should. Women are not a monolithic group. Feminists share values, but we do not have to agree on everything. We don't expect all white men, all socialists or all Chinese people to have the same views or tastes and we mustn't expect feminists to do so either. We must be able to say no and take no for an answer. Some feminists try to force others into giving intellectual consent they do not wish to.

We're free to express our views. We're allowed to be angry. If we're from a marginalised group and we are not being listened to by more privileged feminists, we can tell them in no uncertain terms, persuade and influence or walk away. All of those things are valid. We probably do all three at different times.

Please be aware of using *other people's oppression* as a weapon. Amplify the views of the group you're an ally for, but if you've not experienced the kind of prejudice that a black or trans person has, for example, it isn't your place to use internet bigotry as a front to scream and throw things because you've got repressed anger about your own issues.

If you don't spend much time on Twitter and other dark alleys of the internet, you may not be familiar with some of the civil wars in feminism and the violent word grenades thrown around the clock. There is one approach to feminism operating on the internet right now that states there is a right and a wrong answer and that if you do not agree with the right answer all

you can do is 'sit and listen in the space'. If you will not be
silent then you need to leave or you'll be blocked.

They are the rules of a high-control group. In the Jehovah's
Witnesses, the elders have all the answers. They're given from
on high by the Watchtower Society. The general congregation
can never disagree with what's in the publications and even
discussing a nuance is seen as dangerous. Congregants will
moderate each other and tell each other to 'be careful' if they
question anything, however mildly, even in private. If you're
expressing doubts or have your own theories, another Jehovah's
Witness, probably a close friend, will report you to the elders
who will visit your house. If you persist in 'independent thinking' you'll be disfellowshipped and permanently shunned by
friends and family.

There are ways of thinking in some feminist circles right
now that remind me of being in a cult in a way that makes me
go physically cold. I don't mean that this is a metaphorical cult
like the diet industry. I mean that these rules are those of an
actual, literal cult. Feminists, who should be having passionate
debates and talking through thought experiments, are whisper-
ing their true feelings behind closed doors. Some are barking
at people to fall into line on social media and others are being
cowed by other women who set the rules. Those who shout the
loudest and send people to 'dogpile', or 'drag' others, are not
taking no for an answer when they should.

The right wing often seems to get more done, largely
because its goals are broadly fiscal. If we want to make a hundred dollars together, who cares if we disagree? All we need to
do is find the quickest way to get that sweet hundred bucks.
The left's goals are ideological, so it feels as if we cannot proceed until we have decided on the details of our beliefs and
the best way to carry out our goals. That can never be done.
As the insightful comedian Michael Legge said in his recent

show *Jerk*, 'I'm left wing but it's probably hard for you to tell that right now because I'm not currently arguing with someone I agree with.'

I am not telling any angry, oppressed person not to rage against the machine, even if that machine is staffed by other feminists. I am saying, if you have an element of privilege, whether that be education, time, insight, clarity of thought or access to technology, do everything you can on the days when you're feeling strong to persuade and win people over for the women in the world who have no voice, Twitter account or iPhone. Can we collectively build empathy among women for the sisters who came before us who built us freedoms in a promised land they didn't live to see?

If someone is denying your identity or humanity, I understand that you cannot work with them. Leyla Hussein, the brilliant anti-female genital mutilation activist (featured in Chapter 9: There is No 'Try') is often told that there will be a pro-FGM speaker on a panel 'for balance'. She declines. She won't be on stage with someone who would cut a child's clitoris off in the same way you wouldn't be on stage with someone who is pro-paedophilia or a rape apologist.

If someone disagrees with you in less important ways, can you work with them where you do agree? Can you amplify the issues you feel similarly about? There are two episodes of *The Guilty Feminist* I am especially proud of. One is 'Minefields', and the other is 'Faith'. I assembled a panel of diverse people to talk about gender and religion and we disagreed lots while having an absolutely brilliant time, laughing constantly and loving each other warmly. I don't have to agree with everything you say to try to understand it better and to give ground. I don't have to be convinced by conclusions that you've arrived at from a different life experience to respect you as a human being and understand that you have good reason for feeling as you do. Maybe we're both right. It's possible we're both wrong.

What is happening now is that people are in such violent disagreement on the internet, a place where normal humanity and civility goes for a holiday, that they need to tribe heavily with those who do agree with them. You need your gang for protection. 'At least we all agree. You've got my back if they come after me, right?' Now what happens if you have a small difference of opinion with one of your tribe, or you discover a gaping difference in world view? If you own up to feeling differently now, you will not have your tribe and you will be out in the rabid, dark world of Twitter, alone.

If you engage in internet feminism, lots of people who you think are in your tribe do not really understand or believe everything they claim to. You might not be sure about some things that come as part of your package deal, either. The more people draw swords, the more they need to violently agree with those in their camp who will protect them. This is why we are heading towards an Orwellian ideological hegemony if we do not start to accept that there are different ways of looking at things. Plurality of thought and the ability to set our own intellectual boundaries has never been more important.

We have to stop letting our emotions get the better of us and lashing out when we encounter clumsy language or someone who hasn't fully assimilated what in some cases are very new ideas. It's only by continuing to talk and share and learn and change that we can make any progress at all.

As discussed in the introduction. the world is becoming far more gender fluid and Generation Z will not honour the binary the way that Baby Boomers do or Gen X does to a lesser extent.

Gender has been a stable concept for a long time and it's undergoing a huge revolution. No one can claim they knew this five years ago. It's changing rapidly, and we need to go with it because everything about denying people their right to their own identity shouts 'wrong side of history'. I know I've made mistakes, including on early episodes of the podcast, and I'm sure I'll make more in the future. But when I see someone else making a mistake, I'm trying (and sometimes it's a huge effort) to take other people through the change that I've been through.

I try to reason. I try to explain. I share stories. If you're transgender, non-binary or gender-fluid and this stuff makes you feel devastated, that's totally understandable and you don't have to do any of the emotional labour or heavy lifting. If you're cis, maybe try influencing on behalf of trans people who've been through enough.

Some people are trolling, some won't wish to change their tribal views no matter what, but some just might need a little time and empathy to think things through. We will need empathy too. We are using language and assumptions now that will be completely outmoded in two years' time. I do not know it all and I never will. But I don't think I've ever been won over by someone shouting at me.

Sometimes we do not have the time, energy or headspace to educate people because we have our own issues and we feel they could Google for themselves. If we're convinced that they aren't just making trouble, consider asking them to rethink with something encouraging like, 'There's plenty of stuff online to read. Try these search terms,' and then walk away.

Nobody has to argue with strangers on Facebook. It might feel like you do but no one is forcing you. We're not being allies to oppressed communities we're not members of by screaming at strangers. It's more likely to alienate people who aren't there yet but might be if they don't get frightened away. If it's not our oppression, there's no need to open with something aggressive. Even if we are in the oppressed group, anger isn't the only tool available to us. I've actually had some success asking kind and open questions to those who write to me to tell me that 'feminism is cancer'. Sarah Silverman is a master at this. Check out her Twitter feed. She beats their swords into her ploughshares.

I'm not saying that civility is more important than standing up to fascism. It isn't. Sometimes hostility is the only appropriate response to oppression. Do what you need to do, but be aware rather than reckless and use fury with intention. Feminism isn't a vent to blow off steam because deep down you're angry about other things. Be careful not to undermine the work of those who are making genuine headway in terms of inclusion, influence and zero-tolerance boundary-setting. The pen is mightier than the sword, but the keyboard is a bunker to fire off nuclear weapons and watch people burn at a distance. If you wouldn't say it looking into their eyes, try not to send it to the cloud where it can never be undone.

Sometimes people tweet me with breath-taking hostility and when I reply they say, 'Oh, no – you're doing a great job. Thanks for responding,' and I wonder, why didn't they open with something friendly and then make their point clearly but kindly? It's as if the standard opener on the internet is so hostile, it's almost the custom to start with a furious insult. The push for unanimous agreement is concerning to me in itself. Where does that end? What's the good version of that? That we all end up saying exactly the same things to each other in a loop until a new directive on gender or feminism is sent to us from a university PhD? That's the plot of *1984*, gang.

If you are going to 'call people out', please be aware that it's highly class- and location-based. This is a language and a world view invented and perpetuated by a small bubble of thinkers and is not known to over 99 per cent of the world. I've seen white Western women 'calling out' women of colour in developing nations for not accepting their precise definitions and examples of cultural appropriation and emotional labour. It is intellectual imperialism to impose your specific, contemporary academic views on women from other cultures, classes and backgrounds and imperialism is neither feminist nor liberal.

Personally I do not use terms like 'call out' because it's become a shorthand for the moral high ground. First person to say 'I'm calling you out' wins. It's not an un-useful term but I don't like that kind of tribal language because I'm a 'cult survivor' and I find it 'triggering', by which I mean I lived in a high-control group that referred to a 'pure language' and this kind of code was what kept the dogma alive. I'm not saying don't use it. I'm saying you're your own person. Have a think and then decide for yourself. Use it if it works for you, not because you feel you'll be ousted from the gang if you don't.

We must learn to say, 'No, I do not agree with you,' and find a way to accept hearing no from another feminist, or feminism will not last. Freedom from the tyranny of the patriarchy, access to books, ideas, invention and original thought is what feminism is fighting for. We must never insist that other female minds bow to the will of dogma or all we do is dig a tunnel out of one prison yard into another.

We can learn to say an intentional no, to set boundaries with anyone who doesn't want to take no for an answer but will learn to if we teach them. We can live in honour of Madam C. J. Walker and say no even to those who others idolise and who are usually right. Respect, like money, is not given until it is applied for. No is often an invoice for respect.

Fish are so woke

One of the people who has been most useful in helping me unpack some of the more complicated contemporary feminist issues and someone who knows a great deal about debating without hating is Reubs Walsh, who is transgender and non-binary. She is also a social neuroscientist doing a PhD and one of her fields of study is gender.

Hello, Reubs Walsh. You are an academic?
I'm a PhD student living in Amsterdam but I grew up in England. I'm a Christian, but none of that fire-and-brimstone-and-misogyny bullshit, and I'm a neuroscientist. I study the interplay between the biology of the brain and the social environment, particularly in terms of development and social cognition, so how people understand themselves and each other. I'm looking at how, in particular, adolescents learn to understand other people and how that affects the way they understand themselves. So one of the interesting things I look at there is gender and trans people.

You did the 'Minefields' and 'Faith' episodes with us, which are two I'm very proud of. I met you online because of your willingness to say 'no'. Do you remember tweeting me with an objection to language we'd unwittingly used on the show? How do you remember our interactions and how we became friends? How do you remember the shows?
Yeah . . . Initially I tweeted you because I was frustrated at first by the preponderance of cis, white feminist guests, and to some degree, cis, white feminist topics in a podcast that I found way more open and inclusive in its feminism and its comedy than is often the case. I guess because that's a hard balance to strike. So I tweeted saying I'd love it more if you had more diverse guests, and then we talked about how you might be able to find those people, and I guess I ended up being one

of them! But before that, since you'd shown willing to try and solve that problem, I figured it was worthwhile tweeting when I was somewhat hurt by you using noted transphobe Germaine Greer as an example of a super-feminist. Obviously it was just thoughtlessness, but I was quite upset by it and tweeted in my best disappointed-but-still-optimistic tone, and you basically asked me to continue tweeting when I noticed things that didn't feel inclusive, and the conversations got ever more interesting and intricate and eventually we ended up having vegan food together!

The shows were an amazing experience. It was a really wonderful panel that I was very proud to be part of, me and four utterly brilliant feminist women. I felt like the time we spent planning those episodes generated a real sense of trust and sisterhood among us that allowed us to be really honest and open together and to go into some very challenging topic areas without needing to feel defensive. We've continued to have some really fantastic conversations as well, and supported each other's feminist work, which has been wonderful.

Adolescence is the time when you come into your own gender, certainly sexually. Gender fluidity is really interesting for feminism right now. There seems to be an emergence of the transgender community at the moment. Do you know why that is?
The LGBT rights movement kicked off in the 1960s and I guess a lot of your readers will know what happened. In those days, there was much less of a distinction between what was L and what was trans-masculine, what was G and what was trans-feminine. The main focus at that time was decriminalisation for all queer people. Now

same-sex marriage is becoming less controversial, it has created space in the LGBT community for trans people's voices to be heard.

Do you think sometimes it's confusing to put the T with the LGB since being gay is about who you're attracted to, while being transgender is about your gender identity, which is quite different?

There's a conflation of sexuality and gender by people who are trying to undermine trans people in particular. But LGBT-phobia is predominantly about policing the boundaries of gender. It's about fitting into these narrow boxes which exist in our culture for reasons, I think, to do with controlling political power and retaining agency in the hands of certain people.

What's the difference between gender identity and gender expression?

Gender identity is something that happens inside yourself. Gender expression is about the performative part. It's those things that you do to let other people know what your gender identity is – or as close as you can get. Whereas gender identity is the stuff that is hard to describe that goes on inside you, almost in the background.

Increasingly, I find it implausible that the seven billion people on Earth all fit neatly into one of these boxes. Is binary therefore the convenience of human beings being able to categorise each other quickly: 'I know who you are. I've got it summed up'?

Yes. Learning to put things into categories quickly and without too much thought is a very big part of how human beings understand the world, and indeed, many organisms do this (category-learning) with gender. The important difference being that no other species, including social species, has a gendered culture with cultural signifiers of gender or cultural constructs of gender. A lot of fish in their normal lifecycle change sex one or more times – they have three or four different sexes.

Ah, fish are woke. That's what I've learned.
Fish are woke.

Fish are so woke. #fisharewoke.
Sexual dimorphism isn't something that exists in nature in the way that we see it in human beings, so there's a lot of reason to think human gender has a lot more to do with our culture than our biology. We have natural categories and cultural categories. That's a dog, that's a cat, versus, that's a zoo animal, that's a farm animal. One of the very first categories proposed as natural, along with things like colours (as in red and green), is gender. And it's pointed out that you don't immediately categorise dogs by their gender automatically in the way that you do people.

Well, we always assume animals are male. I've got two beautiful cats and everyone who comes into my flat says, 'Oh, isn't he lovely.' But both my cats are girls.
I always think of cats as girls and dogs as boys.

I'm sure you're not alone. I watched a BBC report about a little girl in Afghanistan where girls can't work and boys can. If your family has six girls and no boys, you're allowed to dress up one of your girls as a boy to go and sell water, for example. This tradition is known as

Bacha Posh. They have to dress as a boy for the whole of their childhood. Everyone knows that they're just boys financially.

Boys for tax reasons.

They're economic boys. This little girl was dressed as a boy and her mother said, 'Oh, she really hates it and she gets teased all the time and she hates having her hair like that,' and the little girl was crying. And I thought, oh, that's being transgender. Everyone's calling you a boy and you're really a girl.

Exactly! I think part of the reason people get stuck is that cis women imagine what would it feel like if they felt they were a man when really it's more like, 'How would I feel if everyone treated me like a man?'

If right now that just started happening to me, how would I respond?

And if you then assert your gender to people, they—

They snigger or they get hostile.

Or say, 'Yeah, Deborah, I know you think you're a woman but you're basically a man so why are you called Deborah? Is it just to confuse people? What's your anatomy like? How do you have sex? How often do you have sex?' And make all of these things conditional for you to be a woman and then still didn't grant you that womanhood. Some people think that trans women are somehow too femme, because of course at first many trans women do luxuriate in being able to express that – but then I've also heard transphobic self-proclaimed feminists sort of imply that trans women, or maybe the imagined cis man who pretends to be a trans woman, aren't really women without wearing lipstick – without a hint of irony, or a touch of lipstick on their own lips.

Do you know why this is such a difficult idea for some parts of the feminist community to understand or accept or have empathy for?
Sure. Well, the first thing I would say is that I appreciate that they self-describe as feminist but this thing, this is not feminism. Reducing women to their bodies is patriarchy. The second thing is, where does it come from? I think the oppression of women is rooted in perceptions about their minds and their brains and the belief that they are less capable than men's minds and brains. And when you look at womanhood in those terms, of course, trans makes perfect sense because womanhood is a thing that happens in your mind and brain and not in your body. But in my experience, trans people don't think women's brains are biologically or cognitively inferior, or even particularly different, to men's brains at anywhere near the rate that cisgender women do, never mind cis men. So it's a nuanced thing but I think it's a nuance that cisgender feminists should be expected to grasp. I think feminists are generally smart people, so I tend to think if they ignore that nuance it's got to be somewhat wilful, because it challenges their world view, rather than because they just don't understand.

Some people say that trans women experienced male privilege when they presented as a man. Some trans women say they remember having male privilege and noticed the shift when they transitioned. Some trans women say they don't feel they benefited from male privilege because the marginalisation of being trans cancels it out.

Personally, I was raised in an environment where people looked at me and thought they saw a boy and therefore encouraged me in academic pursuits in the way they do with boys. In the childhood of trans women the things that are done to us are done on the assumption that we're boys. And some of those things have positive intentions that girls wouldn't experience because we live in a sexist society. That is true. But we still experienced those things as girls. We still watched Disney movies and we didn't identify with the prince, we identified with the princess who lacked agency and whose life's purpose was made out to be marriage.

But there are some aspects, like putting a male name on a CV or a letter and being more likely to get a response from a sexist. I mean, if it's a privilege to get responses from sexists.

It can be if it means you get the job.
Then yeah, that is male privilege but, of course, that does disappear when you transition. Overall, the privilege is on a minus because the world responds to transgender people with suspicion and violence or exclusion. Then there's the dominant social narrative about gender which is sexist and if you identify as a girl, even if you haven't realised you identify as a girl yet, you internalise that as criticisms of yourself.

How can cis feminists reading this book better include transgender and non-binary sisters? How can we better include?
Well, you could not call the male or non-binary ones 'sisters'. That's something.

What do we call them? Siblings?
Yeah. Feminist families.

I think the core of how it could be done is – well, it's intersectionality, isn't it? In the history of feminism, black feminists have said and written incredibly valuable things about why and how race oppression is part of the system by which gender oppression is able to continue to exist.

If you want your feminist methodologies to be more trans-inclusive, instead of looking at what a certain type of white man has and thinking that women should have that too, take a step back and ask what value system is that man using and is it valid? Is it valid to be really pleased that you have a lot of money? Now, it probably is because we live in a society where money is useful but is that how we want to frame our feminism?

So then how do we use that money? Are we using any of it to help and give others platforms?
We have to try to incrementally change the way we think and talk and teach each other about gender so that it doesn't set up this diametric opposition between men and women. And that's something I think often cis feminists find quite difficult because rightly, they are angry with people who reinforce and benefit from patriarchy, which is mostly men. But trans people who don't identify as men are, well, not men, and trans men and even cis men are harmed by patriarchy, and indeed women and non-binary people also get caught up in and potentially reinforce patriarchal standards because they're so woven into how we communicate gender and generally participate in culture.

What can we do? How can we behave? How can we be welcoming?

Well, there are some very simple things. If you're having a women-only space, that's cool but explicitly say 'trans-inclusive women-only' space. And, although I know this is something where maybe trans people disagree with each other more, I think that means anyone whose gender identity encompasses womanhood. Which might mean that phrases like 'women who live full-time as women' need to be dispensed with – non-binary women are still women, but might present in a way that gets read as male and not care – and that doesn't mean they aren't women.

More often now, I hear 'women and non-binary' which I like because I think it's implied that anyone who's welcoming non-binary people is welcoming trans people.

Yeah, I like 'women and non-binary' or even 'cis women and trans people of all genders' because often these spaces are about trying to create a space where the beneficiaries of patriarchy can't swing their privilege around, so that means the people who need to step back are men, or even only cisgender men, depending on the context.

Reubs, you're trans and non-binary. Could you just talk me through how that works? What does transitioning mean?

Gender transition is when you go, 'Oh, hey guys, you know that assumption you've been making? It's not quite right.' Saying to someone, 'My gender assigned at birth isn't actually my gender' is a moment of gender transition. But then it's also a process of getting to know yourself better, which most people go through to some degree. But obviously trans people have a label for it because for us it's a bit more involved and can be a very long, even lifelong journey of self-discovery and an evolving sense of self, plus it's a hassle so you need a word for it – sometimes it involves medical intervention – and always lots of paperwork!

So you transitioned from your gender assigned at birth, which was male, to a non-binary state which is neither male nor female. So, do you prefer the pronoun 'they'?
I do but I have made a pragmatic decision. What makes me most uncomfortable is when my attention is called to it, especially if I'm not in that space of thinking about gender. It's one thing if we're having a conversation about gender but if it's about pizza, and someone says, 'Margaret, has Reubs told you what she, her, they want on their pizza?' then that draws my attention to it. In that situation I'm fine with 'she' because it's easier for other people and it isn't wrong, it's just ... imprecise. 'He' is wrong. 'She' is fine. 'They' is best, but until the world catches up and 'they' becomes quote-unquote normal, then 'she' is probably easier for everyone, including me.

I have a non-binary friend and they say that in a future world where children see lots of gender expression played out by people who have been assigned both male and female genders at birth, they wouldn't feel the need to transition. Is that a possibility, do you think?
I think it is. But in order for that to be the case, we would need to stop coercively gendering children. Babies don't really have a gender. They have body parts but not a gender yet. We don't need to assign people a legal gender at birth; we might not need to assign people a legal gender at all.

I think there probably is some value in gendering babies, even if it's just medical.
But is it medically useful to gender babies at birth? Paediatrically, no. It's useful to know whether someone has active ovaries and/or a uterus, because then you can look out for things like ectopic pregnancy. But some men have ovaries; some cis women don't have a cervix. It is a clinical risk to make assumptions based on external genitalia at birth. It doesn't actually create a difference, medically speaking, at that time. It only creates a difference legally.

There's also femme-phobia, the idea that liking high heels and mascara makes you not a feminist. It's so arbitrary, the way we decorate. In the 1700s, men were wearing powdered wigs and powdering their faces and wearing high heels and these were manly acts.
Yeah, and I would have hated doing it.

Whereas now powdering your face is a feminine act and therefore for a trans woman, a way of expressing herself in that gender space.
Yes, it can be a way for trans women to communicate to other people who they are.

Yes. So if all cisgendered women quit make-up and heels tomorrow, how do transgender women then play in the gendered space?
Why does it matter? Cis men and women can be very feminine or masculine too. The relationship between gender identity and gender expression isn't one-to-one any more. We need to know language. We need to know your preferred pronoun but to relate to people you need a conversation, not just assumptions based on what

they're wearing or how they have decorated. It would be good if it were more common to ask people their preferred pronoun.

If someone walked up to me in a bar and said, 'What's your preferred pronoun?' I don't know how I'd react. Some of the trans women I know would find it hurtful.
But you only have to ask the first time you meet.

There are some trans women who usually pass for cis who I know would find that really upsetting because it would imply that they didn't pass.
Another option is calling people 'they' unless they prefer something else. In the community I was living in in Oxford towards the end of my degree, people called each other 'they' habitually. Where there's a critical mass of non-binary people it just starts to happen by itself.

I think because women are oppressed as well and have been marginalised for so long, it's a bit like saying to black people, 'Let's eradicate the history of race – let's not say black and white any more.'
I don't think it eradicates the history of gender to say that the pronouns we use, by default, should be neutral. I guess the hypothesis you're inching towards is that people who are more hurt by misgendering of their pre-transition life then react against that and become incredibly binary which I think is probably true. I would just like to make it easier for a non-binary person to be able to live their authentic self.

Reubs is someone I happily and regularly disagree with. I have phoned her up to talk things through and we allow ourselves the time and space to craft arguments to each other, which is why I value her friendship. I am excited to invite Reubs on stage to our new series of *Guilty Feminist* debates. A formal debate is a medium that allows rigorous, respectful disagreement and requires us to make a proper rebuttal and not just meekly agree and make everyone happy, as women are trained to do. Let's not be afraid to say no, and not be too proud to be won over by a compelling argument. I am so desperate for the media to move away from televised roast battles which showcase personal attacks for cheap laughs, and into hilarious and meaningful thought experiments, I'm staging it myself to demonstrate that light entertainment can do the heavy lifting.

Enemy Lines

I'm a feminist but sometimes I think the patriarchy does look very comfortable.

I'm a feminist but I've always enjoyed the occasional boys' night out, joshing with the lads. I know it's not really a boys' night out if I'm there ruining it by being a girl, but I get to play in their space and take up three chairs using both my arms and some serious posturing. Some of them are well read, clued up and breathtakingly arrogant. Others are logical to the point where it's socially impractical. Some are camp, sassy and screamingly bitchy. Others aren't as funny as they think they are, but they make up for it with salesmanship. Some want to solve any problem, flat tyre or Rubik's Cube, in their vision. Others want to be psychoanalysed and adored. Some are warm and affectionate and want to deconstruct movies too deeply. A few are nervous and dithering. Many are stuck in relationships that are like broken-down cars, but they refuse to call the AA. Some are functioning alcoholics who refuse to go to AA.

These descriptions could work in different ways for my female friends too (except, if I'm incredibly honest, 'breathtakingly arrogant') – so I don't know what it is about being with boys, really. I rarely crave being in exclusively male company, but when I do, I guess it's a vibe, a smell, a heft, a roar, a bicep, a challenge, a taste of being on the team that has been dared to be daring by all of history. Men can be glorious. I feel like I'm meant to caveat that, but the truth is, some of my favourite husbands are straight white men. I love lots of men and I like lots about men even when they're in big gangs of boy-chaps.

Feminism is a fight and a fight requires an enemy, right? Sometimes our enemy feels nebulous. What is this ninja-like patriarchy that's all around us and nowhere at all? The 'fem' in feminism and the 'pater' in patriarchy can make it seem like enemy lines are drawn between men as the beneficiaries of patri-archal systems, and women who are oppressed by the same. In some circles, feminism has a reputation for being 'man-hating', and I believe this is because fighting for change looks angrier than fighting for the status quo. It's easy to present footage of women shouting outside buildings with placards – protesting male-biased events or institutions – as evidence that feminism is organised, recreational man-hating. I'm not claiming that no feminists hate men. I can't control what women feel in their own time. I'm saying that you've got to hijack feminism for your own ends if you want to use it to despise or abuse men.

So who are feminism's enemies, and who are we told they are?

Swallowing the red pill

Men can be tools of the patriarchy (all puns intended). Men behave in toxic, violent ways and hoard their power and influ-ence the way governments hoard oil. Feminism contests that behaviour and says, 'Women and girls suffer from structural, verbal and physical violence perpetrated by men and boys, and we do not accept that this is society's foregone conclusion.' Feminism must fight for women's right to decide what happens to our own bodies, including if, when and how we grow babies inside our wombs, in a world where almost all the laws have been made for and by men. Feminism is there to skywrite, 'Women have a valid fear of male violence'. It doesn't claim that all or most men are violent predators, because they are not, but feminism has to flag up that men are the only ones who can stop this behaviour both individually and as a culture.

Men are great, and toxic masculinity exists (in all its self-loathing, violent and controlling forms), and those two things are compatible. There are many displays of fury from men right now about the small changes feminism is making. As the creator of a feminist podcast, sometimes I am the recipient of this fury. One morning I received a message from a sixteen-year-old boy in Florida that read: 'Make me a sandwich.' When I replied, 'Sure. What do you want on it?' he replied, 'Well done. You've won feminism, but tell me, why don't you call it "equalism" if it's about equality?' We ended up having quite a nice chat and he did, after some time, admit that it would be better if governments reflected the gender split in the population more accurately.

This was quite a mild and completely predictable heckle from a boychild who'd Googled 'feminism' and wanted some attention from a stranger, but many women receive rape threats and sadistic descriptions of graphic violence from strangers on the internet every day. This has become so ordinary it is exhausting. This is especially true of women who are on television or walk through some other ray of limelight. They don't have to be speaking about feminism, either. They can be talking about a historical artefact, judging a cake-making competition or doing amateur ballroom dancing.

There is a deep fear radiating from some men at the moment. They see that influence and opportunity are being ever so slightly redistributed, and it is as if the fear of having only 97 per cent of the pie, rather than 99 per cent, is making them melt down. It is like someone is breaking into their house and stealing their gang's right to be the sole voice of influence and they are entitled to use any means necessary to scare off the intruders.

Some call themselves 'men's rights activists'. We need to be honest and say that most MRAs aren't life's winners. You don't see Bill Gates Googling a woman with a blog called *Gaby's Got Girl Power* and telling her that she's a fat whore who's too ugly to rape. You don't read about Hugh Jackman trolling schoolgirls who are campaigning to get more female authors on their curriculum – #wolverinesaysfeminismiscancer. Most men who feel emotional and tearful about feminism feel let down by the patriarchy themselves. They don't know who to blame, so they're lashing out, not at the power base but at the ones in warpaint who look like they're from the other side of the wall. A notable exception of a man who's won the game of capitalism and power and still finds time to call Rosie O'Donnell a fat loser on Twitter is Donald Trump, but his middle name is 'notable exception', so that should be no surprise.

Many men's rights activists and their sympathisers have written to encourage me to watch *The Red Pill*, a documentary by a young woman called Cassie Jaye. Jaye was a Hollywood ingénue who was sick of playing the hot blonde killed off by a 'troubled' man in a mask and chucked it in to direct docs with a feminist or social agenda. She looked into the MRAs, expecting to find them abhorrent, but is won over by their point of view and in the end (spoiler in all sense of the word) decides not to call herself a feminist any more.

The film was largely funded through Kickstarter when everyone's favourite misogynist provocateur Milo Yiannopoulos tweeted the link. It was given a load of free publicity because it was pulled from cinemas in Australia and Canada due to protests. I watched it thinking it must have some kind of potent power and was a bit worried I'd fall down the 'rabbit hole' with Cassie.

Guys, it's safe. You will not swallow this pill.

The men she interviews include Paul Elam, a man whose website *A Voice for Men* currently features headlines such as 'Study Reveals Female Rape Victims Enjoyed the Experience', 'October is the Fifth Annual "Bash a Violent Bitch" Month' and 'All Women are Pedophiles and That's All They Are' – but she doesn't seem to push him on this terribly much. He basically claims that this is tit for tat because 'Jezebel started it', and she seems to find that acceptable.

It's worth examining the issues the MRAs are angry about (as outlined in this film) and why they're so sad and sulky about feminism, because the MRAs' constant, furious noise makes a lot of people believe that feminists and men must be enemies.

First, they maintain that men do not have the same reproductive rights as women. Cassie creates a handy flow chart showing that men's rights stop after they decide to have the kind of unprotected sex that risks their partner getting knocked up. After that, the MRAs complain, it's her body and her choice. 'Why don't men have a choice?' the stars of the documentary want to know. The answer to that question is because it is her uterus. You can't decide whether someone else grows a person inside herself or not, whether you're her lover, her husband, wife, best friend or twin sister. It's really a question for her and she's got to trust her gut, because that's where the foetus will be living. I can't stop a chap I'm sleeping with from having a vasectomy. They're his bollocks so they're not my reproductive rights. That has to work the other way around regardless of your well-meaning flow charts.

If men had to get a human being the size of a watermelon out of a hole the size of a tampon, you'd better believe all the rights would be theirs and more. How do I know this? They're responsible for most of the legislation in the history of the world, and women who contributed were working in a pre-dominantly male environment in a bubble bath of male views.

I can only imagine that a sexual partner having an abortion when you want a child must be devastating, but until med-ical science can build cis guys an artificial uterus for foetal transfers, I'm out of ideas for how to fix that. I imagine that a woman having your biological child when all you wanted was a one-night stand is also terrifying, but do you want to live in a world with court-ordered abortions? If you're not up for a woman being tied down while you enter her cervix against her will, this might just be a consequence of sex that grown-ups have to deal with. I suggest wearing a weapons-grade condom *every time*, if you're in any doubt that your sexual partner and you share the same goals on the baby front.

Second, MRAs assert that almost as many men suffer from domestic violence as women, but that there is no media interest or refuges for male victims. This theory of 'gender symmetry' says that men and women hit each other behind closed doors at an equal rate but that men won't report it because society doesn't encourage them to. There are some statistics to back this up,[1] but what Jaye never acknowledges is that the force

---

1 The US's National Comorbidity Study of 1990–92 found 18.4% of men and 17.4% of women had experienced minor Intimate Partner Violence (IPV) and 5.5% of men and 6.5% of women had experienced severe IPV. The 1995 Home Office Research Study 191 in England and Wales found that in the twelve months prior to the survey, 4.2% of both men and women between the ages of sixteen and fifty-nine had experienced IPV. Kessler, Ronald C.; Molnar, Beth E.; Feurer, Irene D.; Applebaum, Mark (October 2001). 'Patterns and Mental Health Predictors of Domestic Violence in the United States: Results from the National Comorbidity Survey'. *International Journal of Law and Psychiatry.* 24(4–5): 487–508. PMID 11521422. doi:10.1016/S0160-2527(01)00080-2. Retrieved 29 June 2014. Mirrlees-Black, Catriona (1999). *Domestic Violence: Findings from a new British Crime Survey self-completion questionnaire* (PDF). London: Home Office. pp. 20–21. ISBN: 978-1-8408-2193-2.

with which men are capable of attacking women cannot be reciprocated. A man in *The Red Pill* describes his wife frequently screaming and throwing things and explains that he would go outside so the neighbours could see that he wasn't the perpetrator. The fact that he could walk past her and get out the door is key – but is never discussed by Jaye.

This is not to say that some men aren't physically weaker than their female partners but in general, men are taller than women, men are stronger than women and they have a higher percentage of lean muscle mass than women. The reason there are so many more refuges and safe houses for women is that they are much more likely to die at the hands of a male partner. Fifty-five per cent of murdered women are killed by intimate partners (current or former).[2] By comparison, about four per cent of men who are murdered are killed by their female partner (and often that is in self-defence). The statistics on Intimate Partner Violence show that women are more likely to throw something from a distance, push or slap, whereas men are more likely to strangle and punch.[3] Of course, none of these statistics are a comfort to the men who are being beaten but force, severity and death are not explored in *The Red Pill* and seem to be forgotten about or not understood by MRAs.

A more sympathetic complaint from men's rights activists is the courts' lack of interest in them as parents. Undoubtedly some men do lose their children unfairly or are granted 'visitation rights' rather than joint custody, which is heartbreaking when they want to live with their children at least 50 per cent of the time. Some women won't put the name of the child's

---

2 https://www.theatlantic.com/health/archive/2017/07/homicides-women/534306/.
3 Chan, K. L. (2011). 'Gender differences in self-reports of intimate partner violence: A review' (PDF), *Aggression and Violent Behavior*, vol. 16 (2), pp. 167–75. doi:10.1016/j.avb.2011.02.008.

father on the birth certificate and, in those cases, the man has no rights whatsoever. These are changes men and women absolutely need to fight for together. The presumption that a woman's place is in the home and a man must be a breadwinner above all else is the patriarchy's favourite song. We need a cultural shift so that men don't miss their children growing up and women don't limit their career opportunities even within happy, heterosexual, co-parenting relationships.

In Sweden, where gender roles are more fluid, parents are offered 480 days of paid parental leave between them – but to take them all, each parent must take at least 90 days. Guess what? When a couple splits in Stockholm, custody is almost always worked out between the parents and the children. Custody cases rarely go to court because there's nothing to 'win', as child support is fixed and most couples have joint custody anyway. There's a culture and an expectation of shared parenting and breadwinning so that even if individual couples vary, the norm sets the thermostat. Sweden is also a wealthy country with great socialised education and that needs to be factored in. So many injustices could be fixed, given time, funding and a willingness to rethink our assumptions about gender roles.

Women and children first

The Red Pill is a deeply flawed documentary that looks at times like a child's school project in its lack of critical thinking, but the one issue it flags that seems incontrovertible is that society finds men more disposable. A 'women and children first' mentality implies that women's lives are somehow more valuable. Millions of men have been slaughtered in wartime, and in peacetime men almost always do the jobs which could be fatal.

We don't think about it very much and we really should.

At the moment I have a house guest called Steve. Steve is a twenty-five-year-old man who fled Syria because the regime running his country created a 'kill or be killed' policy during the war which made his life there impossible. One night over drinks with friends, Steve told me how he got out of Syria and spent a year in the Calais Jungle[4] where he volunteered to be a firefighter. Fires were a regular nightly occurrence due to the shelters being made of wood and fire being the only source of heat. He did this with no experience whatsoever. In Damascus he was an architecture student and when he arrived in the jungle, he was teased for being a 'posh boy'.

I wondered if the women ever fought fires, and he told me that the women and children had their own secure compound built and looked after by volunteers and that there were many fewer fires there. I asked him if he'd ever have taken our mutual friend Charlotte out to fight fires if she'd wanted to go, when she was volunteering in the Jungle. 'Absolutely not,' he said. 'It was seriously dangerous.' Since then I have met female firefighters who were in the Calais Jungle at other times, and there are certainly many women fighting fire around the world right now (and more who wish to but are excluded from doing so), but it is mostly a male profession and it was Steve's attitude that interested me the most.

I asked Steve if he was a feminist and he said that he was. He told me about his mother, who sounds like a kick-ass woman who has facilitated incredible conflict resolution between men in a war zone. Everything about Steve seems impressive, respectful and wise. I asked him, 'Why is it okay for you to do dangerous things and not a woman? Why is your life worth less

---

4 The Calais Jungle was a refugee camp with living shelters, restaurants, shops and houses of worship built by refugees and volunteers. It was dismantled by the French government.

than a female life?' Steve paused. 'I don't know,' he said. 'I've never thought about it. It's just always something I've assumed. If you're a man, you step up.'

Of course, there are issues here with women being lumped in with infants as if we are frail and incapable. There are assumptions about men needing to be brave and strong. The end result, however, is that men are the default gender when life-risking work needs to be done.

Steve and I tried to work out why this was our assumption in 2017, even in cases where technology levelled the playing field. Steve suggested that it was somehow animal and biological, but when we researched it, we couldn't find any usable patterns of protective behaviours in nature that were gender-specific. Lions leave all the work to lionesses and, at times, eat their own cubs. The most they do is protect their territory with a bit of growling. They only fight on their own behalf. Penguin dads club together, like they're in a Scandinavian after-school club, to keep their young warm while the mothers go and feed and look after themselves. Even with primates we couldn't find much gender conformity with sex, violence and protective instincts.

I suggested it was a tendency for men to have superior upper-body strength, but that doesn't explain society's willingness to put men entirely in the line of fire. Steve told me that one of his friends had been on a leaking boat while trying to escape a war zone and the men were told to jump into the ocean so that the boat would sink less quickly and the women and children had a better chance to survive. Clearly his friend had lived to report the story, but his terrifying experience could quite easily have been fatal. I asked Steve if his friend had felt that this gendered expectation was unfair in any way and he said that he hadn't seemed to. It was 'just the form' on boats, he said.

We tried some evolutionary theory. If we take this all the

way back to the savannah, we only need one man to get any
number of women pregnant. If our cycles had synched, one
chap could knock a good dozen of us up in an afternoon. We
need to incubate the baby – which takes the best part of a
year – and then breastfeed, which was probably a two-year job
in those days. By comparison, we needed many fewer men to
hunt protein and parent the tribe's kids. (Remember, we could
easily afford to lose a few men on each hunt, if at least some of
them came back with protein for the winter.)

The reality is, though, I don't have any children. I'm not
breastfeeding anyone. What if I'd been in that boat, in the
middle of the ocean at night with a tall, skinny, twenty-year-
old lad who weighed less than me and so was a better bet for
keeping the boat afloat, had superior upper-body strength and
would be more help keeping the children alive and had more
years ahead of him and so arguably deserved a longer shot at
life? What if he'd been told to get into the ocean? Would I
have taken his place? Would I have said, 'Your life isn't worth
less than mine. There are practical reasons why I should get
out and you should stay in'? Or would I have taken my female
privilege and stayed in the boat?

I'm a feminist but I can't guarantee you I'd have jumped
in the black, cold ocean in the middle of the night. Can you?
It's hard to give up privilege. It's difficult to sacrifice your
own place and easy to justify your position in it. I think
that's what it's like for men in boats of power and influence.
Are you getting out, if everyone assumes you deserve your
place there?

What *The Red Pill* does not mention is that those doing the
killing and making men run are always male too. Women are
rarely responsible for warmongering, bombing, killing and ter-
rorism. Men kill each other at astounding rates. While 78.7 per
cent of homicide victims worldwide are male, a whopping 96

per cent of all homicide perpetrators are male.[5] If men stopped killing, killing would stop. As much as men's rights activists would like to, you can't blame feminists or women for that. We make up 22 per cent of the corpses and only 4 per cent of the killers, and then it's mostly in self-defence.

Men are discouraged from displaying their feelings, which means they often don't get to process them. This results in shame, frustration and pent-up rage, which causes violence. Sometimes they turn the violence on themselves. Men are three times as likely as women to kill themselves and male suicide is an epidemic, growing year on year. The pressure on men to conform to all the old stereotypes of provider and protector and all the new ones of being hands-on fathers and good communicators means they need help that they're clearly not getting. Men are not the enemy of feminism. Patriarchy is the enemy of feminism and the enemy of men. It expects, demands and dictates. While it tells women that they need to be demure, grateful and nurturing, it tells men they need to fight all their fires alone. Sometimes that means we all get burned.

Often a man does something toxic, disrespectful or horribly violent and women on Twitter respond with the hashtag #menaretrash. This is done for tribal solidarity, but it draws enemy lines, lowers the self-esteem of allies and gives MRAs fuel to recruit. It also excuses the terrible behaviour. Men aren't trash. They're living, breathing humans who should behave with empathy. Responding with #notallmen isn't useful either because if you're a guy who's so appalled by the behaviour in question, you'll show solidarity with your sisters before you

---

5 UNODC Homicide Statistics 2013 used tables: 'Homicide counts and rates' and 'Percentage of male and female homicide victims', *Global Study on Homicide* (PDF), edited by Jonathan Gibbons (2013), www.unodc.org. United Nations Office on Drugs and Crime, Vienna. Retrieved 31 May 2014.

seek to clear your name from the worst excesses of your tribe. Take it as read that 'not all men' is implied.

Some men are irredeemably violent, misogynistic and hateful. They must be fought or evaded and nothing will change that. We must, as human beings, stand up for women and do more to change this culture of dominance, battery and homicide. Online platforms like Twitter need to show their repugnance for misogynistic abuse and eradicate this culture. Society needs to cry out, restrain and prosecute. Men need to confront other men and kill these norms.

Some men can be rehabilitated and some can't. Society needs urgent change on this front. Feminism has to fight men who are structurally, verbally and physically violent and it must also fight for men who are being pushed into lonely desolation by the patriarchal pressures to conform to traditional masculine ideals.

Another reason, despite all of these horrendous aspects of male behaviour, that I can never get behind the #menaretrash meme, is my own privilege as a middle-class, straight white woman. Which men are the equivalent of garbage to be tossed in a landfill? Black men serving jail sentences for a crime I'd get away with? Gay men who don't dare to travel to countries I can visit because they'd face the death penalty? Trans men who are beaten up on the street? Men who are perilously close to suicide from a lifetime of repression? Refugees who would drown so I could stay in the boat? Sorry, sisters, but you've got to clarify. Don't be quick to call men pieces of shit and don't chant 'Men are trash'. The patriarchy loves to put us into opposing camps and watch us jeer at each other. The patriarchy loves the binary.

If we won't respect the binary and form ourselves into two orderly camps, how will they know who to oppress? Some men are tools of the patriarchy. Some men are victims of it. Many are both. I want to tell men they're worth more and shouldn't be ashamed and have no need to behave in nasty, disrespectful ways that are mostly displays of self-loathing combined with the need to feel power over someone else to elevate themselves. Men are our brothers, fathers, lovers and sons. Men need feminism to show them that women aren't subservient and men don't need to carry capitalism on their shoulders and put out every fire. We need each other. We need to draw enemy lines with the structures that confine and demean us. #thepatriarchyistrash

Mean Girls

> *'There is a special place in hell for women*
> *who don't help other women.'*
> *—Madeleine Albright*

When discussing the television adaptation of *The Handmaid's Tale* on a Facebook thread, a male friend commented, 'The Handmaids must despise the Aunts more than anyone. They must hate the couples, but if they ever got hold of the Aunts, god knows what they'd do to them.'

The couples are wealthy, infertile overlords who need the wombs of young, healthy women to make their babies. The Aunts are the single women who groom and coach the Handmaids for cruel reproductive services in the dystopian world of the story.

I agreed: 'Yes. That's because we're all sexist. We all expect better displays of humanity from women. Married women might be excused for being under their husbands' thumbs. But single women are meant to be nurturing and compassionate, so a woman like Aunt Lydia is always far more despised by other women than a man in the same position, who we might expect to be cruel.'

A man can sell us out, cut us out and knife us in the back and somehow it doesn't feel as hurtful as if a woman undermines us at the school gate. That's because a woman is 'meant' to be in our tribe. We're in the oppressed group, so why aren't we sticking together?

When I was between comedy agents, I sent out invitations to a show I was doing to try to drum up some interest. One agent wrote back saying, 'I can't consider anyone of the female persuasion right now. That might sound sexist but it's not. It's not me that's sexist, it's the industry.' I was furious. I read the email to a friend, who gasped, 'How can he say he's not sexist?'

'No, the email is from a woman,' I replied. 'Of course it's from a woman. None of the men bothered to write back.'

We laughed. We were angrier with the woman for taking the time to spell out that people 'of the female persuasion' were unwelcome in the comedy industry than with the men who had binned the email on sight for the same reason.

Still, her email was pretty terrible. I'm sure it wasn't her intention, but it almost made me quit comedy. It's exhausting being told that industry professionals won't even see your work on the basis of your gender. It means that no amount of work, talent, investment or smarts will ever get you through the door. And it's especially discouraging when the message comes from a woman. I had another email from a woman around the same time that read, 'We're a bit saturated at the moment – girl-wise.' It seemed as if 'hardly any people like me' was still 'too many people like me' and that 'other people like me' were happy to tell me that.

What's going on when women discriminate against you on the basis of your gender, which is also their gender? It can seem like they're drawing an enemy line in their own camp. I think it's an unwillingness to change or to challenge the system. In the case of the women who wrote me those emails, I believe it was pragmatism. The industry tells them it's easier to sell men, so why make their lives harder by representing more women when they already have some on their books? It's supply and demand. If you're an estate agent and flats are selling like hot cakes but beachfront houses aren't, then as much as you might admire the beautiful five-storey glass-fronted property with a view of the ocean, if it's going to be a huge pain in the arse to shift, you get yourself some inner-city one-beds, grab the commission and put Prosecco on the table.

The problem arises when you're not selling real estate but people. When the system demands that you give unfair advantage to one gender over another, you've got to change that system or at least acknowledge you're giving in to its sexist demands. That agent had – and still has – a good number of high-profile and up-and-coming women on her books, so from her point of view she was 'doing her bit'. However, by telling a woman comedian that the industry didn't have room for her, she almost made the already terrible gender balance in comedy worse, because I nearly packed up and went to another business with a better attitude.

She may feel that her male counterparts aren't making their lives more difficult, so why should she? If a female agent's business goes down, while the guys stay afloat largely repping saleable young men who have a good shot at whipping out the one-liners on *Mock the Week*, then she can't help any women at all. Also, she has to be fair to the women she's got. If there are only so many slots for comedians 'of the female persuasion', she's got to keep her existing women clients in bus fares and kebabs.

My reply to that agent's email was this: 'We are the industry. I'm a comedian and you're an agent. If we're not going to change it, who will?' It's easy to create enemy lines when the opening gambit is the definition of sexism, but I prefer to suggest that we are on the same team and see if I can change minds. I'm a privileged, middle-class white person so I always think it's my job to make us as many alliances as possible. The agent saw my point and said she'd come to the show.

Naturally, she didn't come to the show. She's an agent, after all. But I like to think she might have reconsidered how she'd tell another woman that she wasn't eligible for viewing due to being 'of the female persuasion'. (For the record, I could quite easily have been persuaded to be male at that time, if that were an option.)

I also started to create shows for and by women to demonstrate to the whole industry that they were wrong. I wanted to show them that being a woman wasn't some kind of awful albatross I had to suffer with but an advantage, because my perspective was fresh and women are starved of fun and clever material because the 'industry' had decided that only men – and a few exceptional women – sold tickets. Women on the business side of the industry respond to me differently now that I've stopped trying to shove their male peg into my female hole (all puns intended) and have created my own playing space for myself and other women. Try asking others to reshape your patch of the landscape with you and if they won't, do it yourself and then invite them to have a look. It's hard for others to maintain enemy lines when you cross them with invitations to fun events with wine and crisps.

Friends of mine in professions with more traditional career trajectories have told me stories of female bosses or colleagues behaving in malicious or competitive ways. 'She doesn't like other women', is something that's said frequently. According to what seems to be a rigorous American study, women have lower job satisfaction when they have a female boss – but male job satisfaction is unaffected by the gender of their manager.[1]

That's not as big a surprise as it should be, is it? Let's be real. While most of us know awesome women who mentor, encourage and ally, we also know women who'd cut you off at the knees for a slight advantage. I'm a feminist but I sure know some mean girls.

In the early days of my corporate work, an HR exec in a big company wanted to hire me to deliver a diversity seminar. Only problem was, I'd have to be vetted by a senior partner who 'will hate you, because she doesn't like other successful women'. They made it clear that she was difficult in general but especially hostile to women and saw herself as 'one of the boys'. I was advised to 'tone myself down' so I'd have a chance of being hired by her.

Everything in this woman's working life had told her that there's only one spot at the top for a woman. It's a numbers game. There are plenty of jobs for the boys, but when a woman makes CEO there are articles in industry publications enquiring as to 'how she manages' and what her 'secret for success' might be. What if you're better than she is? What if you're competitive with her and steal her hard-earned credit? What if other people like you more? Why would she ever showcase you when being female in a male-dominated field can be her USP?

Also, we're all trained to be competitive with our own tribe. Many of us are only directly competing with the people who left school or university the same year as us, which explains the success of Facebook. 'She's just sweated through a half-marathon.

---

1 These results remain after controlling for a host of relevant observable factors and persist after controlling for various fix effects: http://www.sciencedirect.com/ science/article/pii/S0927537116301129, *Labour Economics* vol. 42, October 2016, pp. 194–202.

I was thinking I might do a full one.' 'Their kids are so cute. I'm doing a fancy-dress photo shoot with my cat.'

I suspected my presence among the senior partners was a potential threat to her because I might do something to make her look comparatively less wonderful. Maybe I'd undermine her, prove her wrong or people would like my presentation and she'd have to hear that another woman was great.

I asked the HR guy who wanted to hire me why she was so successful if she hated women and was difficult in general. He said, 'Well, it doesn't matter how she behaves, she's the company's biggest rainmaker.'

I wanted to neutralise her fear that I would make her look bad, but I did not like the advice to 'tone myself down' and make myself less impressive. Instead the first thing I said when I met her was, 'I've heard all about you. Geoff said you were the company's biggest rainmaker.' She gasped and then beamed. She wasn't used to hearing nice things about herself because she was so difficult – and she especially wasn't used to hearing compliments from women who she routinely terrified and alienated. I kept my status high and made her feel important and likeable and she approved my seminar on the spot. At the end of the meeting, she grabbed my arm and said softly, 'What else did Geoff say?' She seemed vulnerable, and frankly a little emotional, because someone had praised her behind her back. She'd built her career on being mean and she was very successful but also lonely and unhappy.

Most of the time highly competitive, prickly people of all genders make you feel unimportant because status is relative. They're taking your status because they feel like they don't have enough of their own. If you make them look and feel important, interesting and likeable, especially in front of others, they won't just like you a little more, you'll be one of the only people they'll love and respect.

I once had a man undermine me for hours when I was teaching an improvisation workshop. When I praised something he did in front of the group, I could see him think, 'Well, I thought she was an idiot but she recognised my genius so she must know something.' After that, if he undermined me, he undermined the compliment I gave him. The reason he was minimising me and the session as stupid was so that if he failed, he hadn't failed at anything worth succeeding at. Once I made him feel safe he became a champion of my session, telling everyone how valuable it was.

You've got to be good at identifying what is genuinely good about people. You take a risk if you bullshit someone because you may reveal that you don't mean it. Also you feel awful because the exchange has no integrity. You might want to reserve sycophancy for a short-term necessary win where you really don't respect the person you're dealing with and you don't mind being a little manipulative. Personally I'd only do that if I were in some kind of physical danger, because it has no integrity so it makes me feel bad.

My advice is to take the person who is acting like your enemy and get them talking and doing stuff, then find something you can truthfully admire or show an enthusiastic interest in. Asking their expert opinion on something they know about is a wonderful (and practical) way of making them feel important. I've taught this to interns who've then written to the most senior person in their company: 'Dear Dianne, I've asked around and everyone tells me you're the industry expert in X. I'm a graduate. Could I have ten minutes of your time to ask your advice?' They get emails back immediately. Who doesn't want to hear that everyone in their industry thinks they're the best? They always want more details.

One thing, and this is important, you've got to do it from a place of status (be purposeful in your movements, with the option of stillness) or you just come across as a puppy who loves everyone and that's not complimentary.

The best model for this is someone who makes a living out of their opinions. Gok Wan has to be likeable otherwise you don't want his advice on whether you look good in palazzo pants. But he can never present his opinions as if he's not certain of them because you've got to believe him when he says the cold-shoulder dress is so very you or you won't buy it. He doesn't make anything. He doesn't sell anything. He gets paid because he makes you feel you believe in yourself.

It takes a while to get good at this kind of thing and in some long-term situations, the woman who's determined there'll be no more female senior partners, book club members or feminist activists on her watch does not care what you do or say: she's made up her mind and she's created her enemy lines. This is still your best strategy. Where there's only the smallest ground to be gained, it's yours.

Why go to all this trouble for a woman who's treated you in a hostile manner? First, you get your agenda sorted. That's good for you. Second, you challenge the idea that there's only one spot at the top for a woman and women are enemies trying to snatch it from each other. There has always been and always will be an old boys' club and 'jobs for the boys'. Women need to start helping each other the way men do or we will never make enough headway. We have to start forming alliances, and sometimes that means taking the lead with someone who is prickly or mean. You don't have to stay out of their way. You can take charge of the relationship and demonstrate that feminism can be fun, warm and amplifying. Pretty soon you'll probably hear that they've been saying wonderful things behind your back.

Be aware, where you have an influential spot in your feminist book club, management team or parents' association, how often you make space for newer, younger or less central women. Are you helping other women, or do you sometimes have an edge to you because you don't like someone or you feel that you don't need more competition on your patch? Are you one of the women other women don't like working for? It must be some of us; the numbers don't lie. Have we all, at some point, been guilty of being that mean girl? If you think you might be doing this, put this book down, pick up the phone and make whoever it is feel a little more welcome and a lot more valuable. We've got to start co-creating tribal confidence among women. We are the industry. You. Me. And her.

Enemy lines within feminism … *again*

I was on two panels last International Women's Day and each featured a (different) woman who declared herself to be 'not a feminist'. Both women are much-admired movers and shakers who don't feel an affinity with the word for various reasons. They both lived by feminist values, amplifying and showcasing women wherever they could. Afterwards I wrote to one of them who I'd felt a great rapport with and said, 'I'd rather you were a feminist and said you weren't one than weren't a feminist and said you were. But I'd rather again that you were a feminist and called yourself one.'

That was a daring move on my part. She wrote back and we had a great exchange. The word 'feminism' has connotations that some women dislike and we need to start asking each other why that is, talking it through and getting together on the same team as much as possible. I have no desire to bully another woman into identifying as a feminist, but presenting a welcoming request to get on the team can be a wonderful show of solidarity in itself. Telling women who say they're not feminists that they're wanted in a tribe they've previously felt excluded from can be all that's needed.

Other women feel that they've done it hard and they're damned if they're making it easy for the next generation. But while they may have been the first female advertising exec, that's only because Peggy from *Mad Men* broke ground before them as a copywriter and someone broke ground before her getting into the building at all. You only notice the closed doors. You never notice the open ones.

Other women feel that if they're open about being feminists they'll be seen as using whatever position they have in the world to unfairly advocate for women and 'sneak women in' who don't deserve to be there. Recently I was at a recruitment event and I talked to two male recruiters about this phenomenon. One of them was a young African American guy and he said, 'I have the same feeling. If I've hired too many black people in a row, I think that I'd better hire some white people so I don't look like I have a secret black agenda.'

We looked at the other guy who was white and asked, 'Do you ever worry you've hired too many white guys?' He laughed loudly. 'It's never occurred to me,' he said. 'If I hire a woman or a person of colour, though, I give myself some brownie points. Diversity targets!'

Where we feel we might be judged as 'having a feminist agenda' if we make room for good, strong, qualified women, the white guy gives himself a cookie and the day off.

We've got to reassess our enemy lines. Sometimes we're on the same side and we don't even know it. Men aren't the enemy. Other women aren't the enemy. But the power structures have a vested interest in having us polishing our duelling pistols for each other when we should be dismantling the very machine that's making capital and sport from our oppression. I can think of no better person to illuminate how and why we can do better than the wonderful Bisha K. Ali.

Oppression Olympics

One of my dearest friends is also one of the first people I turn to when I feel I'm getting out of my depth on both subtle and dramatic enemy lines: Bisha K. Ali, comedian, writer, activist and regular guest co-host of *The Guilty Feminist* podcast.

Hey Bisha, do you have an 'I'm a feminist but' for us?
I'm a feminist but when the boat starts sinking, I definitely want to be the first on a lifeboat.

Can you tell us who you are and what you do?
I still haven't figured out who I am – so thank you for starting this by sending me spiralling into a navel-gazing existential crisis. For now, let's say I'm a writer and a stand-up comedian. I'm also a feminist, a second-generation immigrant, a woman, a gamer, a nerd and a terrible daughter. Four of those put me on the receiving end of public ire. The last one is my own burden to bear.

This chapter is about enemy lines. Who or what do you think the enemy of feminism is?
Come on, Deborah. The answer is all men. Hold on, let me go lock down my entire internet presence.

I'm kidding, of course. The enemy is the kyriarchy. Forgive me if I'm repeating something that's already been said – but for those of you hearing the term for the first time, the kyriarchy is 'best theorized as a complex pyramidal system of intersecting multiplicative social structures of super-ordination and subordination, of ruling and oppression.'[2] Clear?

If the patriarchy is Frankenstein's Monster, then the kyriarchy is Dr. Frankenstein. If the patriarchy is the rock that smashes through your window, the kyriarchy is an earthquake avalanche. If the patriarchy is a thread of silk used to garrotte us, the kyriarchy is a web of silk that falls over you, suffocates you and leaves you a lifeless husk.

One more. .

If the patriarchy is the spoon, then the kyriarchy is *The Matrix*. Except, there is a spoon. Well, sort of. Actually, the spoon in *The Matrix* and the *Matrix* trilogy as a whole has plenty of analogies that are perfect for explaining both the patriarchy and the kyriarchy. In fact, much to the chagrin of the MRAs who have tried to steal *Matrix* references for their cause, The *Matrix* trilogy is almost certainly an overt allegory for coming out as transgender under the kyriarchy as it is today.[3] Long live The Wachowskis.

And if you haven't seen *The Matrix*, put this book down and go watch it. Sorry, Deborah. My nerdery comes first.

It would be easy if we could point to an enemy, eliminate it, tend to the wound and heal. Unfortunately, the wonder of systemic sexism, white supremacy, hetero- and cisnormativity is that it has its grip and cannot be extricated cleanly. It's born of a legacy of colonialism and historic power structures that have been dominant for, well, at least a couple of years.

---

2 *Wisdom Ways: Introducing Feminist Biblical Interpretation* by Elsabeth Schussler Fiorenza (Orbis Books, 2001).
3 'Some thoughts and disagreements on. *The Matrix* as a trans allegory' by Jennifer Harrison (2017): https://medium.com/@GeneticJen/some-thoughts-and-disagreements-on-the-matrix-as-a-trans-allegory-9f0754121f85.

It benefits many people who have very little incentive, except morality and kindness, to change the system that gives them free passes and opportunities. Those systems actively hurt others. They hurt you, they hurt me, they hurt people with a range of different lived experiences and identities and impact each of us differently. The sticky part is, you, and me and many others definitely *actively* benefit from some of those systems more than others. What a mess.

My point, which I have dragged you through a bunch of sci-fi references to get to, is that the enemy isn't any one thing – and I don't think we need it to be one decisive enemy. It's a given that homophobia, misogyny, transphobia, and hate are always the enemy. But I don't think that's all that our fight is.

Our job is to stand up behind those who ask for our solidarity and say – we have your back, we will not take your voice, and we will give you the resources that we have at our disposal to help realise the change that you need. The fight is to be self-critical, be reflective, actively work on our empathy and knowledge, and for the love of the fucking universe – *listen* to those who get hurt while we benefit. Then do something about it. I believe this fight to be a moral imperative.

What does 'intersectionality' mean to you?
For me in a practical sense, what intersectionality is, it's an awareness and therefore taking action on that awareness of the fact that everyone is privileged to a different degree. So, for example, I'm not disabled and I do not know what it's like to live in a body that's not my own – but I can take into account how the world that we live in is structured around people existing in a certain way.

I studied economics at university and the phrase that you use when you're looking at economic models is *ceteris paribus* which means 'all other things being equal'. So, I'm in the position that I'm in, and change one element, would my life get worse, will it be harder? So, for example, I'm Bisha K. Ali. All other things being equal, but just change one variable. So, change my skin colour, make me a white person. Would things get easier for me? Un-fucking-doubtedly. Everything else in my background is exactly the same, but I'm white, it's going to be easier and that's what we're looking at.

That, therefore, is a marker for how the system is set up to make certain people succeed and other people fail and it's looking at that and being able to single out those elements and say, okay, why? How is the balance towards those people who, all other things being equal, having that element will make you more powerful or might give you more advantages. So, those are the intersections we need to look at.

What is 'white feminism'? When people talk about that, what do they mean?
I think there's a lot of confusion about actually what people mean. White feminism is the flattening out of all women's experience and saying that all women suffer in the same way and white feminists are the ones who get to say what that is. That's what white feminism is: the idea that when white women have as much influence and power as white men, the problem is solved. We'll get to yours later. Get in line.

It's like trickledown economics. It's a fallacy. It'll get better for the rest of you once it gets better for us at the top. Which also creates a hierarchy, saying, 'We're at the top.'

How do you deal with trolling?

It depends on my mood. The mute button is my go-to response. If I'm feeling feisty, I'll screenshot the abuse and post it on my channels, too. If I'm feeling like I have a little more time in my day, I may even respond and see if the person sending me disgusting abuse is okay. My empathy for the perpetrators of abuse (specifically towards me) fluctuates.

In 2017, I uncovered a minor international public art scandal in Calgary, when a photograph of me and a number of other comedians appeared in an art installation. A local artist (taking publicly funded money) claimed he'd taken pictures of local homeless people but in fact he'd plagiarised the images. It made the national news in Canada and very briefly in the UK. From my perspective, I was irritated on behalf of the numerous photographers whose work was used without their consent and whose copyright was breached, but for me personally, it was an exciting adventure in which I got to be the protagonist in a quirky indie thriller for a few days. The Mayor of Calgary initiated an investigation as a result of my super-sleuthing (which went viral as a result of a gif-heavy Twitter thread I send out into the universe) and the city took down the installation.

As a result, a number of people felt that they should tag me into their conversations about what an attention seeker I am, how fame-hungry I must be, and how you could *barely tell* it was my face. It was a seven-foot poster of my face, but sure, you could barely tell. I didn't mind that, though I'd have preferred to have not been tagged into the conversations. You don't call up the person you're whingeing about and have them on the line while you complain about them to your mates, do you? It's rude.

Rudeness, however, I am used to. A much darker edge comes with being a woman who exists on the internet, in a public space. I had a number of vile, unwelcome messages, that ranged from 'attention seeking whore', to 'feminist cunt'.

One gentleman caller in particular had it out for me. While the majority of the incoming messages died out within a week, he was relentless. A few weeks passed, and he messaged me to remind me that I'm a 'useless bitch'. More time passed, and the messages continued – escalating to use racial epithets (you can guess and you'd be right) and then a few weeks ago – 'Would you like a video of me naked and cumming?'

And then, there it was. A full frontal video of this man naked, masturbating, and I assume doing what he threatened. I didn't check to see if he was telling the truth about the second part.

Is this 'trolling' or something more? It's certainly illegal. So now it's a crime that I have to go and report and spend my time on? And if I don't, this guy goes around doing this to other women (some perhaps much younger than me, or who don't have the same tools that I do to deal with something like this)? Now the weight of this guy's dangerous and damaging behaviours sits with me, and I have to make a bunch of decisions? I have films to write, gigs to play, self-esteem to repair. In this case, I dealt with it by reporting it to the website I received the messages over. They did nothing. Then I had a writing deadline, and I didn't get the chance to report it to the police. Back to life as usual. I suppose you could say that I dealt with him by normalising him. Which isn't healthy or useful, either.

So how do I deal with trolling? It varies – day to day,

and troll to troll – but victims of this malicious, gross behaviour don't owe anyone shit. Don't let anybody tell you otherwise.

Talking to Bisha always reminds me that the word 'victim' doesn't come attached to frailty. You can be injured and silenced, then regroup and find your army. The Florida high school students marching on Washington and demanding gun reform are victims of a tragic, brutal invasion, but their demands are anything but cowed and their dignity and power are remarkable. Strength is so much more easily found in numbers. Feminism can help us unite against our oppressors if we will just link arms.

There is No 'Try'

I'm a feminist but one time I went on a Women's March and popped into a department store to use the loo and on the way back, I got distracted trying out face creams and when I came out, the march was gone.

Radical pragmatism

If I'm in a train carriage with two seats to myself, and I use one for my handbag and I've got my feet up and I'm spread out, then my wishing that the pregnant woman in front of me had a seat isn't helping her. Telling her I believe pregnant women should have seats, and that I'm one of the good ones who thinks pregnant women shouldn't have to stand, doesn't take the weight off her feet. I have to move my stuff, budge up and actively share. If there are two pregnant women and one who's ill, then I have to stand up.

The more I realise my own privilege, the more I realise that 'not actively being racist' is not enough. Not feeling racist and wanting people of colour to have the same advantages I have doesn't help right the institutionalised power imbalance. If people who lack empathy have more get-up-and-go than those who want a fair world, then things can only get worse. It's not enough to feel like a good person: we need motivation to put things right.

Being a good person is rarely about what we don't do and what we don't feel. Feminism isn't about wishes. It's about actions. Doing nothing is doing something. It's supporting the current injustices. Doing nothing and saying nothing is tacit support.

If I really want a fairer society for women, including myself, and especially for others who have less, I've got to do stuff. It's intimidating, though, isn't it? Go online and someone might accuse you of hashtivism. Go to a march and you might get swallowed by the crowd. What good are you really doing out there? What if you say the wrong thing? What if you run out of steam? How do you know how to organise, inspire and make real change? How do we try if we're not sure we will succeed? As that famous feminist Yoda says, 'Do or do not. There is no try.'

Some activists work within the system and some are looking to take it apart. You have options. Are you naturally pragmatic or radical? It is my firm belief that we need both. Many things we take for granted today were radical fifty or even twenty years ago. The decriminalisation of queer people, desegregation, interracial marriage, equal marriage for gay people, women owning property and women being allowed to vote or participate in democracy were all once highly radical ideas.

The suffragists were pragmatic, non-violent and a constant presence for forty years. The suffragettes smashed stuff up, got arrested and made all kinds of noise. Generally radical voices propose ideas loudly and relentlessly until those ideas start to seem less ludicrous to society. Often they riot, chain themselves to railings and lie down in front of horses and steamrollers to draw attention to their cause and start changing people's minds. Pragmatists can't start bargaining with the powers that be or drafting laws until society is won over to the *idea* of change. By the time legislation is being written by pragmatists, the radicals have started shouting about their next preposterous demand that won't become possible for a good decade.

I'm naturally pragmatic. I like to see things through from beginning to end and enjoy negotiation more than conflict. I would not be a convincing radical. The other side of that same coin is that I have the privilege to be pragmatic.

I benefit from the current system more than some of my radical counterparts who want to burn the whole thing to the ground and start again because the whole system makes their lives unbearable. Some radical activists will no doubt identify that I have more room on the train than I need or deserve and think me budging up a bit to let someone else sit down is nowhere near enough when some women aren't even on the train. They want to push the train off the tracks. Probably I will get more radical as I get older and angrier. The more activism you do, the more injustice you witness, the angrier you get and the more radical you become. Right now, I need to work from the place that is authentic to me and not use privilege as an excuse to be sedentary. Whatever you can do, do that. Here are some thoughts, ideas and inspiration from four of my favourite activists.

Becca Bunce

Becca, do you have an 'I'm a feminist but' for us?
I'm a feminist but I unwind by watching *Keeping up with the Kardashians*.

Could you tell us about yourself?
I am co-director/co-founder of the award-winning and

law-creating IC Change campaign which is working to get the UK government to bring in a life-saving law for women – the Istanbul Convention (on preventing and combating violence against women and domestic violence). There is another dimension to my work. As a disabled woman, disability has changed and challenged my understanding of feminism at times – and it has been helpful to work with groups such as Sisters of Frida (a disabled women's collective) to ensure disabled women are represented in feminist spaces and beyond.

You and your friends went part-time in your paid work to make a practical, political, feminist change. Could you explain how and why you did what you did?

Three years ago, my friend – and feminist force of nature – Robyn Boosey dropped a (seemingly) innocuous question over Facebook chat: 'Do you fancy doing a change.org petition with me? It's to get the UK government to ratify the Istanbul Convention on ending violence against women.'

In that moment, we were unaware that we had co-founded and become co-directors of a volunteer-run campaign. A short time later, Rachel Nye joined us to co-direct (and went on to bring her power and expertise to the What Women Want 2.0 campaign). Together with a fantastic, dedicated team we built a coalition of over fifty supporting organisations, and two years later Parliament was firmly in our sights as we mobilised thousands of people to support the successful passage of a Private Member's Bill.

Why are we campaigning for what might be seen as an obscure international law? The answer for us is that it is obviously – and desperately – needed. We'd all volunteered, worked in or been supported by women's services. We'd seen women be let down by a system that does not work together, meaning that women could not get access to the services they needed. Or when they did get support from one bit of the system, another bit would let them down. So you can get into a refuge, but there is no secure long-term housing to go to. There isn't a twenty-four-hour rape crisis helpline. Women's lives were being endangered by not having a joined-up, strategic approach to ending violence against women.

The Istanbul Convention offered change. It was designed by people who knew the systems and what was needed to make sure they worked. It recognised that domestic violence, FGM, so-called honour-based violence and forced marriage are all part of gender-based violence. It provided a roadmap for us to make sure women can live free from violence and the fear of violence. The law from the UK side was drafted by people who had worked for women's organisations, academics who had specialised in violence against women, and was based on the experiences of thousands of women's lives.

Can you tell us more about this law?
The Istanbul Convention is the most comprehensive legal framework that exists to tackle violence against women and girls. It sets minimum standards for governments to meet when tackling violence against women. When a government ratifies the Convention, they are legally bound to follow it. So if the UK government ratified the Istanbul Convention, they would have to take all necessary steps it sets out to prevent violence, protect women experiencing violence and prosecute perpetrators. The UK government would also have to ensure that there

is sufficient monitoring of violence against women. The monitoring point can seem dull, but if we don't monitor an issue it is difficult to make a case for why it needs attention and resources.

Ratifying the Istanbul Convention will mean a lasting national commitment to tackling violence against women and an increase in women's safety in the UK. It is a pragmatic law that does not just sit on paper, but translates into real action. Ratification of the Istanbul Convention will mean that women and girls in the UK will be guaranteed the right to live lives free from violence and the fear of violence. Crucially, the Istanbul Convention will help guarantee that we won't have vital services disappear, but rather we will have a strong infrastructure of support. This infrastructure will allow women to thrive, rather than fight to survive.

UN Women have named the Istanbul Convention 'a gold standard' for tackling violence against women. Human Rights Watch have called it 'groundbreaking'. And it has won awards for its brilliance.

What was the outcome of your campaign?
We made a law! Spearheaded by an incredible MP, Dr Eilidh Whiteford, and bringing together a coalition of organisations, IC Change secured a Private Member's Bill through Parliament. This law means that every year the government has to tell Parliament what progress they've made towards ratification and give a timetable for what they are going to do next. This may seem like a small thing, as it doesn't actually make the Istanbul Convention law yet. But it gets the issue back on the agenda after the government has repeated the same line about why they hadn't ratified for *years*.

One of the funny things is that we were repeatedly told that this *would not happen*. Private Member's Bills have a low success rate and frankly no one thought we would get any traction, particularly with such a complex issue. Private Member's Bills require MPs to show up on a Friday, when they'd normally be in their constituencies. We needed to get them to show up twice.

It can seem like a complex campaign, but for an international law to happen in the UK, you often have to make domestic laws first so that we comply with international law. The government had got stuck in the process. We are making sure that they stick to their promises and deliver the Istanbul Convention for women and girls in the UK.

I find when I go to a march I don't know what to do after that. What can I do that's practical and sustainable? How can people help if they have limited time and money but want to make a difference?

There isn't a right answer to this. It is doing what you can, when you can. With any action I think it's helpful to start small but think big. For some people, digital action such as signing petitions or emailing MPs may be the most accessible way to engage. For others, it's getting involved with the community around you, seeing what they are up to and what support they may need. For some, craftivism may be a gentler way to engage, while others may find direct activism is the best for their needs.

The best bit of advice I got about activism is that it is a relay race – we hand on the baton. IC Change started with a petition and has grown from there. But the campaigning for the Istanbul Convention goes *way* back. Experts – women's organisations, survivors, human rights advocates – campaigned to make sure that this law was put on the table. They campaigned to get the UK government to promise to ratify (by signing in 2012). They had campaigned for ratification – and other countries are campaigning across Europe. And these campaigners play a role in the wider, global movement to help end gender-based violence.

Don't put pressure on yourself to solve issues spanning thousands of years in an afternoon. Start small. Find what works for you. And do what you can.

How does anger play into activism? Where is it helpful and where does it hinder getting the results you want?
I can only really answer this from my perspective, as everyone has different motivations and different ways of reacting to anger.

Anger can be a useful emotion to channel into activism. To be honest, it is normally a frustration or a negative experience that sparks the motivation to create change. There is a lot to be angry about right now. Anger is a natural response to injustice. Anger can be really powerful. And sometimes it can even feel freeing. But for me it can also lead to burnout – physically and mentally. So I try to balance it with a sense of love and optimism – and a good dose of humour.

I've found it easy to be consumed by the anger, or to feel like nothing can change. What has sustained me has been seeing that change is possible – and to look to the people out there creating change for inspiration.

Anger can also be powerful in building a movement and galvanising a community. It is a point of connection and can help a group of individuals to reclaim power. It can also be a hurdle when presenting a message to someone new to your cause. It can be alienating, and can prevent long-term behaviour change in those you are trying to influence. And critically it can cause burnout within the community.

We are all living in a patriarchal society, which is also racist, ableist, xenophobic, transphobic. These structures mean we've all been conditioned to an extent by a dominant culture. If we are trying to influence someone else to change their behaviour, just telling them they are wrong is not going to work. Rather, it could push them to become more defensive of their stance and less likely to consider a different way of thinking.

None of us can escape the fact that we've been an arse to someone because of learned behaviours at some point in our lives. To be clear, I'm not saying we should accept the unacceptable. There are lines and boundaries. I'm saying we are all human and do make mistakes. We have to consider this in our activism.

Even though we feel people should know why something is unjust, often they don't. I'm aware that a lot of people have never heard of the social model of disability.

How can we get small groups of people together that sustain? I feel I work better if I know that others are counting on me, or there's some camaraderie in it. Is that key for you? Do you know if that makes a difference to effective activism?

IC Change has had at its core a small group of activists that has worked with other small and large groups – and individuals – all of whom we saw as part of the campaign. We all played a role. Each action accumulated into a wider pressure that made a law, and will hopefully make a few more laws as we go.

Robyn always said we have not won if we win the campaign but lose our friendship. This was crucial. There were challenges and times when things became strained. But it meant we had to talk about it. Difficult conversations on race, religion, disability – conversations about envy and impostor syndrome. And many conversations where we told each other (in our own way of saying it) that we thought the others were awesome – which can sometimes be hard to hear!

We also made time for being ridiculous or silly. Whether campaign actions (we delivered a motivational mix-tape to Theresa May) or simply the selfies we sent each other while hiding in a toilet, bleary-eyed after a major campaign moment. Humour got me through where caffeine and sugar couldn't.

Saying that, *don't forget snacks*. People sustain, but we also need to be sustained! The worst moments and decisions inevitably came from 'hanger' and exhaustion. The best happened with cake.

What specifically could we as *Guilty Feminist* podcast creators, listeners and readers do together to change the world and make it a fairer, more empowered place for women? How do we make a movement?

Get involved. Whatever you can do, do it. There isn't one feminist campaign. There isn't one thing that will change it all. But there are lots of people working towards gender equality. Look around, look at what campaigns or actions you want to get behind. Perhaps even challenge yourself to understand why someone else thinks their campaign is important and educate yourself on the issues they are talking about. And then commit to taking action – simple, small steps such as I will sign a petition, or talk to my family about this issue or donate regularly to an organisation that is taking action.

How can we use whatever privilege we have to advance feminism?

A good place to start is acknowledging what privilege we have. The next bit for me is not then getting obsessed with individual guilt about the privilege, but making sure we actively challenge to dismantle these structures. This doesn't mean being a 'voice for the voiceless' – people can speak for themselves – it is about hearing the challenges people say they are facing and actively working to change them. It is about not having all-white panels. It is about challenging when people ask if a disabled person can really be up for the job. It is not sitting in silence or being complicit in the discrimination against other people. Challenging this is painful, but not as painful as being on the receiving end of systematic discrimination.

You mentioned disability before and are a disability activist. How does feminism intersect with disability?

Audre Lorde said this best: 'There is no such thing as a single-issue struggle, because we do not live single-issue lives.'

I can't divorce being disabled from my feminism. Let's start with disability not being a tragedy. It is a fact. Equally my impairments don't give me special powers or take away from me. They actually make me pretty standardly human.

So why are we not anticipating this very human phenomenon of being disabled in how we set up our everyday life? Why is it buildings aren't accessible? That it is difficult to get a job? Or people are shocked that I am able to be an activist?

We need to think about who is making the decisions and what relationship we have to power.

In Virginia Woolf's *A Room of One's Own* she talks about a woman having to be escorted by a man to the library in a university college. This seems outrageous. For most women the idea of having to be escorted somewhere that men have access to feels like part of history. Yet being escorted through buildings is a reality for disabled people in many public places or buildings they use in their everyday life. It is the only way you can access the building. Taken in through a side entrance. The decision to enter or leave mediated through the permission of others. And that's if you can get into the building.

If you think of the impact on disabled people from going to work to getting a coffee, from having lunch with a friend to getting your shopping – this is the everyday. Never mind places of power, such as the Houses of Parliament, which, as a disabled person needing step-free access, there are parts you cannot get to – parts of the building the public can freely walk to if they can negotiate steps. Your access to power – and to hold power to account – is constantly mediated through the willingness of someone to escort you.

We need activism around disabled women's rights. In the UK we have seen a systematic degradation of disabled people's rights through changes and loss of benefits and funding. These changes have made it harder, or outright prevented disabled women from living independent lives, and the loss of benefits puts them at risk of isolation and dependency on others.

It is this isolation that feeds into the statistic that disabled women are twice as likely as non-disabled women to experience domestic violence. This isn't the only statistic to be angry about. Thirty-five per cent of disabled women are paid below the National Living Wage compared with 25 per cent of non-disabled men and 29 per cent of non-disabled women. Disabled men face a pay gap of 11 per cent, while disabled women face a gap twice as large at 22 per cent. Disabled women with a mental health problem die on average thirteen years earlier than the general UK population.[4]

Challenges are met by realising that we can all play different roles. IC Change has shown me that if we behave inclusively, rather than trying to just add people in to current systems, it is possible that disabled people can lead as well as getting involved on a team.

I've heard a lot about the social model of disability. Can you explain it?
I think the social model of disability is useful for activism, as it talks about what we can change. The social model of disability says that people are disabled by the way society is organised, rather than the person's impairment, health condition or difference. It looks at ways of removing barriers in society that restrict disabled people. This can mean rethinking the built environment, how institutions and systems work that we interact with, or changing the attitudes that we face these with.

So I'm not disabled because I cannot breathe under water, unless you force me to live in a fish tank.

---

4 Statistics from: http://www.sisofrida.org.

That's not a bad analogy! All human beings have access needs. When you are disabled, this is more apparent because the environment and systems we interact with haven't been designed with disability in mind.

Most people don't look at disability that way, so people are likely to be sharing 'inspiration porn' memes or say horrendous things to me when we meet. This can be tough to hear as a disabled person.

However, I have to remember that I went on a journey of understanding too. Sometimes I will have to take others on that journey with me – other times I have to decide to opt out or challenge. I don't always get that call right. Often it comes down to prioritising my energy at the time. Like, I have the energy, I will work to make things more accessible – not just for me, but for the next person who will interact with a space or system.

Where can we do more to include disabled feminists if we're not disabled, especially if we are running feminist events?
Make inclusion a priority. *Plan ahead*. Don't try to add accessibility in. Start by thinking about accessibility as soon as you are planning an event. Sisters of Frida in partnership with the RSA have a guide on their website about how to approach accessibility and questions you will need to think through. If you have a budget, hire someone to consult on accessibility. There is a great hashtag #AccessibleOrganizingMeans that came from inaccessibility at the Women's March with some sensible, easy-to-implement ideas. Remember access isn't just for people attending, but also for speakers and organisers!

However, if you have an event up already then something really useful is to just tell people what access there is and what there isn't. Let people know if they can access any areas for socialising as well as the main event. Or if they need to come through a different door. Put it on all of your event information, whether on Facebook and Eventbrite or on a flyer. And have a single point of contact for questions, as there is nothing more infuriating than calling an event organiser and the venue, and repeatedly being sent between the two until the event is sold out or you give up trying to go.

I would prefer to know something is inaccessible and choose to access another event, than use a lot of energy to go to something I then can't get into. Nothing is ever fully accessible, as it is possible that people can have competing access needs (such as whether there are bright lights or low lights). Even with considering competing needs, it is possible to make things more inclusive and accessible.

Last year I was invited to the reclamation of the empty Holloway Prison – a place where many suffragettes were locked up and force-fed – by radical intersectional feminists Sisters Uncut. The prison had been closed down and women had been sent to larger, more industrial prisons far from their families, which meant many couldn't afford to visit them. I think you'll understand the government's reason for this decision when I tell you that Holloway is prime real estate, and they wanted to sell the building for a profit so some rich investors could get richer by turning the space into luxury flats. Sisters Uncut were rightly repulsed by this and decided to occupy the building to demand the government reconsider their position and turn the building into facilities for local women. I was struck by how dignified, dedicated and diverse the women were and how large they were living in their defiance of injustices. I will never forget the youthful speakers, the silent vigil, the rooftop release of coloured spray paint into the sky and the pedestrians who stopped to hear stories about women who had died inside the prison due to abuse or neglect. I spoke to Mo Mansfield of the Reclaim Holloway movement, which includes Sisters Uncut in its collectives, about how they're changing the world, with radical action, unfettered anger and laser-focused goals.

Mo Mansfield

Can you explain what Reclaim Holloway is?
Reclaim Holloway is a coalition of local residents, campaigners, prisoners and ex-prisoners and interested organisations who collectively fight for the Holloway Prison site to benefit the local community of Islington and the people formerly incarcerated there.

Our principles are abolitionist feminist (we do not support the expansion of the criminal justice system and we do not work with those who profit from it) and intersectional (we leave no one, and no struggle, behind). It fits within the history and legacy of the land as a site of imprisonment, and the voices of the generations of women held there.

Prisons are ineffective, dangerous and life-threatening, and they perpetuate the structural oppression faced by marginalised groups. The majority of people held in prison are poor, and there is significant over-representation of black and minority ethnic groups. We believe that the criminal justice system should be radically downsized and defunded. Funds should be invested in communities, early intervention and other means of community justice and accountability. This is public land – our land – and it should not be used to generate skyrocketing private profits for developers that shut out the community, particularly low-income people and people of colour who are being increasingly priced out of the area as well as being over-represented in prison populations.

I went to the Sisters Uncut (radical feminist activists) occupation of Holloway and it was amazing in its dignity, determination and diversity. How important was it that they took a stand in the way they did? How did it change things in terms of profile and government response?

The Sisters Uncut occupation was an inspirational demonstration of what is possible, and that is exactly what people need to see with their own eyes. They put into practice our shared belief that the Visitor Centre could be used for community good right now. Their occupation drew attention to the ridiculousness of a public building needing to be protected from the community. Through their week-long provision of a community space they proved that instead, given a chance, the community could be protected and connected to each other by the building.

The Ministry of Justice, the current landowners, have from November 2015 been dismissive of people's efforts to use the Visitor Centre. Sadly the occupation did not shift their position. However, it did draw attention to the campaign and reached a much wider audience, and inspired many along the way.

Did Reclaim Holloway come out of that bold act, or did it already exist as a separate entity?

Reclaim Holloway was set up with the aim of keeping the land under the control of the community and prevent-ing the construction of more prisons, in response to the announcement that the prison would be closed which was made in the Spending Review of November 2015.

Reclaim Holloway is inspired by earlier campaigns

focused on Holloway, in particular the 1970s campaign Alternatives to Holloway by the campaign group Radical Alternatives to Prison.

The initial impetus of the campaign came from grass-roots activists Reclaim Justice Network and Women in Prison, and we held public meetings with local housing activists Axe the Housing Act. Reclaim Holloway quickly grew as a coalition built on the determination that the Ministry of Justice should not use the money gained from the sale of Holloway to build more prisons.

What results have you had so far, and what results are you still hoping for?
Islington Council have said that they would like to see the site being used by the community while the development and planning process is going on, which is likely to be another two years.

We have established a group for women who were in Holloway to develop their voice around what they want to see in a future Women's Building on the site.

Our biggest struggles are likely to come when developers enter the picture and use their vast resources to water down the vision for what could be achieved for the community on the site.

In particular we are concerned that a Women's Centre will be approached as a tokenistic appeasement that doesn't address the issues facing women or women's services. We understand a Women's Building to be a place where women can be creative and innovative as well as supported. A place that's open to the public; a place of celebration of the feminist movement.

We are hoping that the campaign will begin to reach a wider audience, and in particular that support and understanding for a Women's Building will inspire people and reach a critical mass.

How can people take radical actions that make genuine change in the world about injustices that anger or inspire them? What advice do you have for those who wish to make change?

Angela Davis said, 'You have to act as if it were possible to radically transform the world. And you have to do it all the time.' She described radical as 'at the roots'. We strongly believe that change must come from the roots, from the ground up. This means fostering solidarity and raising the voices of those with direct experience of the harms we want to change.

Change can happen quickly, but more often it takes a long time; we feel it is important to take a long-lensed approach. We are inspired by campaigners who went before us, particularly Radical Alternatives to Prison. Mariame Kaba describes hope as a discipline that must be practised every day, and while we are realistic about the challenges we face, we must also foster hope in ourselves and in those around us.

We must be honest about the system's resistance to change, and desire to co-opt the most radical proposals or ideas. Holloway itself is a great example of that, as now we are in the centenary year of Votes for Women and the suffragettes, and their radical resistance has been sanitised. People call for statues and commemoration, when on the very same site we are engaging in a land battle, in trying to provide support for women deemed too poor or not worthy enough to be even incarcerated in north London, let alone live and thrive there.

What's your 'I'm a feminist but . . .'?

I'm a feminist but I've imagined a future where I win the lottery more than a future without the patriarchy.

I met Leyla Hussein on a *Guardian* panel about feminism. I was drawn to her golden light, unstoppable energy and quality sense of humour, all of which give her a magnetic force. She told me about the Dahlia Project, the only counselling programme for victims of female genital mutilation in Europe, and I was impressed and inspired. She explained how it helped women understand the physical and psychological trauma of having their clitoris cut off with a knife as children, and how it killed the practice within families by de-normalising the violence. Last year she told me that unless she could raise £20,000 she was going to have to close the project within a few months. She needed £50,000 to keep it open for a year. I knew we couldn't let it close down. It sounded like a lot of money, but Leyla told me that £180 would pay for a full course of group therapy for one woman, including childcare. Fifty pounds would pay for just the childcare. Those numbers sounded more manageable. I told her I thought I could raise £20,000 but didn't want to promise the whole £50,000. I asked friends, corporate clients and podcast listeners if any of them could afford £180. For many women that's an unaffordable amount, but for many others it's not. Sometimes you give a random amount of money to a charity and you don't know where it's going. Would women with good incomes give up a luxury or share some of their savings to know that one woman was going to receive counselling? Or what about £50? This was a more manageable amount for many, and again, they knew what it was buying and who'd be receiving it. The UK had recently released new ten-pound notes featuring Jane Austen. We asked on the podcast if anyone would be prepared to give their first Jane Austen tenner in a #Jane4Dahlia drive. I still feel a little teary saying that, with Gift Aid included, we've raised £82,000. Sometimes activism needs money. And sometimes sisters will generously share their cash with those who need it. That's nearly enough for this year and next. Although we have stopped asking on the podcast, people haven't stopped giving. I asked Leyla why she's an activist and how she does what she does.

Leyla Hussein

Leyla, how did you become an activist and what is the Dahlia Project?
I didn't plan on being an activist, I just wanted to protect my daughter from harm and patriarchy. Dahlia was born based in my experience in therapy. I constantly had to explain what FGM was to my therapist – it was exhausting. So I wanted to create a space where FGM survivors didn't explain, only shared their experience, and where FGM was recognised as a form of abuse.

What motivates you to do more than see the problem but actually try to fix it?
I never try to fix. 'Influence for the better so it gets fixed' is my motto. My daughter and the women I work with totally motivate me and misogynist men definitely keep me on my toes.

How do you begin to do something like this? What first steps can people take to change the world if they see a cause they want to champion?
To make any change you need to accept that there is a problem and that your approach isn't the only way. The feminist movement is full of people whose approach has become 'My way or no way'. Being open is key.

Why is money important to the sort of changes you wish to make in the world, and how do you go about raising it?

Money is super-important, and we shouldn't feel guilty about asking for it. That was a big lesson I had to learn. Girls are brought up not to value ourselves, so we feel we always need to work for free and if we get any money, we need to be grateful. Investing in me and the women I work with is truly important. The support from other women on this is truly amazing as I've experienced it few times.

How does being a woman of colour affect your activism?

Being a woman of colour doesn't just affect my activism, it affects my everyday life from the moment I wake up. As soon as I step out of my door, I carry labels imposed by society – angry black woman, sexualised and objectified by the media. Or a middle-class white woman would clutch her handbag on the suspicion of me potentially stealing it from them. With the name Leyla Hussein there's an added layer of being labelled a terrorist. I guess all those enforced labels affect and influence my activism, but I don't waste my time trying to convince ignorant people I'm not any of these labels. All I can do is live by my actions by trying to create an environment where we can all be in a place of empathy and peace, while calling out the bullshit that's wrong with the world.

How can people help the Dahlia Project?

Please share it with your friends and on social media; donate money, donate your time.

What's your 'I'm a feminist but . . . '?
I'm a feminist but instead of reading Manal al-Sharif's book *Daring to Drive* based on Saudi women's right to drive, instead I was watching *Love Island* and it felt so good.

Before Christmas 2017 I was invited to speak at a protest in front of the House of Commons. The activist who invited me was eighteen-year-old Amika George, a secondary school student who'd identified a problem: girls were skipping school because they couldn't afford sanitary products; and a solution: that the government should provide supplies the way lavatory paper is readily available in school loos. As I headed for the stage, I saw a sea of young faces, excited, cold. Girls waving signs and shouting into the night. These teenagers, students and under-25s wanted to change their world. These young women are not taking no for an answer. They're not accepting 'Not right now.' They gave me faith that feminism is in the best possible hands. They're not waiting for experience to visit itself upon them. They're out there making it for themselves. They don't think wisdom comes as a package deal with age. And they're right. Amika and her dynamic, decisive, delightful friends and allies Scarlett Curtis and Grace Campbell put on a protest that made the news. They are my hope. Never tell me that millennials and Gen Zs are thoughtless and spoilt. Bring on the avocado toast and share it around. They deserve it.

I wanted to talk to Amika because she saw a problem that particularly affected girls, had an idea to fix it, rallied troops and saw the whole thing through. At the time of writing, it looks as if it will become policy in the UK very soon. That's how you show democracy who's boss.

Amika George

Hi Amika. First, could you tell us what problem you saw and what you've done to tackle it, and what outcomes you've got so far and hope to get?

I was totally stunned when I saw a report on the news that there were children in the UK who weren't able to afford menstrual products. It really shocked me that period poverty was so rife in the UK that children, my age or younger, were choosing to miss school and rather stay at home to bleed, or would have to make their own protection using socks stuffed with tissues or newspaper or ripped-up clothes. Even though this story horrified everyone, the government was simply not doing anything about it, and this really infuriated me!

So I started a campaign called #FreePeriods to pressure the government to take action: I put together an online petition and made a pledge to raise awareness about period poverty as much as I could. I wanted everyone to know that this was happening under our noses, and vowed to talk about periods until people got sick of hearing about all things bloody, and try to smash the ridiculous, outdated stigma surrounding menstruation.

Over 139,000 people have added their name to the petition, and we organised a #FreePeriods protest to get the government's attention in December, which was incredible – over a thousand people came waving the most clever and creative banners and signs I've ever seen, and we had really inspirational speakers there who rallied the crowd.

We need the government to make a statutory pledge to eradicate period poverty in schools by providing free period products to girls from the lowest-income families.

We need more education in schools about periods, for all genders, and we need to realise that periods are *nothing* to be ashamed of!

Could you tell us about what made you activated? You saw the problem of period poverty in schools, but what made you say 'This has to change and I'm the one to do something.'?

It came from identifying a real injustice that made my blood boil, and seeing that the government wasn't trying to help these children made me even angrier and more determined. Mrs May's government has pledged billions to Brexit and Trident, and thousands to MPs' second homes, but aren't motivated to give a paltry amount of funding to make sure that all children stay in school. I thought, 'Why shouldn't I try and change this?' I feel that, if we can, young people need to have each other's backs; we need to stand up for each other and fight when we need to.

Did you start this when you were seventeen? It's so young to be thinking about others and devoting time and energy that could be focused on school, fun, romance and, frankly, yourself. When I went to the protest you'd organised I was amazed at how young the crowd was and how motivated. What's up with Gen Z getting angry, active and changing the world?

Gen Z are amazing!! There are so many young activists out there who refuse to accept the status quo and we refuse to turn our eyes away from injustice; we want a better world, and if the powers that be don't see what we see and act on it, we aren't fearful of taking matters into our own hands. Personally I believe that it's the young people today who really understand how to motivate, inspire and mobilise. We know how to capitalise on the powers of social media and how to garner support where it counts.

I started the #FreePeriods campaign from my bedroom in April, and I haven't looked back. Yes, it's so difficult to balance everything – A Levels, university applications and interviews, going out, seeing friends, parties – with campaigning, which can sometimes feel like a full-time job. But if it's something that is important to you – and for me, it's more than a mission, it means so much more, because I'm often contacted by children who tell me how they struggle *every* month when they can't access menstrual products, and how much they look forward to seeing a change, and I realise I can't stop: I must keep fighting for them because it can be life-changing for these children.

If other people are reading this, daunted by your achievements, how can they begin? What manageable steps can they take to begin something for a cause they believe in?
A good way to highlight a cause that means a lot to you is to write about it, either in a blog or as a contributor within a publication. It's a small way of telling the world why it means something to you. See if you can get a small group of supporters together to help spread your message.

I could be a whole lot better at this – I don't use it enough! – but go on Instagram and Twitter to tell people why you're supporting your cause and update your feed regularly with what you're doing about it and you'll find that slowly people will start to take notice.

How can we help you right now or in the future?

Talking about periods is so important! Tell *everyone* about your periods, tell them about the blood, the clots, the cramps, the chocolate! We need to normalise the conversation around menstruation and there's a lot of work to do around that. Even today, an email landed in my inbox from someone who started their period at 15 and, because she'd had practically no education around periods, when she found a clot in her pad, she thought she had a disease and might be bleeding to death. That really upset me. We need to talk about periods in schools, with our friends, with our brothers, and we have to let people know that periods are nothing to be ashamed of. We need to be celebrating the wonder of our bodies, not hiding them away!

As an Asian woman, I don't think we are taught to challenge enough, and that needs to change. It's ironic because the issue of period poverty is really prevalent and damaging in some Asian communities in countries such as Nepal and India. Just this weekend a twenty-one-year-old Nepalese woman died after being banished from her home because she was menstruating. There's so much work to do in these countries to change the archaic and culturally ingrained, superstitious beliefs about menstruation.

This weekend, one of the widest-read newspapers in India covered the #FreePeriods campaign and since then, my inbox has been swamped with messages from across India, from men and women, saying how period taboo is damaging the educational progress of children and how that taboo just has to be eradicated. School dropout rates are alarmingly high, and menstruators are ostracised from society all because they bleed, and that's so wrong!

What's your 'I'm a feminist but ... '?
I'm a feminist but everyone at home knows never to make their tea in the powder-pink, fine bone china mug with yellow daisies on it. It's mine.

Brené Brown, who studies the data of happiness, says that everyone with a capacity for joy has a gratitude practice. Grateful people are optimistic, calm and draw people to them, which is terrific for making a movement. We need to be grateful for what previous generations of feminists created and changed to make our world so much better.

However, a content person has never changed the world. No social change, technology or innovation has ever been invented by someone who was content with the status quo. The chair is a piece of technology, and whoever first thought of sitting on a tree stump was probably told by others that there was nothing wrong with the ground, and as it was good enough for everyone else, why did they need to go making things so complicated? People fear change and try to keep things as they are because the unknown is frightening. Also if you're benefiting from the current system you may not want anyone messing with it. Change requires dissatisfaction. If your life is relatively privileged it's tempting to be satisfied with the way things are, but doing nothing is supporting injustice.

A life made up of 80 per cent gratitude and 20 per cent dissatisfaction creates a great activist. It's the spirit of Maya Angelou. Watch her videos. As much as I miss her, sometimes I'm glad she went during the Obama administration and didn't live to see what's come after it. She's done her part. It's our turn now. When we are together we can make change happen. We need to organise, make our requests clear and if they're not granted, remember that democracy literally means 'the power of the people' and turn those requests into demands.

Politicians are people we pay to do a job. We trust them to spend our collective money and make good choices on our behalves. If you'd paid someone to look after your elderly nan and you popped in unannounced and discovered the carer had taken the money you'd given them to pay for your nan's food and electricity and spent it on drones to bomb other nans, you wouldn't just say, 'Oh well, what can you do? This guy's on a four-year contract. No point firing him. I'd just have to hire someone else, and they're all as bad as each other.' You'd have a word. You'd do whatever you could to make a change. This is the exact situation we are in in austerity Britain. Feminism can't exist in principle. It needs the oxygen of action. We are its life force. If not us, who? If not now, when?

I'm a Feminist But ... But ...

Okay, this is the dessert course. Let's get all the guilt out on the table before we go. Despite the increased balls-out career confidence (and the fact that I've just used 'balls' as a metaphor for courage); despite the fact that I can be grateful for, and even admire, bits of my own body in the right light; despite the fact that I've jumped out of a plane to show gravity it can't fuck with feminism; despite the fact that I often apply for respect and sometimes that application is approved – the 'but' still hangs there ...

Think of all your hypocrisies and paradoxes and the ways you aren't thinking or acting like a feminist. 'Buts' make great punchlines, but do they erode something important? Should I get rid of them at the risk of making podcasts and books 25 per cent less funny for the same money?

I'm a feminist but I've thought forensically about this when I could have been drafting an important letter about gender equality to the Prime Minister: I think there's a hidden feminism in almost all our guilty secrets. The reasons we are drawn to things that appear at odds with our quest for equality aren't always as they first appear. There are examples of this everywhere. Here's some I did earlier. Do try this at home.

Disclaimer: some of the things are heteronormative precisely because they're mainstream 'guilty pleasures'.

Weddings

> *I'm a feminist but I spent more time*
> *shopping for a wedding dress than I've*
> *spent on protesting in my life.*

Brides can be notoriously particular, demanding and emotional about their 'big day'. Some are even accused of becoming 'bridezillas'. None of this seems very feminist, on the face of it. The marriage tradition itself is the Patriarchy Special with a side of People As Property. Get past that to a place where it's a consensual union of two lovers who wish to formalise their relationship in a cocktail of romance, stability and financially efficient living, and the wedding itself is surely the superficial time-waster. Why can't you just go down to the registry office with a few friends in something you already have in your wardrobe? Why do you have to spend hours forcing your best friends and your fiancée's sister (who you don't even like) into uniforms like taffeta soldiers with wild-flower helmets?

Even more inscrutable: why would a person who's never noticed a seat back in her life, suddenly care deeply about there being a length of ivory taffeta ribbon on a hundred and fifty reclaimed wooden church chairs?

It is superficial. It is narcissistic. It is actual madness. How can it be anything except the opposite of feminist?

Say Yes to the Dress is a reality TV show that is no more than some fixed-rig cameras in a bridal gown store. The whole show is brides-to-be trying on dresses and sometimes they don't even buy them. I love watching it, and for a long time I couldn't work out why. How could I possibly care about truculent, mawkish strangers sobbing over tulle?

Then it struck me – I'm watching women be central to proceedings and demand perfection without apology.

I'm not suggesting for one second that Bridal Gowns equal Feminism. Clearly not. I am saying there's a hidden power in the process because it's one of the only socially acceptable spheres of almost entirely female (or fabulous gay male) influence. Some women become 'bridezillas' because it might be the only time in their life that they're in complete control of everything in their domain and they can, at least sometimes, even get their own mothers to back down and bow to their wishes.

When I watch *Say Yes to the Dress* I'm watching young women, working-class women, plus-size women, racially diverse women given space, given time, given the power of command. Women literally put on a pedestal in the middle of a beautifully lit, multi-mirrored oasis with staff running to fetch and carry anything they desire. A woman is given permission to wait till she's laced into a ballgown worth more than her rent for a year and then says, 'I don't like it. It's not me.' At that point, her female friends and relatives who are sitting and watching proceedings like a film star's entourage, agree that she should trust her instincts and the dress should be banished.

Here is a woman who cannot be frock-blocked. I am watching an empress. I am watching a woman behave with the same certainty and capriciousness as a mediocre man in middle management. She's calling the shots, and not just on her dress but on his suit and their flower arrangements and the colour of the cars and the first chord that will play as everyone turns to look at her and gasp as she walks down the aisle – as she takes her moment without hesitation, without feeling obliged, even once, to say, 'I just had a thought and I don't know if it's worth mentioning'.

I am watching a woman say, 'Look at me. See me take up time. Wait while I walk down the aisle as slowly as possible so everyone can see my poise and beauty. See me take up space with the train on my dress which inhabits more floor than I need so you understand this space is mine. See the height of my veil. Taste the champagne I chose because it was my favourite. And notice the length, sheen and colour of the fucking chair ribbons. I have collated every detail of this room, these people, this day. Because if all other days are days of deference to men and people-pleasing and the demands of children and boorish work colleagues who talk over me, this day, this space, this dress is wholly mine.

'And no, Max, you can't ruin it with a purple Ferrari between wedding venues, because this isn't your day. You've had ten thousand years of history. You've had 3,650,000 days. This one is mine. I'm a woman *and* you will watch me take control so comprehensively and unreasonably you'll want to name a monster movie after me, not the other way around. I take control of it *not* because I care more about pink tea roses than political influence, but because roses is all that's on offer.'

My conclusion is not that we should lean in to the wedding obsession, it is rather that weddings are further evidence that women are brilliant at producing highly detailed operations and managing the emotions of a throng of people. If society routinely allowed women as much space and deference in other areas of life and endowed them with *carte blanche* influence, they would relish it and get spectacular results. When society offers tribal confidence, women's self-confidence soars. Wedding trappings might be a superficial distraction, but they are also, for some women at least, a temporary power grab at the threshold of a life of capitulation.

Romantic comedies

> ***I'm a feminist but*** *I secretly love the movie* Pretty
> Woman *and, in truth, am open to the idea of*
> *Richard Gere paying to enter me on a grand piano.*

Feminist 'guilty pleasures' often include a raft of romcoms in
which the woman is rescued by the love of a good man. The
genre is fraught with implications that a single woman is not
complete on her own and that a man is the secret to happiness.
We watch them scornful of our soft spot for romance and critical of our tolerance for the anti-feminist messages.

Why do we watch them? More than that, why do we
revisit favourites in moments of heartbreak, boredom or self-
indulgence? What are we getting out of a fictitious run to the
airport? Are we really hoping to be rescued heroines rather than
autonomous heroes?

I'm a feminist but I still haven't seen *Persepolis*, though I did
manage to find time to rewatch *Dirty Dancing* in order to do
research for this chapter. I swear it was work . . . Oh, Johnny . . .

Here's the thing: every romcom I love has a powerful,
demanding, autonomous woman at its big, pink, marshmallow, cupid heart. Let's take *Dirty Dancing* out of the
anti-feminist corner where it doesn't belong. On the face of
it, it's about a young woman who finds her sexual awakening
through an older, more experienced male dance partner. Her
name is Baby. He teaches her to dance with a high-handed,
patriarchal attitude, they have the sex, her father finds out and
disapproves and she, for a while, is buffeted between trying to
please these two men in different ways.

All that is accurate, but I don't think that's why many girls
and women are drawn to watch it over and over. Yes, Patrick
Swayze has an exceptional torso and a piercing stare and the

pelvic writhing to proper choons is compelling, but that's not what propels the story. Baby drives every part of the narrative. She is brought to the summer camp on a family holiday and takes a risk by defiantly going into the staff dance hall. She discovers one of the dancers needs an abortion and in a pre-Roe v. Wade world, finds a way to both fund the illegal procedure and cover the unwillingly pregnant woman's shift while she's out of commission. She literally takes dancing lessons to facilitate a feminist act.

Her teacher is the imperious Johnny, who has little time for her, judging her as a rich kid who has had all life's opportunities handed to her. She tolerates his arrogant teaching style to a point but when he shows her too much attitude she stands up to him and applies for respect. That's when things change. People remember Baby saying to Johnny, 'I carried a watermelon' because it's a relatable, embarrassing slip in a moment of sexual tension but we should also remember her shouting at him, 'I'm doing all this to save your ass and what I really want to do is drop you on it!' She initiates the sex. She defies the hotel owner and stands up to her disappointed father, who finds her loss of innocence intolerable, by pointing out his hypocrisies: 'You told me everyone was alike and deserved a fair break, but you meant everyone who was like you.' She stakes her claim to her own authenticity: 'If you love me, you have to love all the things about me.'

The last time she is named, she is no longer 'Baby'. Johnny introduces her to the audience as 'Miss Frances Houseman' – named after Frances Perkins, the first woman in the US cabinet and headed for academic and socialist greatness. Without Frances Houseman, there is no plot. She engineers everything. That's why we love to watch her dance. She is calling the shots just like Sylvia is in charge of Mickey in their lip-synched song and dance number. 'How do you call your lover boy?' 'Come here, lover boy.' Johnny wants sex. Baby wants to dance. Guess what they do? *Dirty Dancing* with a submissive leading lady would have died a death. We imagine ourselves in her dancing shoes because she's leading every step (and she's pressed up against an incredibly impressive torso).

A more difficult example to reconcile my feminism with is *Pretty Woman*. It glamorises and sanitises sex work and is a classic Pygmalion story of a working-class woman plucked out of her difficult circumstances and educated for finer things, making her unsuited for her earlier occupation in the process. I do not think that's why women are drawn to it. Vivian is a force of nature. She picks Edward Lewis up, getting in his car and literally taking the wheel. She negotiates a fee, playing hardball. She draws firm emotional lines in the sand, walking out the door when she feels taken advantage of. On top of all that, she returns to a fancy Rodeo Drive store where she has been disrespected and shows the saleswomen who work on commission what they missed out on: 'Big mistake. Big. Huge!'

The thing is, she never really is educated by Richard Gere's character. She crashes his parties, but when she misuses the fancy cutlery, sending a snail across a restaurant, she finds it funny rather than mortifying. She operates with immense confidence and no shame in his world. He is far more changed by her than she is by him. This is why it is a classic Pygmalion tale. Most people know the movie version of *My Fair Lady*, in which Eliza returns to Henry Higgins and finds his slippers. In George Bernard Shaw's original play, she tells him to sod off and marries Freddy on the street where she lives. Henry Higgins ends up alone and ruined for life without her because she's the only real thing that's ever happened to him.

Edward does rescue Vivian at the end of *Pretty Woman*, but she gets the last line when she says of her princess-saved-from-a-tower fantasy, 'She rescues him right back.'

I'm not implying that *Pretty Woman* isn't problematic in a million ways, or that indulging in more romcoms is the most feminist thing we could do with a wet Saturday afternoon. I am saying that our favourites usually feature whirlwind women who are as autonomous as possible within their permitted circumstances (of age, class and financial restrictions). I can think of poor romcoms where the woman's a bit vapid and sappy, but they're not classics and they're not the favourites.

One of the reasons romcoms are maligned is that they are a female genre, so they are written off as fluff. In truth, this is probably because most of them have a female hero or shared male and female heroes.

Movies that seem, on the face of it, to be a cut above romantic comedies in ambition and scope are often horribly lacking in female autonomy. Take *A Few Good Men*, a clever legal drama with a stellar cast and a brilliant script. The title is a reference to a woman in a man's world. It opens with Demi Moore's character, a diligent, extremely committed military lawyer, rehearsing a speech to her boss. She wants to be chosen as lead counsel on a high-profile murder trial. She believes there is more to the case than meets the eye and she is ready for the investigation and experienced in the courtroom. Her boss denies her request because she is too diligent and so likely to slow the case down. A junior officer, in the form of Tom Cruise, who's only been qualified a year, and has plea-bargained all of his cases in a cocky manner, is given the job she wants. That sounds like a set-up for a story in which Demi's character comes into her own and usurps her male counterparts, proving that she should have been given the job all along.

In fact, she proves her boss right, making mistakes in the courtroom, playing support to Tom Cruise and telling him, open-mouthed, that he's an exceptional lawyer on a date she's

asked him out on. He decides to push Jack Nicholson to say
he unlawfully ordered the Code Red because, in his arrogance,
Nicholson believes he can run his naval base in any way he sees
fit. She tells Cruise not to go there if he doesn't think he can
get the senior officer to admit fault. He shoots, he scores, he can
handle the truth. She continues to be impressed. The end. It's a
great law movie, but as far as autonomous women go, give me
Pretty Woman or *Dirty Dancing* any time. You may find those
films patriarchal or flawed in other ways but they are about
women who set boundaries, make choices and instigate change.
Women don't watch romcoms because we are vapid romance
hounds and even if we do, romance is love and love is better
than guns. We watch them, at least in part, because we see
ourselves represented there as autonomous, three-dimensional
humans and so few other cinema genres grant us this.

Catcalling

> *I'm a feminist but I am perfectly capable of*
> *hearing a man shout, 'Hey, sexy!' and thinking*
> *'That's awful – still got it' in one clear thought.*

Women confess things to me, because I do *The Guilty Feminist*
podcast, by email and when they meet me. I am a sort of
Catholic priest of feminism. Often women confess that they
sometimes, and only in the right circumstances, feel validated
by a catcall. Clearly they don't say this loudly because they don't
want to encourage men to do it. Most of us, when we enjoy a
random stranger endorsing our attractiveness, feel ashamed of
this. Why would we want that? Aren't we part of the problem?
Are men right to say it's just a harmless compliment?

If you've ever felt validated, you're not alone. It is clearly
problematic to endorse or encourage sexually aggressive and

unsolicited behaviour, but if we've ever felt a secret satisfaction at discovering the wolf whistle was for us, it's important to ask why rather than squash down the question until it ferments into shame.

Most catcalls are designed to sexually intimidate and to make women feel like we are objects to be lusted after and that our worth lies in our ability to be penetrated. I've experienced this, and it's scary and embarrassing. I've rerouted my journey home because of men like this depersonalising my sexuality and making me feel like part of a subclass of people who exist to serve an animal sexual urge, but not an animal that bothers with a sophisticated or alluring mating ritual.

A man in my London neighbourhood of Camden Town recently shouted, 'Fuck me! I would!' at me, despite the fact that we hadn't made eye contact. A male Adélie penguin brings little rocks to the object of his desire to put in her nest. If she likes the rock, she'll be open to mating with him. There are some men in my area who are offering less than a penguin who has a brain the size of a peanut. It is too low a bar.

I've also experienced a different sort of unprompted praise. I was walking home from the gym one day, in what I imagined was a fairly unattractive, slightly sweaty get-up, and a cool-looking guy leaning in a doorway looked me up and down and said, 'Groovy chick.' I smiled at him and he smiled at me and I kept walking and he didn't say anything further. He didn't try to hit on me. He didn't need anyone else to know that he'd said it. It made me feel good. Like I was nice to look at and he'd made assumptions that I'd be fun to talk to – and he wanted me to know that. I went home feeling like a romantically viable 'groovy chick'. The difference between this man and the 'Fuck me! I would!' guy was this – one personalised me and one depersonalised me. They were not the same thing in different doses. They were opposite forces.

One day a man shouted from a car as I crossed the street, 'You're very sexy!' His tone of voice said, 'I just thought you should know', not, 'I want to see you squirm'. I don't know how he could tell. It was midwinter and I was in a huge coat and it was raining. It wasn't intimidating at all. It made me laugh. As I walked home I thought that my ability to take pleasure in this was probably in large part because the patriarchy has sent me messages all my life that my fuckability is the most important thing about me, and this unthreatening expression validated that. I also thought, 'One day I'll be catcalled for the last time.' I've asked older women and they've confirmed this. Apparently old men usually catcall younger women.

Part of what makes me occasionally reassured by unthreatening catcalling is that the man doing it is, in some way, validating my fertility (mistakenly in my case, as mine is rubbish!). Men, for no reason (except that the patriarchy seems to have nature on speed dial), can be fertile till they die clutching a telegram from the Queen. It feels to me, personally, that there is something deeper here than cultural conditioning; something biological in being reminded that you're still a desirable sexual mate.

Is there a hidden power for women in this? There is a power in knowing that your body, your presence, your style, your gait has the ability to change someone else. That without saying a single word or doing a solitary thing you can make a stranger look twice. To revisit romcoms, there is a reason why Hugh Grant is sexy in *Four Weddings and a Funeral*. It is because he's a funny, clever, good-looking guy with his friends but becomes weak in the presence of beauty. When he's across from Andie MacDowell, her presence alone reduces him to a stuttering mess. She's a force, without lifting a finger. In a world where female upper-body strength will come runner-up almost every time, if our face, our perfume, our indifference reduces men to the position of being the one wanting and longing for our presence, then it can feel like it's the power position, even if, in practice, it hardly ever is.

The trouble with telling men who catcall this is that each and every one of them will say, 'I'm doing the good kind of catcalling. The personalised Moonpig – all about making you feel sexy in an unintimidating manner – sort.' Most of them aren't. If you're a man reading this, don't do it. Many women don't like it in any form, and the ones who do only like it very occasionally when it feels safe and monogrammed – and you have no way of knowing how to do that and no one knows how to teach it. Please don't worry about women 'missing out on compliments' – there's a surplus of guys out there who've got us covered and most of them are doing it so badly it puts us off the ones who secretly make us feel good. Having said that, if you're reading this and you ever leant in a Camden Town doorway and told a brunette in gym clothes and a ponytail that she was a groovy chick, thanks – (she's a feminist but) she knows.

Make-up and dress-up

> *I'm a feminist but if I were told using liquid eyeliner would knock six months off my life, I'd need to know how long I was going to live before I gave it up.*

Make-up and dress-up seem like a frivolous waste of time and money. Why do I assume I have to draw on my face every day? What's wrong with my regular-coloured lips? Why do I care what I carry my stuff around in? Surely I only need a bag to get me from Important Feminist Location A to Necessary

Location of Equality B, so I do not need a variety of receptacles in shiny fabrics with multicoloured trims to distract me from the task.

The patriarchy and capitalism – like a sketch comedy double act – have made it a woman's glittery burden to decorate herself for their delight and greed. Being judged not just on the shape, size and age of our bodies and faces, we are charged with the onerous responsibility of augmenting and accessorising. Yes – we can withdraw from the race and that is a noble choice. Some women are not femme, have never been femme and have no desire to be femme and rightly reject anything that might be colloquially called 'girly'.

Those of us who are drawn to fashion and liquid eyeliner often feel a bit sheepish about it. Some men see femme women as vacuous and exclusively decorative. Some women judge femme women as superficial and unfeminist – even betraying the sisterhood by pandering to the male gaze.

Is there a hidden power in attention to grooming or even flamboyant self-decoration? Hell, yes. It's authorship. I've already explored this in Chapter 5: The Power of Yes, but it's worth unpacking further here because femme gender expression is so commonly derided by men and women, even women who enjoy it.

If gender is performative then women win all the Oscars. Some days I don't know how the patriarchy let us have make-up. They usually get all the good stuff. Make-up can reveal, conceal, highlight and accentuate. It can be playful, creative, self-nurturing and decadent. Most guys have no option for make-up without ridicule. That means they wake up in the morning, look in the mirror and think, 'Well, that's as good as I'm going to look all day.'

How did we end up with concealer and bronzing shimmer cream? Objectively it sounds like something those in charge would keep for themselves, and that's because it was something men once had on tap. Open a fashion history book – from warpaint to powdered wigs to beauty spots and remedies for under-eye bags, men were right in there at the cutting edge of beauty. This went out of fashion for everyone in Victorian times when Queen Victoria thought it was too much fun. When she was up at Balmoral mourning Albert for some years, women started to mutter in public loos and drawing rooms, 'She doesn't seem to be coming back ... Shall we just have a little touch of this and that?' Women took it up again. Men never did.

Many of the world's most flamboyant fashions were also a gaudy male domain, but we ended up with the fun stuff when the music stopped in Sartorial Pass the Parcel. This means the options that are dictated to men are incredibly limited. Most women can choose to have one tube of fabric around our legs or two. If a man chooses one he risks actual violence. If he's famous – David Beckham, Jaden Smith – one tube of fabric around his legs will make front-page news. It is so arbitrary it's madness, isn't it? Boys' top-half options are almost as dull. And shoes? Can he do a wedge? A kitten heel? A peep-toe? A slingback? He'll struggle to carry any sort of handbag. What do men do with all their stuff? Keep it in their admittedly superior pockets or ... leave it at home?

Feminists tend to applaud girls who go to parties dressed as Spiderman rather than Princess Elsa from *Frozen* – partly because they're going against the grain and seeking a symbol of pragmatic power rather than accessorised objectification. Fine. Good. But there is an implication that male traits are better than female ones. Both Spiderman and Elsa have magi-cal powers and use them for good and not for evil. Spiderman uses violence but Elsa does not. Why is it better to be in a Spiderman suit than a dress, if that's what Elsa and her crew are doing? Two tubes are better than one tube, because men are superior to women.

Personal rejection of femme expression is fine of course, but contempt for extreme femme clothes and make-up can be misogyny (sometimes internalised). Femme accessorising is an important part of some women's transition into the female tribe. Many grown trans women who've recently come out describe themselves as teenage girls playing with acrylic nails and patent leather boots for the first time. Let's not diminish the power of the dress-up box. It's a place where we can alter our identities day to day, hour by hour, to express what we feel. The patriarchy fears it, because it dares not look in the mirror as often as we do. Maybe because it will catch sight of its own soul and be horrified. Maybe because decorating your face, your waist, your pencil case is uniquely human. Self-decoration individualises us and there's a power in knowing exactly who you are and taking her out on the street.

Rap music

> *I'm a feminist but* *sometimes to put myself in the right mood before a* Guilty Feminist *show, I listen to Eminem's 'Lose Yourself'. 'Look, if you had one shot, or one opportunity to seize everything you ever wanted, in one moment . . . Would you capture it or just let it slip?'*

So many of my listeners tell me their secret feminist shame is hip-hop. Hip-hop is usually performed by men who look like grown-up orphans the patriarchy hung out to dry because it doesn't do childcare. Why do some feminist women love hip-hop when the lyrics celebrate male supremacy and denigrate women as 'bitches and hos' to be fucked, beaten and left? Some hip-hop lyrics depict women as chattels, gold-diggers and othered objects which have no thoughts or life outside the male gaze, and as victims of male violence.

This horrible posturing is a billion-dollar industry. Supporting it and disseminating it isn't doing anything for the sisterhood. Why do we like it? Is there an unseen heft in it?

Yes. When I see women singing along, they're not in the objectified position. They're swaggering, legs apart, arms open – having a go at being the king of the fucking world who doesn't give a shit about anything or anyone except his own dominance. It gives us a few minutes to imagine what it'd be like if we could play the alpha. There's no real desire to dominate and conquer; rather a dalliance with being in a position to give zero fucks because adoration, cash, fame and rhythm is on our side for once. It's like role-playing being a Greek god. It answers the question, what if my gaze shrank others down to size? How does (pretend) power feel? 'This opportunity comes once in a lifetime.' Or at the very least once in a bathroom mirror getting ready for war.

I am now actively seeking out feminist hip-hop and have commissioned a feminist hip-hop musical to celebrate the centenary of the Representation of the People Act which gave certain women in the United Kingdom the right to vote. This musical, *Suffrageddon*, is being co-created by some extremely talented composers – Omahrose and Mark Hodge and two amazing rappers – RoxXxan and Oracy – who have shown me that I don't need to rely on Eminem for my pre-show feel-goods. British women of colour are bringing the revolution in their beat and rhymes and if we seek out the sentiment to go with the swagger, hip-hop is as feminist AF.

BDSM fantasies

> *I'm a feminist but sometimes I fantasise*
> *about being sexually dominated by famous,*
> *fictitious misogynist Don Draper and, in*
> *truth, I believe that if he were to meet me, I*
> *could make him whole and heal his pain.*

Many feminists are troubled by being turned on by sub-missive sexual fantasies or role play. We fear they indicate our true nature, that we are something to be conquered and diminished. I am talking now about more than a Tallulah Bankhead-style shamelessness about being a sexual being or some mild dominance and submission fantasies, both of which I've written about in previous chapters.

Rape fantasies are especially contentious and some feminists have suggested that it's misogynist to have them or discuss them as they contribute to rape culture. I have read articles calling for women to rebrand them as 'ravishing fantasies'. A failure to acknowledge how common rape fantasies are seems far more likely to cause shame and self-loathing in those who have them. That shame can result in low self-esteem and an inability to talk about or report actual real-life rape. If no one's admitting their fantasies, girls and women might assume they're alone and somehow deviant or perhaps even deserving of rape. For this reason alone, it is important to admit that they are common. In nine surveys of women's rape fantasies (pub-lished between 1973 and 2008), between 31 and 57 per cent of women admitted to having rape fantasies about once a month.[1]

---

1 The most recent report is: 'The Nature of Women's Rape Fantasies: An Analysis of Prevalence, Frequency and Contents' by Jenny Bivona and Joseph Critelli (*The Journal of Sex Research*, 2009).

The most common feminist response to this seems to be an apology for the fantasiser. 'It's only a fantasy. All fantasies are harmless.' Sometimes it is suggested that it's a way for women to absolve themselves of the shame about sex foisted on them by a Madonna/whore attitude they've grown up with. Or it is posited that it's a way to tap into the excitement of fear, which is close to arousal, as if these fantasies are the equivalent of a roll-ercoaster ride. Occasionally experts publish reports reassuring worried Googlers that their fantasies are 'healthy and normal' and no indication that they 'want to be raped in real life'.

Approximately one in five women report having experienced some sort of sexual violence. Rape is a real threat for men, too, but the chances of an individual man being raped are, statistically, much lower. Anecdotally my male friends tell me they don't walk home after dark with their keys between their fingers, glancing over their shoulder, ever alert. I do. Many women I know do too.

So many of my female friends have told me about being raped on dates and at parties or brazenly sexually assaulted on public transport. Some have frozen. Some have screamed. Some have gone to court and won. Some gave up before the case went to court because they feared their lives would be ruined by what would be dragged up. Some of them haven't reported it at all. Rape and sexual assault are a common reality for every woman I know.

Is there an uncovered power to imagining the worst thing that can happen to a woman? Can there be anything feminist in mentally conjuring up the act that's the most horrendous physical manifestation of the patriarchy's desire to reduce and overpower women? Yes. We are the author of our own fantasies. A fantasy allows you to author your worst fear. The fantasiser controls the video game and neutralises the trauma of rape by finding sexual arousal in it and reclaiming consent. It's not 'nearly rape'. It's the opposite of rape. It's the reclamation of submission by knowing every beat before it happens and out-smarting the violent aggressor by taking his power to hurt; by finding pleasure, not pain.

Rape fantasies aren't a hallmark of my interior life, but I do think dominance and submission are two of the sexiest words in the English language and I'm clearly not alone. Women weren't reading *Fifty Shades of Grey* for the prose.

These desires are probably in part to do with sex being a place both to take and to relinquish control in a visceral, carnal way. They're also manifestations of scenarios we fear in real life but which, in a fantasy, we can turn into a Choose Our Own Adventure and own. When I should have been having my sexual awakening, I was in an extremely patriarchal religion: instead of having my first kiss, I was being chastised by older men. Not long ago, women couldn't inherit property because we *were* property. Many of the structures and attitudes from that era remain and we live with the residue. Is it any wonder that sometimes we want to sit in the driving seat of those power structures and take pleasure from the pain?

'Only part of us is sane ... The other half ... loves pain and its darker night despair ...' This dual state is human.[2]

Sometimes we forget that we are allowed to take a half hour off from the full-time job of being a feminist and participate in being human. The darker night of despair can be ours. Men have most of the wealth, almost all of the power and lots of decadent, iconoclastic play spaces. We're allowed anything in our heads.

2 Rebecca West, *Black Lamb and Grey Falcon: A Journey Through Yugoslavia* (Macmillan, 1941).

I'm a Feminist And …

'm allowed to walk into rooms with panache in a body I love, move regularly and know well.

I can say yes to the full expression of myself. I can say yes to taking responsibility to change my patch. My patch is familial, local and global.

I can say no. I can create boundaries and draw myself up to my full height and hold hands with other feminists to make walls.

I can be fearless and use emotion and words to create the space that women deserve. I get to be heard. I deserve to be seen. I can be central and I can share the stage with other women, especially those who will never be offered it by the patriarchy.

Owning my paradoxes and laughing at them releases them, and any shame I carried for them, with it.

I'm still the same person who once lied about her weight on a light aircraft, endangering my own life and the lives of the pilot, the other passengers and a Border Collie that was along for the ride.

I'll always not be perfect. Every day of my life I'll wake up and not be perfect. I'll always do and think less-than-feminist things until the day I die. And that's no excuse not to be bold and more demanding.

This is a landmark time. If we don't stand up now and ask for more, create our own worlds and structures, learn to say 'no' and mean it, when will we have this opportunity again? We need to correctly identify the enemy. It is not our own body. It is not our lack of ability. It is not the most truthful manifestation of who we are. It is not our ideas. It is not men. It is not other women. It is definitely not other feminists. We are fighting deliberate injustice and thoughtless oppression and we need to start with our own actions.

When I first got to London, I was told I'd have to become a more assertive driver because I was used to driving in an Australian beach town. Londoners were rude and aggressive drivers and unless I was prepared to cut into the traffic decisively I'd never get out at all. I was nervous because I had been hired as a nanny and I had to drive other people's children through this ferocious scene in my employers' Land Rover. You know what? I discovered that this was a stereotype. Londoners were polite drivers who were only too happy to give way.

After about six months of successfully navigating my way around London I got a boyfriend, called Tom Salinsky. (Reader, I married him.) One day I drove his car and I tried to pull out onto a main road and I couldn't. No one would let me in. After several aborted attempts, I ended up backed down a cul-de-sac, confused and shaken. Tom said, 'You can't drive this car like you drive the Land Rover, you know. Like a tank down the middle of the road.' I was shocked. 'I don't drive the Land Rover like a tank down the middle of the road,' I replied.

'Yes, you do,' he said. 'And everyone gets out of your way. This is a little VW Golf and no one is going to move for you in this.'

I thought everyone else was polite. Turns out, I'm an arsehole.

That's the same for posh, white, tall men called Toby. They don't know they're an arsehole. They think you're polite. They've never driven any other body. They're used to people getting out of their way and leading them to the best table and shutting up when they speak and introducing them to important people. They genuinely don't know that it's harder for someone driving the body of a 5'2" black woman. They've never looked out that window. I feel a little guilty for driving the Land Rover the way I did, but I wasn't truly culpable until I knew.

At that point, I switched it up. I let other people in 55 per cent of the time. I learned quickly that I had to let them in with authority and generosity because they'd dither in my presence. Deference to structurally given status needs to be managed by the one with the unfairly gifted power. I had four-wheel drive privilege. Intersectional feminism is like this. Once it's been pointed out, you've got to start letting other people in. People let Land Rovers go first because they know they'll come off worse in a collision. You don't need a lot of confidence to drive a Land Rover. I pulled out nervously the first time, expecting the worst, and discovered that the road made it easy for me. The other drivers endowed me with privilege because they made assumptions about me. Let's start noticing and acknowledging which doors are open to us and issuing invitations to women who might find them shut. Let's go through those doors together.

There has probably never been a better time to be a woman since we lived on the savannah. I used to assume that things would be even better for women a hundred years from now and better than that a hundred years from then – but lately that easy assumption has turned into a faltering hope. Virginia Woolf said a hundred years ago that in a hundred years' time no one would notice if a novel were written by a man or a woman. It would simply be written by a person. How wrong was she? Are my hopes for women a century from now going to seem as naive as Woolf's are to me?

Hope is the chasm between things as they are and things as they could be. The canyon between the actual and the possible. Hope requires imagination. It is predicated on a careful awareness of things as they are – and a shedding of denial.

Some women insist, 'We have equality! What are you complaining about?' The courageous act of hope isn't required if you don't look down from the tightrope of the patriarchy but instead pretend that your feet are firmly on safe ground. But it doesn't mean you're any less likely to fall. The gravity of power abuse will have its way.

Hope is predicated on dissatisfaction. A content person never changed the world. A satisfied person has never seen a Goliath and dared to craft the perfect slingshot. But hope without a plan of action is the doorway to depression. Every time we turn what is into what could be we turn our hope into change. We must learn to change our hopes into actions and when that is done, hope again, act again.

Hope that we can help women to have better lives – then volunteer at a rape shelter. Hope that women of colour can be heard in a noisy world – then make it our job to amplify their voices. Hope for more women in leadership roles – then mentor girls and women we know and love and pump them with confidence and any opportunities that are in our gift or could be if we hoped they were and changed things so that they would be.

That seems like too much for people like you and me to do.

We are only us. We can hope – but can we dare? Sometimes I think, no. Not me. It's too hard. I'll be criticised. I'll get it wrong. I don't have time. Where would I begin? Then I remember that my life now is the direct consequence of the hopes of the long-dead women before me. We live their hopes every time we walk down the street unchaperoned, uncorseted, uncensored. We live the hopes of our great-grandmothers every time we decide if, when and how to have a child and each time we don't die in childbirth because they hoped for the medical advances that are our normal.

We live the hopes of the suffragettes and the demands of Maya Angelou. Not all of their optimistic predictions have come true, but their strenuous resistance has transformed into our way of life. We live in a world where a woman can run New Zealand and take maternity leave. We live at a time where a woman in Saudi Arabia can drive a car and a girl in Nigeria will be immunised against polio.

We are the breathing, living manifestations of the hopes of women who are not breathing any more. We must hope for ourselves, our daughters and the women a hundred years from now. We are the thing with feathers and now we must spread our wings and fly.

We need to learn to laugh at our guilt and the paradoxes we live with so that they do not slow us down. We've got no time to waste, lots to do and given that we will die with a full inbox and a love of Don Draper, we need to start living as if none of that mattered. Personally, I hope to die at 110 on stage recording my podcast in a stylish bed-jacket, my last words, 'I'm a feminist but my favourite memory about the day we finally ended the patriarchy was what I was wearing.'

We are able and allowed to be imperfect every day and still cry …

Once more unto the breach, dear friends, once more;
Or close the wall up with our female dead.
In peace there's nothing so becomes a girl
As modest stillness and humility;
But when the blast of war blows in our ears,
Then imitate the actions of the tiger;
Stiffen the sinews, summon up the blood . . .
I see you stand like greyhounds in the slips,
Straining upon the start. The game's afoot:
Follow your spirit, and upon this charge
Cry 'God for women, feminism and Saint Angelou!'

Acknowledgements

All the thank yous to my magnificent editor, Sarah Savitt – a woman with much insight, endless patience, a glorious feminist spirit and an impressive clarity of vision.

Thank you also to Tamsyn Berryman whose work on this book has been tireless. She has the patience of any number of saints and the eye of a hundred eagles.

Thank you for the non-stop efforts of Clara Diaz, Kate Doran, Hillary Tisman and Grace Vincent, and all at Virago who have made an actual, real-life book happen.

Thank you hugely to my saintly, skilful, powerhouse of a literary agent Zoe King and the rest of my brilliant sanity-inducing team including the dynamic Abby Singer, the golden Siobhan Bachman, the unstoppable Ruth Cairns and the terrific Chris Lander.

Thank you to my family and tent poles – the wise and mischievous Gina Decio and the relentlessly loving and rigorously supportive Tom Salinsky. Thank you both for making the ridiculous possible. Love and appreciation also to the Sedgwicks for always being on my team, which has given me the audacity to try things I might not have dared to – and Steve Ali for joining our family with an open heart and a golden, brave spirit – bringing perspective and kindness wherever he goes.

Thank you to my mother and father and sister and brother who made me feel special and important growing up, which is why I believe my thoughts are worth sharing in the first place. Thank you to my other families – my family in-law and my long-lost, newly-found biological one who've made me feel so welcome. And much gratitude to my urban family – we've chosen each other and carry each other through failure, success and what lies in between. We support each other through the worst excesses of privilege. Let's keep doing that.

Thank you to the brilliantly talented Linda Cooper for the cover photos and the extraordinary Yuan Li, Milliner to the Feminists, for the fascinator.

Thank you to Philip Kidson from The Mindful Place for insight and clarity when there's only fog and frenzy.

Thank you to all the co-hosts of the podcast who bring so much of their seething talent, killer material, comedy godliness, dynamic energy, joyful attitude and strident, hopeful, guilty feminism. They are Sofie Hagen, of course, and Yassmin Abdel-Magied, Lolly Adefope, Bisha K. Ali, Aisling Bea, Kemah Bob, Catherine Bohart, Jen Brister, Desiree Burch, Margaret Cabourn-Smith, Zoe Coombs Marr, Jessica Fostekew, Geraldine Hickey, Claire Hooper, Rosie Jones, Athena Kugblenu, Cariad Lloyd, Nat Luurstema, Mae Martin, Rose Matefeo, Shazia Mirza, Aparna Nancherla, Celia Pacquola, Sara Pascoe, Rachel Parris, Carrie Quinlan, Jessica Regan, Jamila Rizvi, Abigoliah Schamaun, Alice Sneddon, Alison Spittle, Jess Thom, Sindhu Vee, Felicity Ward, Myf Warhurst, Cal Wilson and Susan Wokoma, and I know there will be many more wonderful women to come.

There are too many guests to mention and I fear leaving someone out but I appreciate every great joke, brilliant insight, championed cause and love left on the stage and captured for ever online. You've made this what it is and what it is, is brilliant.

Index

Muriel's Wedding (film), 152
My Fair Lady (film), 302

Nanette (Hannah Gadsby Netflix
   special), 189, 193–4
neuroscience, 224
New York Magazine, x
New Zealand, 319
Nicholson, Jack, 304
Nigeria, 319
Nightingale, Florence, 31–2
Nye, Rachel, 270

Obama, Barack, 101, 102, 106
Obama, Michelle, 81, 101–2, 103, 178,
   214
O'Donnell, Rosie, 240
Oliver, John, 150
Omahrose (composer), 311
Oracy (rapper), 311

Pankhurst, Emmeline, 168–9
parenting, 6, 9, 247; childcare, 20,
   21, 22, 24, 33; gender roles in
   Sweden, 244; in hunter-gatherer
   societies, 20; MRA complaints,
   243–4; and women's choices, 24, 35
patents, American, 17–19, 31
patriarchy: and augmenting/
   accessorising, 308; change as
   painfully slow, 9, 31, 33; and
   contraceptive pill, 22–5, 26; 'Cult
   of the Body' indoctrination,
   40, 41–6, 47–55, 56–8, 59, 60–7;
   cultural brainwashing by, xiv–xv,
   xvii, 34, 40, 41–6, 47–55, 115–16;
   as enemy of feminism, xvii, 238,
   248–50, 259–62, 316; excuses
   for exclusion of women, 33–4;
   fuck-the-patriarchy version of
   feminism, xvi; 'gender symmetry'
   theory, 242–3; historical 100
   per cent male quotas, 13–16,
   30; history of, 19, 21–5, 40; and
   homogenisation, 27; idea of only
   one spot at top for a woman, 254,
   257; love of the binary, 249–50;
   male fear of women's gains,
   239–40; male pronouns, 9; and
   male violence, 238–9, 243, 248–9,

313; marginalised groups/voices,
3n2, 9, 27n, 30–1, 103, 146–52, 154,
170, 175, 192–9, 217, 229–35, 282–5;
and marriage, 297; meaning of
term, 3n2; men let down by, 31,
240, 248, 249–50; and the plough,
21, 23, 25, 40, 41; power structures
and economic models, 3n2, 11–13,
22–6, 30–1, 32–4, 40–6, 173–4,
259–62, 275, 316–17; and property
ownership, 21–2, 40; and radical
feminism, 6–7; and religious
heritage, 3–4, 43–4, 47–8, 52, 56,
74; smashing of by microclimates,
144–52; and trans people, 229,
231, 232; undermining of women,
119, 120, 121–4; Venn diagram
of privilege, 26–30, 81, 110–11,
249, 316–17; white men's tribe of
ownership/influence, 17, 18, 22,
30–1, 32–3, 34; and white women,
16–19, 34; and workplace structure,
72

Paw Patrol (animated television
   show), 123–4
pilots, female, 92
Pincus, Gregory, 23
Planned Parenthood, 23
poker, 83–8, 89–91
political rights, 8, 13, 14, 17, 32
Pretty Woman (film), 300, 302–3, 304
property ownership, 21–2, 40
public land, private development of,
   281, 282–3, 284

queer community, 27, 29, 30,
   112–16, 143, 178, 225–6, 268; living
   the truth, 118, 119, 131–2, 133;
   second-wave feminists, 8; use of
   term 'queer', xiv; *see also* sexual
   orientation
quotas, gender: in Germany, 12;
   historical 100 per cent male, 13–16,
   30; opposition to, 12–13, 16

race and ethnicity: cultural
   appropriation, 65–6; and election
   of Trump, 177–8; and feminism,
   154–5, 157–8; interplay between
   race and gender, 5, 17–19, 25,

racism – *continued*
29–30, 81, 110–11, 152, 154–5, 157–8,
177–8; language usage relating
to, xiv; National Negro Business
League, 205–6; *see also* colour,
women of (WOC)
racism: and election of Trump,
177–8; intersectionality concept,
9, 29–30, 81, 110–11, 116, 152, 231,
262–3; and marginalisation, 27n,
65n, 153, 154–5; and Murdoch, 173;
slaughter of indigenous peoples,
11; slavery and colonisation, 11,
17; and suffragettes, 8n4; and
unconscious bias, 28; US voting
rights, 15
Radical Alternatives to Prison, 284,
285
rap music, 310–11
rape, 126–7, 312–14
Ray, Charlotte E., 17, 98
Reclaim Holloway movement, 281–5
Reclaim Justice Network, 284
The Red Pill (Cassie Jaye
documentary), 240–4, 247
Reed, Judy W., 18
Regan, Jessica, 179, 180
religion: Lanyer's satire on, 166–7;
patriarchal heritage, 3–4, 43–4,
47–8, 52, 56, 74; *see also* Jehovah's
Witnesses
reproductive rights, 9, 238–9, 241–2
Rock, John, 24
romantic comedies, 300–4, 306–7
Room (film), 59
Roxxxan (rapper), 311

Salinsky, Tom, 316–17
Sandberg, Sheryl, 82
Sanger, Margaret, 23–4
Saudi Arabia, 319
Say Yes to the Dress (reality TV
show), 297–9
Sedgwick, Ned, 145n
sex and sexuality: coercion,
126–8; contrary instructions
on, 128; domination, 130–1, 314;
intrusiveness of penetration, 129;
issue of 'consent', 126–8, 129; rape
fantasies, 312–14; saying no, 128–9;

stereotype of women not wanting
sex, 129; submissive fantasies/role
play, xv, 130–1, 312–14; women's
sexual appetites, 129–31
sexual orientation, xiii, 112–16;
Australian referendum on equal
marriage, 189–91; homogenisation
due to patriarchy, 27;
intersectionality concept, 9, 29–30,
81, 116; language usage relating
to, xiv; LGBT rights movement,
225–6; living the truth, 131–2; *see
also* queer community
Shakespeare, William, 165, 167;
Henry V, 179, 180–1, 320
ShaoLan, 79
Shaw, George Bernard, *Pygmalion*,
302
Silverman, Sarah, 222
Simon, Sam, 139n
Sisters of Frida, 270, 280
Sisters Uncut, 281–5
skydiving, 125, 153
Smith, Jaden, 309
socialism, 5, 8
South America, hunter-gatherer
societies in, 19–20
Special Operations Executive, 121
Spiderman, 309–10
stand-up comedy, xv, 93–5, 98, 102–3,
184–7; Hannah Gadsby, 192–8; as
male environment, 110–16, 134–6,
149, 251–3; Zoe Coombs Marr,
110–16; shows for and by women,
156–7, 253; Susan Wokoma, 156–7
Stanley, Jessamyn, 30, 59–66
Steinem, Gloria, x, 35–6, 154, 168
Stewart, Jon, 149–50
Stiles, Patti, 95–6, 97–8
stories and narratives: about black
women, 143; female microclimates,
xiii, 140–2, 144–52; female stories
as human stories, 142; finding a
voice, 171–82, 185–92, 209; hero as
vehicle for empathy, 144; Phoebe
Waller-Bridge, 158–64; white men's
stories in Hollywood, 142–4
Stynhach, Andriy, 22–3
Suffrageddon (feminist hip-hop
musical), 311